THE
UNTOLD
WAR AT SEA

THE
UNTOLD
WAR AT SEA

America's Revolutionary
Privateers

Kylie A. Hulbert

THE UNIVERSITY OF
GEORGIA PRESS
ATHENS

© 2022 by the University of Georgia Press
Athens, Georgia 30602
www.ugapress.org
All rights reserved

Designed by Kaelin Chappell Broaddus
Set in 10.5/13.5 Adobe Caslon Pro Regular by Kaelin Chappell Broaddus

Most University of Georgia Press titles are
available from popular e-book vendors.

Printed digitally

Library of Congress Cataloging-in-Publication Data

Names: Hulbert, Kylie A., 1984– author.
Title: The untold war at sea : America's revolutionary privateers / Kylie A. Hulbert.
Other titles: America's revolutionary privateers
Description: Athens : The University of Georgia Press, [2022] |
Includes bibliographical references and index.
Identifiers: LCCN 2021028331 | ISBN 9780820360706 (hardback) |
ISBN 9780820360713 (paperback) | ISBN 9780820360720 (ebook)
Subjects: LCSH: United States—History—Revolution, 1775–1783—Naval operations. |
Privateering—United States—History—18th century.
Classification: LCC E271 .H87 2022 | DDC 973.3/5—dc23
LC record available at https://lccn.loc.gov/2021028331

Contents

Acknowledgments

*T*he life of this historian is often filled with fleeting moments of the past, letters and log books, court records and the journals of the Continental Congress, and a plethora of other eighteenth-century sources. In the midst of these papers and pages, mentors, colleagues, friends, and family have bolstered and motivated me. This book would not be in your hands were it not for their unwavering support.

The seeds of this project were planted during my first year of graduate work at the University of Georgia. I benefited from exceptional scholars who championed this author and this project from the outset. My never-ending gratitude belongs to Peter C. Hoffer, who challenged me to hone my prose and my contribution to Revolutionary scholarship. Woody Holton granted me the opportunity to learn from the best as his graduate research assistant at the University of Richmond and he stayed on for the long haul. I appreciate his insights and support more than he knows. Benjamin Ehlers and Stephen Berry rounded out my dissertation committee as staunch advocates of the project who brought their own unique perspectives to the table. All of these powerhouse historians taught me the importance of the stories historians tell.

The top-rate team at the University of Georgia Press, spearheaded by Mick Gusinde-Duffy and my project editor, Jon Davies, made this a smooth and relatively seamless process, despite my novice status. My thanks to them all, as well as the readers who posed important questions and offered insightful and constructive criticisms, all of which made this a better and stronger book.

Research is vital for any historian and I was lucky to have support in conducting mine for this book. My thanks to the Willson Center for Humanities and Arts, the Graduate School at the University of Georgia for a Graduate Student Research Award, the Department of History at UGA, Greg and Amanda Gregory, and the College of Arts and Sciences at Texas A&M University–Kingsville. My thanks also to my exceptional fellow panelists and audience members at the Society for Military History and the Omohundro Institute's Conferences, who allowed me to share my ongoing research and posited thought-provoking questions and observations.

The work of a historian is often solitary in nature, but that does not mean we are solitary creatures. The coterie of colleagues and friends I have gathered over the years is second to none. My thanks to them for their support, whether during long overdue phone calls, in exceedingly detailed e-mails, or on much needed walks. My special gratitude to Chris Phillips and Joseph Beilein, who answered the call when I needed aid in deciphering handwriting and found access to an integral source. I know if I am ever in need I can count on you all. If this book—and these words—make any sense, the man to thank is Greg Wu. Writing is a process and a craft, I always tell my students, and I began learning my craft in Mr. Wu's ninth-grade English class.

While these privateers have taken me into the past, my family keeps me firmly rooted in the present. The Hulbert clan of Apopka, Florida, took me into their fold from day one, and I am forever grateful to be a part of their family. My sister, Lindsey, and her Kuczma clan are the life of the party. Our family vacations offer a much-needed respite from historical pursuits. My parents, Jack and Peggy Horney, are, simply put, the absolute best. Their love and support are beyond all measure. I thank them from the bottom of my heart for all they have done.

Over the course of this project, Matt Hulbert and I have created our own family. I may be biased, but in my view, it is perfect. Our three children— Eleanor, Grant, and Beatrice—bring sunshine, joy, and happiness into the world and into our lives. I love every moment I spend with them, and I love every moment I spend with Matt. I am incredibly lucky in this regard. Matt is a juggernaut: an award-winning historian, an amazing father, and an extraordinary husband. Words fail to express what he means to me. Suffice to say, his mark is on every page and on my heart. I could not have accomplished this endeavor without Matt, and I would not share life's adventures with anyone else. This book is for him.

THE
UNTOLD
WAR AT SEA

A song of privateering ventures dedicated "to all the jolly tars who are fighting for the rights and liberties of America." *Manly. A favorite new song, in the American fleet*. Salem: Printed by Ezekiel Russell, [1776]. Courtesy of Phillips Library, Peabody Essex Museum, Rowley, Mass.

Introduction

*I*n the early months of 1779, Captain Hugh Hill and his crew aboard the American privateer *Pilgrim* sailed the waters of the Atlantic in search of prizes. The captain kept a keen eye out, scanning the horizon for an enemy vessel and a potentially big payoff. On February 13, a ship sailed into view. Hill and his men prepared for an engagement, sensing success might be within their grasp. The privateer attacked and seized the *Nuestra Senora de Merced*, commanded by Matthias Sagarra, en route from Spain to London, England. Hill was duly commissioned by the Continental Congress, and under this authority he ordered his prize sent into port at Beverly, Massachusetts. There, in the Maritime Court of the Middle District, the owners of the *Pilgrim*—Samuel Cabot of Beverly and Stephen Cleveland of Salem—brought suit.[1]

On behalf of Hill and his crew, Cabot and Cleveland claimed the *Nuestra Senora de Merced* was "the property of and belonging to some of the Subjects of the King of Great Britain," not including Bermuda, Providence, or the Bahamas. Therefore, because the ship belonged to enemies of the United States in an open state of war, it was a lawful and legal prize. The libelants' story asserted Sagarra refused to allow the Americans to search his ship, and he quickly threw important papers overboard. Using "false papers and false pretences," Cabot and Cleveland argued Sagarra had attempted to deceive Hill by claiming the *Nuestra Senora de Merced* was the property of Spanish subjects. Their privateer had successfully taken a vessel, and they aimed to profit from its seizure.[2]

A few months later, in March 1779, the court heard Matthias Sagarra's version of events. He iterated his argument that the vessel and its cargo were not in service of Great Britain. The captain himself averred he had cargo in the hold, in addition to monies received from an exchange of goods at Cadiz. Sagarra charged Hill and his crew with an "illegal and groundless capture." The owners of the *Nuestra Senora de Merced* had "suffered great damage," and due to their unsavory actions, Hill and his privateer crew had kept Sagarra from completing his voyage from Cadiz to London. Sagarra sought nothing less than the complete restoration of the vessel and its cargo.[3]

The jury impaneled for this case heard testimony from both sides and examined the evidence presented. On Friday, July 9, 1779, at nine o'clock in the morning, the jury returned with its verdict. The group of twelve men determined the ship and its appurtenances, along with certain pieces of cargo, did belong to subjects of the king of Spain and ordered their return, but the remainder of the cargo not included for the claimants was indeed legal and lawful prize due to Cabot, Cleveland, Hill, and his mariners.[4]

The Massachusetts court's verdict did not satisfy either party, and both appealed the case to the Continental Congress. On November 6, 1779, nearly nine months after the *Pilgrim* had captured the *Nuestra Senora de Merced*, the Court of Appeals handed down its decision. The commissioners outlined specific pieces of cargo deemed lawful prize as they appeared to belong to British subjects, including "one half pipe of wine" and nineteen barrels of cochineal (insects used to make a natural dye), all of which amounted to a reduced prize compared with the original verdict handed down by the Massachusetts court. The court ordered the vessel and the rest of the cargo returned to Sagarra for his use. To make matters worse for Cabot, Cleveland, and Hill, the court instructed them to pay Sagarra $1,056 to cover his court costs. The *Pilgrim* succeeded in taking a prize, but the fruits of the venture were not what they had once seemed.[5]

The story of Hugh Hill, the *Pilgrim*, Matthias Sagarra, and the *Nuestra Senora de Merced* opens a window on the significant role privateers played during the American Revolution. Sailing in the waters of the Atlantic and the Caribbean, privateers effectively harassed and damaged enemy commerce, though they did not always practice their craft in an honorable way. Almost any vessel navigating open waters was fair game, especially if the ship carried valuable cargo. Considering the long-standing tradition of privateering, the colonists' decision to take to the waves in 1775 was not surprising. Indeed, to merchants, sailors, investors, and outfitters, privateering was a logical part of wartime operations. At a moment when the British Royal

Navy dominated the seas and the Continental navy was barely out of port, American privateers took on risk and adventure in hopes of securing victory over their enemies and bringing home valuable prizes. Their actions clearly made an impact on American war efforts, and their stories were hailed in the early years of the conflict when American victories were few and far between. Nevertheless, these seafarers' story remains largely untold, eclipsed by the Continental army and navy, militias and minutemen, Founding Fathers and mythical heroes of the Revolution, *until now.*

The American Revolution was a crucial moment in the history of privateering. Yet both historians and popular authors alike have tended to focus on the role of the young Continental navy, led by the likes of Esek Hopkins and John Paul Jones. Indeed, very little appears in print, academic or mainstream, regarding the operations of ocean-faring former colonists who took to the high seas to protect their economic and political interests, to harass the British, to make a profit, and to influence the outcome of the war. *The Untold War at Sea* addresses this gap by reexamining the American Revolution in an Atlantic World perspective through the lens of privateering.[6]

The majority of existing literature on privateers focuses either on the elite men who supported the practice or on the effects of privateering itself. One of the earliest full-on studies of American privateering, Edgar Stanton Maclay's *A History of American Privateers*, published in 1899, concentrates on the role of these raiders in both the American Revolution and the War of 1812. Though Maclay relates a number of interesting stories about numerous privateer vessels, his work suffers from a lack of citations and an inherent bias toward the "commendable . . . conduct" of American privateers who supposedly "showed themselves to be not only daring, but gentlemanly." Written more than fifty years later, William Bell Clark's *Ben Franklin's Privateers: A Naval Epic of the American Revolution* examines Franklin's efforts on behalf of American prisoners. Franklin's main purpose in outfitting privateers, Clark maintains, was to seize as many British captives as possible and use them in deals of exchange. Writing several decades after Clark, Robert H. Patton, in *Patriot Pirates*, tells the story of privateers by emphasizing the main players of the Revolution such as Silas Deane, George Washington, and Benjamin Franklin; in the process, Patton ironically does very little in the way of investigating the lives of actual privateers. As such, no true social history of these Americans exists.[7]

While merchants-turned-privateers did indeed play a significant role in the war, their impact goes beyond the numbers and effects of their ventures. Their lives and experiences took them to ports both domestic and abroad; they sailed on the high seas of the Atlantic and beyond. The Revolution of privateers was not the Revolution touted so often in history textbooks. Their Revolutionary experience included a far greater geographical scope than any Continental soldier or militia combatant, from the backwoods of South Carolina to the streets of New York or Boston, could even imagine. By incorporating the story of privateers into the greater Revolutionary narrative, the fabric of the war becomes richer. Privateers add a layer of complexity, highlighting patriotic fervor and self-interest. While they derived their authority and right to take prizes from commissions granted by the Continental Congress, as the saga of Hugh Hill and the *Pilgrim* illustrates above, their decisions and actions were not always guided by the principles outlined therein. Hill, and other commanders like him, made choices for the benefit of themselves and their crews—choices that did not always align with the goals of the cause at large.

While Continental soldiers were considered part and parcel of the emerging nation, privateers occupied a category that was similar to, yet completely separate from, their other martial counterparts. They sailed under the American flag and claimed to support American initiatives and goals, but their actions did not always match their avowed promises. As noted, privateers drew their authority from commissions granted either by Congress or state governments, but their loyalty and interests did not always coincide with those powers. Indeed, those bodies did not always protect or promote the privateers they commissioned. If a privateer venture went south, the Continental Congress oftentimes washed their hands of the issue or claimed the privateer had operated outside the given directive.

In the immediate present, the state did not have many options. Without a strong navy, leaders of the Revolution grappled with the question of how to engage the British navy—the greatest sea power in the world. Privateers presented a solution, one that cost the Continental Congress very little in terms of expenses but could yield great returns for the cause. However, by relying on private maritime citizens—that is, those who officially outfitted, fiscally supported, organized, or engaged in privateering ventures under their own volition—the state, despite its best efforts, could not always control the exploits of those privateers. Thus when the time came to form a respectable, recognized nation, the Congress faced the issue of what to do with those sailors, captains, and merchants who had accomplished a great deal for the Revolution, but who did not fit neatly within the positive, triumphant narrative the Founding Fathers were eager to propagate.

Following the war, the rebellion had to become a distinguished Revolution. The creation of this new United States required a founding mythology that relied on heroic figures such as George Washington, Nathanael Greene, and John Paul Jones. Unlike Continental troops and sailors, privateers were often operating outside the purview of what we now consider the mainstream war. Privateers who inhabited a grey area during the war could not remain. Because their actions and experiences were unfamiliar and unique unto themselves—exploits in the far reaches of the Atlantic, engagements away from the main armies, a complicated court process to receive prize money and recognition—they were erased from public memory without much resistance in the postwar period. Merchants-turned-privateers returned to their prewar practices. No battlegrounds remained, and no memorials stood to remind the public of their efforts and sacrifices. These combatants having fulfilled their purpose during the war, the state needed them to disappear in its aftermath. And they remained forgotten until the next war, when the state called on private maritime citizens to take up arms once more. Yet the War of 1812 was different in that the nation was already established, so privateers could remain as part of that war's history. Eventually, though, the practice itself became obsolete and was ultimately outlawed.

One historian has suggested that sailors were actually a "transnational" group who "helped to form the early United States during the age of Revolutions." Another has contended that these seafarers were some of the first to grapple with ideas of American citizenship. Privateers were part of that process. Whether exploring foreign ports or caught up in legal cases abroad, these men had to justify their actions while representing an unseasoned new nation that did not always even recognize them as official representatives of their cause. Brian Rouleau's study examines the role mariners played in creating a global empire that began with America's struggle for independence. The history of privateers is militaristic indeed, but they were also among the first Americans to truly engage with foreign nations politically, economically, and socially. Thus, their history is an integral part of maritime culture at large, particularly if one accepts a recent definition of "maritime" as not only the water, but "that which border[s] or touche[s] the sea ... continuity between land and ocean." Privateers bridged those worlds as their experiences took them across the Atlantic and back home again to Admiralty Courts on land run by men who did not always understand the ways of the water.[8]

From the beginning of the wars for empire, the Atlantic and the Caribbean in time of conflict were the hunting grounds of privateers. In societies where commerce depended on the sea-lanes of trade, pirates and privateers were often found preying on enemy merchant vessels. At a time when large navies did not patrol nations' waterways or the waters of their colonies, sovereigns sanctioned, and sometimes helped finance, private armed vessels for war in an effort to disrupt the trade of their foes. For England, pirates and privateers sailed the waters of the English Channel into the Atlantic Ocean beyond. Though, as one historian notes, the term "privateer" was not widely used until the seventeenth century, the practice of privateering as it is known today rose to prominence in England during the reign of Queen Elizabeth I (1533–1603).[9]

At various times, Elizabeth publicly and privately commissioned men such as Sir Francis Drake, Sir Walter Raleigh, and Sir John Hawkins to aid in the war against Spain after 1585. Elizabeth was a shrewd monarch with tight purse strings. Lacking sufficient funds to wage an all-out offensive war, the queen was often on the defensive. Frequently, she was forced to rely on her subjects for aid, and they responded by organizing hundreds of private cruises. English merchants viewed private ventures as an opportunity not only to make a profit, but also to take an offensive stance against England's enemies. The Royal Navy participated in engagements, to be certain, but as Kenneth R. Andrews notes, "Privateers far outnumbered the queen's ships throughout the war" against Spain. These privately outfitted vessels played a significant role in the conflict and took part in joint efforts on occasion with Her Majesty's fleet. Yet many of the queen's newly christened privateers were former pirates. This grey area created a problematic distinction between the two or, rather, a problematic lack of distinction. To this day, pirates and privateers are often conflated.[10]

Historians define privateers as state- or government-sanctioned merchants specifically outfitted to engage and attack enemy shipping. Pirates, on the other hand, were illegal sea raiders operating outside of any government, men motivated purely by self-interest and profit. Privateers were supposed to be patriotic and loyal to their commissioner, while pirates were beholden to no one but themselves. Privateers had to bring their prize into port and present their case to an Admiralty Court; pirates took what they pleased. Privateers were often converted merchants who operated only in times of war and necessity; piracy was a way of life during war and peace. At least, these are the hard-and-fast definitions as they exist in theory. In practice, the difference between these groups was frequently more complex.[11]

English privateers, and by extension North American colonial privateers, honed their trade in the late seventeenth and early eighteenth centuries during numerous European wars. The Anglo-Dutch Wars (1652–1654, 1665–1667, 1672–1674), the Nine Years' War (1688–1697) and the War of the Spanish Succession (1701–1713)—known as Queen Anne's War in the North American colonies—witnessed privateers taking to the seas in great numbers. Captains from Massachusetts and Rhode Island received letters of marque and commissions to sail against the Dutch during the on-again-off-again wars. Samuel Moseley of Dorchester, for example, sailed the ship *Salisbury* along the New England coast in 1674 as a deterrent against Dutch privateers and craft intent on attacking Nantucket. In 1675, a joint venture between a colonial privateer and a French vessel resulted in the capture of several Dutch privateersmen who were forced to surrender and taken to Boston as lawful prizes.[12]

During the Nine Years' War—also referred to as King William's War—privateering continued apace in the British North American colonies. The lieutenant governor of Bermuda outfitted and commissioned a vessel "to seize pirates or sea rovers" during the conflict in 1689. Two years later, the governor of the island granted commissions to two privateers who ranged far along the coast of the colonies, all the way to the waters off New England, where they captured the *Three Brothers*, a vessel from Cadiz carrying "prohibited goods." Rhode Islanders continued their privateering tradition after a fleet of French privateers attacked Block Island in July 1690, and in New York, Lieutenant Governor Jacob Leisler began commissioning privateer vessels in May 1690. Captain William Mason returned to the city by September of that same year with six prizes in tow.[13]

Captain Peter Lawrence, a veteran of King William's War in Rhode Island, seized the opportunity to continue his privateering ventures during Queen Anne's War and outfitted a vessel in Massachusetts in 1702. Thomas Larrimore, who likewise had served on several privateer vessels during the previous conflict, took up the position of privateer captain in July 1702 and capitalized on the circumstances of war by taking his first prize less than two months later. Throughout these European conflicts of the late seventeenth and early eighteenth centuries, British colonists employed privateers to engage, deter, and defeat the enemy. While merchants found their trade interrupted and sometimes cut off by rival vessels and fleets, these businessmen recognized the potential profits of privateering and took to the high seas.[14]

Anglo-American colonists gained still more privateering experience during the War of Jenkins' Ear (1739–1748) and King George's War (1744–1748). During these conflicts, North American colonial cities outfitted and sent their greatest number of ships to sea up to that point. Following King George's June 1738 authorization for letters of marque, John Jones of Boston received a commission for his vessel *Young Eagle*, commanded by Captain Philip Dumaresq, in the summer of 1739. The commission was granted by the colony of Massachusetts, from whence the ship sailed along the coast of Spain and among the Canary Islands. Great Britain, Spain, and France all encouraged the outfitting of privateers, which were a major component of their wartime efforts; Anglo-American ships numbered in the thousands during these wars alone. Rhode Island privateers the *Castor* and the *Pollux* cruised in tandem beginning in the summer of 1742 and took three Spanish vessels within the year. Overall, the colonies sent more than three hundred privateer vessels to sea, including the brigantine *Ranger* out of Boston, which engaged with a French privateer off Cape Breton in 1744.[15]

By the outbreak of the Seven Years' War (1756–1763), British North American colonists were more than well equipped to aid in efforts at sea against France. Building upon their experiences in previous European-colonial conflicts, Anglo-American privateers took up the call to arms and operated alongside the Royal Navy. In Rhode Island alone, 20 percent of the male population climbed aboard privately armed vessels. British men-of-war stationed in the colony of New York lost numerous sailors to privateers anchored in the harbor. Men serving on board said vessels dodged press-gangs and sought greater returns. In 1756, the official declaration of war against France caused celebrations in the city, where privateering reached a fever pitch. New York sent out 26 privateers in the course of that year, bearing 350 guns and 2,700 men. Overall, the port received 381 captured enemy vessels by war's end, more than any other British American port.[16]

Thus, as the opening salvos of the American Revolution sounded, privateering was almost second nature to merchants and seafarers of North American coastal towns. The process of outfitting and manning privateers began early in the conflict—this was a colonial military tradition, a logical extension of what colonists had learned and accomplished in the previous wars of the eighteenth century. They understood the nature of the privateering business and the legal system necessary to condemn prizes. By the time of the American Revolution, these colonists were prepared to face the British Royal Navy by utilizing the skills they had acquired during earlier wars. American privateers turned the tables on their British enemies.

Privateers aided in the American war effort in numerous ways, from capturing prizes with essential supplies to harassing British merchants' ships
so effectively that a number of these businessmen actually began calling for
an end to the war from their offices in England. Many of those who participated in privateering made personal choices and sacrifices, whether for
the cause, for opportunity, or for the profit they hoped to secure. Regardless of their motives, American privateers were crucial to the Patriots' success during the Revolution. These mariners operated in a world driven by
position and profit—a world where a man's status derived in part from his
social standing; a world run by men, for men; a world where the outcome
of war would determine what sort of men would rule North America. This
was a world where pride, honor, and tradition played crucial roles. Privateers
chose not to serve in the traditional sense; rather, they engaged with the enemy in ways characterized as unbecoming of a gentleman. Oftentimes, they
were labeled as pirates.

Due to their sometimes less-than-savory methods, privateers were often overlooked upon their return home. Engaged in legal proceedings over
prizes and prize money, their experiences in the postwar United States were
vastly removed from that of their Continental navy counterparts. Privateers
were perceived as greedy or unpatriotic in their efforts to recover money
owed or accolades due. Only when privateers' activities served a specific wartime purpose—for example, as supporters of the small naval force during the
War of 1812 or as substitutes for the Confederacy's lack of a traditional navy
during the American Civil War—were memories of these men and their patriotic endeavors resurrected, only to be forgotten moments later when their
martial stock waned.

Privateers were clearly an important component of the American war effort, especially during the early years of the Revolution. While the Continental Congress struggled to construct a navy, privateers provided a quick fix
to the question of the war at sea. Following the British blockade in 1775 and
prior to the signing of the Declaration of Independence, privateers brought
the battle to Britain's doorstep. The precise number of vessels engaged from
1776 to 1783 is difficult to pinpoint with complete accuracy. That said, esti-
mates range from 1,151 to 1,697 to over 2,000. The number of sailings was
most certainly in the thousands, with the year 1781 possibly having seen the
highest number of commissioned vessels at 550. Approximately 52,000 sailors embarked on privateer ventures during the war, and their efforts resulted

in the capture of at least 600 British vessels. Though an element of risk was involved in outfitting a privateer, the potential for return of profit was great indeed, with the average prize valued at $45,699. Privateers of the War for Independence plied their trade in an attempt to aid the war effort and bring much-needed supplies and goods to the colonists.[17]

In addition to these patriotic aims, American privateers were highly motivated by another important factor: profit. The Continental Congress issued commissions authorizing these private enterprises, but nothing was owed to that governing body upon privateers' return to port. While patriotism and pride supposedly inspired troops of the Continental army, privateers were often cast as the antithesis to republican virtue. The ultimate goal of their ventures was to seize as many vessels as possible and return home with a profitable prize. Despite privateers' possible positive impact on the war effort, they were easily pegged as entrepreneurs and investors exploiting the chaos of war.

All of these components color the cast of characters engaged in privateering ventures and efforts. Whatever their motivations or experiences, privateers performed as key players in the Revolution. Their stories provide new opportunities to reexamine the oft-touted narrative of the War for Independence. They, too, have a place and a role in the spirit of 1776. Privateers were a different type of combatant with their own set of skills. They sailed in foreign waters. They traveled and fought on foreign soil. Their exploits took them to exotic islands and European locales. These men operated on vessels specifically outfitted for war, resulting in experiences unlike those of other Revolutionary fighters. Their encounters contained elements of risk, adventure, patriotism, and self-interest. Privateers warrant a reconsideration of the war many Americans think they know—they reveal there is more to the story than Thomas Jefferson and the Declaration of Independence, Paul Revere and his ride, Washington and his winters, or the victories of Saratoga and Yorktown.

The on-the-ground activities and experiences of privateers are central to this reexamination of their role in the American Revolution. Privateer operations offer the opportunity to pursue another avenue of inquiry into the Revolution's greater impact and influence as a global conflict. By examining their ventures, the scope of the conflict expands. The experiences of the "typical" combatant in the war are no longer confined to the soil of North America. Engagements are not only between British regulars, German mercenaries, and colonial Patriots. With the addition of privateers, the fighting includes international crews operating in international waters on an international stage. These merchant marines understood that the war not only consisted of battlefields on American soil, but required foreign support and aid. Foreign recognition was imperative. The process of revolution and winning independence was global in nature, and privateers operated at its core. Rather than being unfamiliar and unknown, their experiences are an integral part of the narrative this project illuminates by reintegrating their story into the popular patriotic account.[18]

The Untold War at Sea is structured to follow the tenure of a privateer as he experienced the war: from the docks to life aboard ship, from engagements and battles with enemy vessels to the American prize courts, and, ultimately, to war's end, where the public waited to hand down judgment and create a narrative of the war that belittled the efforts of privateers. These phases are reflected in a popular song from the Revolutionary period titled "Manly. A favorite new song, in the American fleet." Hence, the chapter titles are derived from verses of this song.[19]

Chapter 1, "Hardy Sons of Mars," catches up with privateers before they leave the docks. The Continental Congress took months to grant permission and write commissions for the outfitting of privateers. With these documents in hand, privateer owners and outfitters next faced the process of financing, equipping, and manning merchant vessels converted for the purpose of harassing and taking enemy ships. The call for privateers, however, promised profit for those willing to take their chances at sea.

Chapter 2, "A Privateering We Will Go," journeys into the waters of the Atlantic; it examines the daily lives of privateers aboard their vessels and in foreign ports. Privateers made repairs to their ships, dealt with unexpected damage, and fished, bartered, or bought supplies for their long journeys. They found or created entertainment on board and onshore, and they exchanged important information as they explored various ports.

Chapter 3, "When Cannon Balls Do Fly," engages readers with the stories of chases, battles, prize taking, the spoils of victory, and the consequences of defeat upon the seas of the Atlantic World. Privateers encountered European enemies and allies as they sailed the waters of the Atlantic in search of their prey; sometimes, they became prey themselves. They experienced different treatment as prisoners of war, particularly since the British oftentimes viewed their actions as akin to those of pirates rather than legally commissioned commerce raiders.

Chapter 4, "Make Your Fortunes Now, My Lads," returns with privateers to the colonies as they brought their prizes into court. Once again, the Continental Congress takes center stage as it attempted to create a functioning

Admiralty Court system. The experiences of privateers within this unstable legal institution illustrate the difficulties they encountered upon their return home.

Chapter 5, "To Glory Let Us Run," focuses on the various perceptions of privateers during the war. Though some colonists openly supported the efforts of these mercenaries at sea, many more touted their actions as piratical. Privateers took men from the war effort, both on land and on the waters; their presence crippled the manning of the fledgling navy. European powers had to contend with privateers and their brazen actions in foreign ports and waters. Though their efforts clearly had an effect on the British economy, privateers simply did not fit the postwar narrative of triumphant Patriots.

Collectively, the day-to-day lives of these men as they traversed the Atlantic Ocean expand the scope and impact of the American Revolution beyond our current geographical, political, and social understandings of the conflict. While scholars work toward internationalizing the Revolution, *The Untold War at Sea* posits that privateers were an integral part of what made the Revolution global in real time. Their journeys took them far beyond the shores of the colonies into an Atlantic World where allies, commerce, patriotism, identity, and pride all crossed national boundaries, where the process of revolution itself was international. It is high time we followed them. Because ultimately, as the following pages will show, when the engagements and efforts of privateers in the Atlantic World are brought center stage, our understanding of the American Revolution as a world war continues to grow.

CHAPTER I

Hardy Sons of Mars

*T*he oars of the longboats cut silently through the waters of Narragansett Bay on the night of June 9, 1772, as Rhode Islanders approached their quarry: the British vessel HMS *Gaspee*. Captained by Lieutenant William Dudingston, the *Gaspee* was known for terrorizing the coasts of Rhode Island, taking guilty and innocent colonial merchant vessels alike in an effort to quell smuggling and the illegal marine actions of the colonists. The British meant to send a clear message to the colony of Rhode Island. Its inhabitants were to follow British maritime legislations or face severe consequences—consequences that would be meted out by the likes of Dudingston and the *Gaspee*. Alas for Dudingston, he underestimated the colonists; he failed to see how his actions alienated and angered merchants and sailors. Thus, when the *Gaspee* ran aground while chasing the colonial vessel *Hannah*, Rhode Islanders seized their chance to rid themselves and their colony of the hated ship for good.[1]

Rhode Islanders quickly convened a meeting at which they decided to stage a surprise attack on Dudingston and his vessel. Outfitting at least seven longboats captained by experienced commanders, the colonists shoved off from the shore and headed toward the *Gaspee*. As they approached the hull of the British ship, the watch caught sight of them and demanded that they identify themselves. Abraham Whipple, captain of one of the longboats, offered a cheeky retort, after which one of his crew fired upon the watchman and initiated the assault. In short order, the colonists had boarded the *Gaspee*, commandeered the vessel, and captured the crew as well as all their possessions, forthwith sending them to shore, where they would be dealt with accordingly. Flames illuminated the night sky as the *Gaspee* burned upon Narragansett Bay. Rhode Islanders watched from the shore as the symbol of British tyranny and oppression went up in smoke.[2]

The burning of the *Gaspee* was not an action of privateers per se, as none of the longboats were commissioned vessels sent out by the colonial government. However, the event is significant as it highlights the motivations and willingness of merchants, captains, and sailors to take to the seas to protect their colonies and their investments. Rhode Islanders would not simply accept British vessels' oftentimes, though not always, unwarranted attacks on colonial shipping. They would meet fire with fire when the occasion arose. Port towns would be ready to outfit and arm privateer vessels. When an official call to arm privateers went out three years later, the coastal colonists were ready for action.

The Continental Congress did not issue this summons lightly or quickly. The cohort in Philadelphia spent long hours, days, weeks, and ultimately months debating the pros and cons of allowing the commissioning and outfitting of privateers. Privateering was a long-standing tradition, but it was mainly associated with war and armed conflict. The British North American colonies had not yet declared independence in 1775. Opponents feared Great Britain might view a direct appeal for privateers as an offensive action, an instigation of war. Champions of the cause, such as John Adams, contended privateers were the colonies' best maritime hope until a Continental navy could be established.

The debate among delegates highlights the tenuous position privateers occupied in the opening moments of the Revolution. It also foreshadows their commemorative vulnerability in the wake of American independence. On the one hand, when they proved helpful and necessary to the cause, privateers were seafaring heroes who took the conflict directly to Great Britain. On the other hand, when they ran afoul of the law or took matters into their own hands—as the residents of Rhode Island did with the *Gaspee*—privateers were unwelcome troublemakers. Though the Continental Congress issued rules of conduct for privateers, it lacked the power to enforce those rules once vessels left port. And unlike the Continental army and navy, which in theory functioned within a strict hierarchy and answered to the Congress, privateers were often free to act as they saw fit once they received congressionally approved commissions. In short, Congress turned privateers loose to make war by any useful means necessary. Yet from the start, the unconventional qualities that made privateers so effective—partly the result

of the means through which they were commissioned and regulated
Founders—ultimately set them on a course that would make them ur
the nation's triumphant founding narrative. The Continental Congress's first
steps toward privateering were momentous indeed, not only for the war at
hand in 1775, but also for the future fight to establish its legacy.

On December 4, 1775, Elbridge Gerry, a member of the Massachusetts Provincial Congress, sat down to compose a letter to John Adams, who was
serving in the Second Continental Congress as a representative of Massachusetts. Gerry apprised his old friend, "A privateer is fitting out by Private
persons at New Port to mount 14 guns & I hope soon to give an account of
several by this Government and many more by Individuals." "The late Act &
Resolve for fitting out armed Vessels in this Colony, I apprehend will have
a good Effect," Gerry continued, "having already animated the Inhabitants
of the Seaports who were unable to command much property, to write in
Companies of twenty or thirty Men & go out in Boats of 8 or 10 Tons burthen which they call 'Spider Catchers.'" These spider catchers targeted British ships entering the harbors and ports of Massachusetts Bay, engaging in
some of colonists' first acts of official resistance on the seas.[3]

The "late Act & Resolve" to which Gerry referred was passed by the Provincial Congress on November 1, 1775; it called for "encouraging the Fixing
out of Armed Vessells, to defend the Sea Coast of America, and for Erect-
ing a Court to Try and Condemn all Vessells, that shall be found infesting
the same." Gerry, the composer of the act's preamble, justified this declaration by citing the abuses and actions taken by Great Britain and the rights
of the colonists of Massachusetts Bay to protect themselves from such encroachments, by force if necessary. The preamble highlighted the need for
maritime protection from the "career of Devastation & Slaughter ... [and
British ships and troops] infesting the Sea Coast with Armed Vessells, and
daily Endeavouring to distress the Inhabitants by burning their Towns, and
destroying their Dwellings." As such, Massachusetts was the first colony to
officially authorize privateers, followed two months later by New Hampshire, whose representatives voted to appoint a judge of the Court of Admiralty and granted a commission for the privateer *Enterprise* commanded by
Captain Daniel Jackson.[4]

Massachusetts and New Hampshire were following the lead of the Continental Congress. In November 1775, the Congress had received a letter

from George Washington inquiring about the procedure for disposing of vessels and goods the United Colonies had taken from the enemy. Washington informed John Hancock and the delegates that several captures had been made: "These Accidents, & Captures, point out the necessity of establishing proper Courts without loss of time for the decission of property, and the legallity of Seizures, otherwise I may be Involved in inextricable difficulties." A committee was appointed to investigate, and it informed the Congress on November 25, "The good people of these colonies, sensibly affected by the destruction of their property, and other unprovoked injuries, have at last determined to prevent as much as possible a repetition thereof, and to procure some reparation for the same, by fitting out armed vessels and ships of force." The committee also reported a rumor that commanders of British ships had received orders from His Majesty, King George III to attack seaport towns that might support rebellion.[5]

Falmouth was one of the first cities on the losing side of this order for death and destruction; James Warren informed Adams that the British "cannonad[ed] Falmouth, Casco Bay, and that Wallace, the pirate at Newport . . . insisted on the removal of the troops from Rhode Island, or he . . . [would] destroy Newport." In an attempt to address these attacks, the committee presented resolutions designating any vessel carrying any kind of provision or aid to the British as "liable to seizure . . . [and] confiscation." These determinations also ordered that any vessel cruising against the enemy must be commissioned by either the Continental Congress or by someone appointed in the United Colonies. Though the committee offered these resolutions, the Continental Congress did not immediately draw up commissions. Indeed, it would be another four months before the delegates wrote an official proclamation concerning privateering. While the Congress prevaricated and squabbled over questions of procedure, committee work, and protocols, the colonial governments took it upon themselves to protect their coasts and actively brought the fighting to British men-of-war and merchant ships.[6]

In Massachusetts, word spread of "a privateer . . . [that had] taken two prize schooners and a sloop, laden with fish and oil from Halifax for the besieged army in Boston." Another ship, the *Dolphin*, captured a sloop carrying "wood, potatoes, &c. which . . . [was] sold." Local newspapers printed the latest reports of privateer actions and captures. On December 11, 1775, the *Boston Gazette* informed its readers, "Several vessels loaded with fuel, provisions of various kinds &c. bound to Boston, have been carried into Salem and Beverly." The article ended with additional news: "Last week a privateer from Plymouth, took several small craft bound to Boston, with provision and fuel." Rhode Island's *Providence Gazette* reported, "A Ship from London, and a Brig from Cork, bound for Boston, were last Week taken at the Eastward by our Privateers." The ships' cargo included coal, vinegar, pickled cabbage, beef, butter, oats, tripe, peas, potatoes, tea, and more. These goods and supplies helped the colonists prepare for the impending conflict and motivated merchants and sailors to take to the seas.[7]

The Continental Congress was aware of privateering efforts in the colonies. President John Hancock received a letter from James Otis, dated November 11, 1775, conveying the following information: "Captain Robbins, from Ireland, was taken, on Tuesday last, by one of our boats, and carried into Beverly. This vessel is loaded with provisions." James Warren notified Samuel Adams, "Our Privateers more than answer our Expectations. since the Grand Prize I wrote Mr. [John] Adams of several other vessels [that] have been taken." On December 30, 1775, the Congress heard word of a privateer commanded by Captain Simeon Sellecks, who had recently taken a prize amounting to £1,500—a haul he ceded for use by the Continental Congress. Then in the early weeks of February, news arrived of a venture of several vessels that attempted to take arms and ammunition in New York.[8]

Yet not all privateering efforts were successful. Josiah Quincy wrote George Washington from Braintree, Massachusetts, "Since the sudden and unexpected burning of the Houses upon Dorchester Neck, I have been repeatedly and earnestly solicited by my distressed Friends and Neighbours, to make an humble Representation to your excellency, that, *our Habitations* are *equally* exposed to be destroyed by our Enemies." Despite the colonists' efforts of resistance, Quincy stated, "Two or a Dozen arm'd Cruisers . . . are constantly going out in Pursuit of our Privateers."[9]

In meetings of the Congress, John Adams ardently argued for action in the cause of independence and beyond: "There was no doubt, of our Ability to defend the Country, to support the War, and maintain our Independence. We had Men enough, our People were brave and every day improving in all the Exercises and Discipline of War." Adams wrote to James Warren inquiring about the number of "whalemen, Codfishers, and other Seamen belonging to . . . [the] Province" available for enlistment in either Continental or provincial ships, "or of privateer Adventurers in Case a Taste for Privateering and a maritime Warfare should prevail." Though Adams was greatly in favor of establishing a Continental navy, and he invested the majority of his maritime efforts in that direction, he also contended, "We ought immediately to give Permission to our Merchants to fit out Privateers and make reprisals on the Ennemy." The time to take action was the present, and the Congress's inability to make quick decisions frustrated Adams and exasperated the merchants whose vessels were constantly harassed, chased, and seized by British ships.[10]

Richard Smith, a representative from New Jersey, noted in his diary that Samuel Chase, a representative from Maryland, announced his intention on February 13, 1776, to "move tomorrow for Orders to Admiral Hopkins to seize all Ships of Great Britain and to recommend that all the Colonies . . . fit out Privateers." Alas, there is no mention of the notice in Smith's diary entry for February 14, nor is there reference to it in the Journal of the Continental Congress for that Wednesday. It seems Samuel Chase postponed bringing forth the issue, but this does not mean his fellow delegates were not aware of the matter. Josiah Bartlett, a representative from New Hampshire, wrote to John Langdon on February 21, "I am this day informed that a petition to the Congress, is Signing fast by the Inhabitants of this City, for Leave to fit out privateers . . . to indemnify them for the Losses they have Sustained." Bartlett confided in Langdon that he understood the Philadelphians' plight, remarking, "Indeed it seems very hard that Brittain is Seizing all american vessels and the americans are not permitted to return the Compliment." Bartlett also believed that other members of Congress had changed their minds on the privateering issue and would support a measure in favor of outfitting and commissioning ships.[11]

While the question of commissioning privateers remained tabled, Congress resolved on February 26, 1776—"after long debate"—that no vessel be allowed to sail to Great Britain, Ireland, or the British West Indies until the delegates so ordered. The following day, Pennsylvania representative Robert Morris presented letters from Bristol. These included a copy of the bill allowing for the seizure of all American ships—a "very long and cruel" bill, according to Richard Smith. On Friday, March 1, the petition from the citizens of Philadelphia, which Bartlett had heard rumored, was presented to the Continental Congress; the entreaty asked for the right of privateers and letters of marque to attack and seize ships of Great Britain and its domains. However, the delegates took no immediate action. A week later, Oliver Wolcott, a representative from Connecticut, wrote home to his wife, "A Petition from a Considerable Number of Merchants of this City lys before Congress Asking for Letters of Marke and Reprizal."[12]

In the New York Provincial Congress on Wednesday, March 13, 1776, the representatives considered the matter of privateering. Francis Lewis, a delegate from New York serving in the Continental Congress, had informed his constituency that "the subject of commissionating private ships of war and letters of marque, was in contemplation in Congress." He requested the representatives' opinion in order to speak for the feelings of the state. The Provincial Congress deemed "such a measure . . . very right and proper . . . and requested [Lewis] to inform the other Delegates of their opinion in this particular matter."[13]

That same day, while in committee in Philadelphia, Richard Smith noted in his diary that Chase presented "on the Petitions for allowing Privateers to cruize ag^t the English . . . a Sett of Propositions and Wyth a Preamble." Thomas Johnson of Maryland and Thomas Willing of Pennsylvania opposed the measure, while Edward Rutledge of South Carolina spoke out against privateers but supported letters of marque. Rutledge knew privateers were vessels specifically outfitted for cruising against the enemy and taking prizes, while letters of marque usually applied to armed merchant vessels that were carrying cargo to a destination and guns in case of an incident. Perhaps Rutledge favored letters of marque as an attempt to protect colonial shipping. Smith claimed that "many delegates were strongly for the Thing but the Determination was left till Tomorrow." Once again, Congress postponed deciding the question of privateers.[14]

While Congress continued to debate and postpone, postpone and debate, the colonists continued to outfit their own privateers, following the wartime tradition and attempting to protect their ports, homes, products, and profits. Major Joseph Ward shared good news with John Adams in a letter dated March 14, 1776, from camp at Roxbury. Notifying Adams, "Our Privateers continue successful," Ward also ventured, "Every appearance & the general state of things, affords, I think, an encouraging prospect; and if we persevere I cannot doubt but we shall soon see our Country in Freedom Peace & Safety." An article in the *Essex Journal* on March 15 announced the arrival of a prize "sent into Portsmouth by Capt. Manly . . . 240 tons burthen, having on board 6 double fortified four pounders, 2 swivels, and three barrels of powder." "Her cargo," the report noted, "consisted of 170 butts of porter, 11 packages of medicines, with large quantities of coal, sour krout, &c." The next day, Congress met in committee to address the question of privateers.[15]

The first day of discussion and debate included John Jay's proposition probing the process of determining friend from foe; meanwhile, Benjamin Franklin believed the first step should be a declaration of war. On Sunday, March 17, 1776—a day off for Congress—Oliver Wolcott informed Samuel Lyman of the petition and forecasted, "The report will doubtless be a general license for that purpose [to outfit privateers]. By the late pirating act, the Colonies are entirely cast out of the Kings protection, in an explicit manner. It behoves us therefore to take care of ourselves." The following day, with Congress meeting in committee again, delegates presented the following resolution: "Leave is to be given to commission Privateers and Letters of Marque to cruize on British Property." The vote was divided with New Hampshire, Massachusetts, Rhode Island, Connecticut, New York, Virginia, and North Carolina in favor and Pennsylvania and Maryland against. The other colonies were "not sufficiently represented" for a vote.[16]

The support of New Hampshire and Massachusetts is not surprising, as both colonies had started outfitting privateers months earlier. Ireland and other British dominions were excepted despite the protests of Chase and Smith, who believed it to be "very absurd to make War upon Part only of the Subjects and especially after the Irish Parl^t had declared decisively ag^t [the colonies]." The next step included reading through all articles on privateers and referring to a small committee to write a preamble, which was later read, revised, and "put . . . off till Tomorrow."[17]

The declaration on privateering was finalized on Saturday, March 23, 1776. The resolution began with a preamble of Great Britain's offenses, including "an unjust war" waged against the colonies and prosecuted by British troops "with their utmost vigour, and in a cruel manner." British soldiers were guilty of "exposing the helpless inhabitants to every misery . . . and not only urging savages to invade the country, but instigating negroes to murder their masters." The preamble also noted that the king had rejected overtures of peace and reconciliation from the United Colonies, Parliament had passed an act prohibiting all trade with inhabitants of the colonies, and the English government was contriving to strip the colonists of their liberties and rights under the English constitution. A few months later, the Declaration of Independence echoed these sentiments.[18]

The Congress, therefore, proclaimed five resolutions in regard to waging maritime war, including privateers and privateering ventures. First, inhabitants of the colonies could "fit out armed vessels to cruize on the enemies of these United Colonies." Second, any vessel belonging to inhabitants of Great Britain and taken by a commissioned vessel was deemed a lawful prize. As such, the ship should be condemned for the use of the owners of the armed vessel. Third, any vessel belonging to inhabitants of Great Britain taken by a vessel of war of the colonies was forfeited. After payment to the sailors, one-third of the profits from the ship's sale was for the officers, and two-thirds was reserved for the United Colonies' use. Fourth, the resolutions stated that any vessel outfitted at the expense of a colony should be

divided in a manner determined by the assembly of that colony after seamen and mariners received wages. Fifth, any vessel of Great Britain or vessel
carrying supplies for the British armies was lawful prize and should be condemned in a Court of Admiralty within the colony. The court should determine what charges and expenses came from the capture and trial; those expenses would be paid out of the prize money prior to the division of shares.[19]

That day, John Adams wrote to Brigadier General Horatio Gates, "You
will see by tomorrow's paper that, for the future, we are likely to wage
three-quarters of a war. The Continental ships-of-war, and the Provincial
ships-of-war, and letters of marque and privateers, are permitted to cruise on
British property wherever found on the ocean." When Major Joseph Ward
heard of the resolutions, he wrote Adams, "I take this to be a leading step to
Independency, anything short of which is trifling (in my humble opinion)
and unworthy of America." The day after the resolves in Congress, William
Whipple wrote to Josiah Bartlett, "We have gone on sine you left much as
Usual. have at last finish'd the Privateer Business after spending two days on
the Preamble. the whole was compleated Yesterday and order'd to be printed.
I shall forward them to you as soon as they come from the press." John Dun-
lap of Philadelphia printed a broadside with an extract from the minutes
of Congress, and the resolves appeared four days later in the *Pennsylvania
Gazette*.[20]

Upon learning that George Washington had forced British general Sir
William Howe and his troops to evacuate Boston, Adams later penned a
letter to Cotton Tufts urging him to find a way to defend Boston Harbor
against further British encroachments. "For as Privateering is begun and
Trade will be opened," Adams wrote, "nothing will draw into our Country so many Prizes, so much Trade and Wealth as an impregnable Harbour."
He was convinced that Boston Harbor would "become the Principal Rendezvous ... of Privateers ... as well as a Principal Mart." Robert Morris ap-
plauded the Congress in fitting out vessels, but he also asserted, "They have
stopped rather short of the Mark, by not including West India Property."[21]

Nine days later, the Continental Congress prepared commissions for privateers. The commission granted "license and authority" to the commander
of the ship. It also gave the name, burthen, tonnage, and armament of the
vessel, as well as the ownership and place of residence, followed by the number of men outfitting it. Commissions gave permission for craft "to attack,
seize and take the ships and other vessels belonging to the inhabitants of
Great Britain, or any of them, with their tackle, apparel, furniture, and ladings, on the high seas." Privateers were to bring captured vessels into the

Blank privateer commission granted by the Continental Congress.
Courtesy of the Library of Congress, Rare Book and Special Collections Division,
Continental Congress & Constitutional Convention Broadsides Collection.

nearest port, where the Court of Admiralty would determine their status as lawful prize. A bond also ensured proper conduct and practice by the crew of the ship. The commission was to "continue in force until the Congress . . . issue[ed] orders to the contrary." The next day, April 3, Congress resolved that blank commissions with the president's signature should be sent to the assemblies or committees of the colonies "to be by them filled up and delivered to the Persons intending to fit out such private Ships of War, for making Captures of British Vessels and Cargoes." The colonial governments would execute the bonds and then return them to Congress; a vessel weighing one hundred tons or less owed a $5,000 bond, and a vessel of greater weight owed a $10,000 dollar bond.[22]

That same day, Congress reviewed and accepted instructions to privateers drawn up in committee. The directives informed commanders that they could take any ship or vessel of Great Britain, including those carrying supplies, troops, or ammunition for the British armies. Vessels carrying people intending to settle in the colonies, or hauling supplies for the American cause, should pass by unmolested. Privateers would bring all prizes into the nearest port and before the appointed court. The commander or one of his officers had to bring the master, pilot, and one other significant person from every ship seized to the judge for interrogation, in addition to any and all important papers taken with the vessel.[23]

The captain was responsible for keeping any captured vessel intact until the court passed judgment and deemed the ship lawful prize. Cruel treatment or harassment of prisoners was not permitted; any offender would face punishment. Congress ordered each commander to keep the assembly apprised of captures and to send details, ships' logs, and intelligence when possible. Landsmen had to comprise one-third of the sailing contingent. Prisoners could not be ransomed, but they should be dealt with as the Congress or colonial assembly determined. Lastly, Congress informed the commander that he should follow any future instructions given. Should he disobey any of these instructions, his commission would be forfeit, and he would be responsible for any damages.[24]

John Hancock, president of the Continental Congress, sent letters to the various colonial assemblies informing them of the decision to commission and outfit privateers. In his missive to New Hampshire, Hancock informed the assembly, "While the British ministry are taking every step that cruelty and revenge can dictate for the destruction of American liberty, it is incumbent on these United Colonies to exert their utmost efforts to defeat them." He explained, "[Congress has taken action] in hopes of checking, in some degree, an evil which they cannot, at present, remove and acting on the same principle of self-preservation and retaliation which they have hitherto adopted." The letter included blank commissions, bonds, and instructions for the assemblies and conventions to fill. Congressionally approved privateering had officially begun in the United Colonies.[25]

* * *

The first step in outfitting a privateer consisted of finding financiers willing to foot the bill for such an adventurous investment. The war between Great Britain and the colonies significantly affected port towns and their inhabitants, particularly merchants and their trade operations. Some mercantile families were highly successful slavers prior to the outbreak of war. Due to their operations, they had the means—ships, captains and crews, and capital—to take on the risks and rewards of privateering. With the slave trade now temporarily closed to them, these tradesmen found themselves turning to privateering in an effort to keep their businesses running and make money besides. Rather than allow ships otherwise sitting in the harbor to decay from disuse, many merchants weighed their options and decided to take on this commercial enterprise. Entrepreneurs viewed the endeavor as an opportunity to invest their money with the potential for a large payout. Privateering could be very lucrative, but it was also a great gamble. Investors and owners had to be wary lest they lose their shirts in the process. The number of investors in privateers is difficult to pinpoint with accuracy, but privateering clearly affected a large swath of society from local sailors, carpenters, and shipbuilders to prominent merchants and even members of the Continental Congress.[26]

The Brown family of Providence, Rhode Island, was one such leading merchant clan who tried their luck on the high seas. Building upon a legacy of sailing, commercial enterprises, illegal trade during the Seven Years' War, and success in the slave trade, Nicholas and John Brown turned their attention to outfitting privateers following congressional authorization and commissioning of ships. In 1776, the Brown brothers sent three ships to sea: *Yankee Ranger*, *Diamond*, and *Sally*. Alongside the ship *Montgomery*, the *Yankee Ranger* brought in three prizes sailing from the West Indies laden "with rum, sugar, coffee, cotton, and oil." The sloop *Diamond*, commanded by Captain William Chace, sailed off in July under orders from John Brown to "proceade to Sea as Soon as possable"; *Diamond* was to "Crews off Burmudose, the Bay of Mantancis Cape St. Anthoneys or Crooked Island Passage." There is record of two prizes *Diamond* took during three different cruises, though more might have been lost to time. *Sally* sailed for three years; it took two known prizes. Privateering is estimated to have earned Rhode Island £300,000 sterling in the year 1776 alone. The Brown brothers continued investing in and outfitting ships for privateering ventures throughout the war. While they participated in other ventures to earn money, privateering turned necessary revenue, which allowed the brothers to reinvest and build their broader business over time.[27]

In Portsmouth, New Hampshire, John Langdon also turned his attention toward privateering. Langdon initially served as a representative in the Continental Congress. However, when he learned he could be appointed agent of prizes for the colony of New Hampshire, he was willing to resign his position in Congress in order to be eligible for the role. The Congress thought it unfitting for a representative to hold a lucrative office while serving constituents. Friend and fellow representative William Whipple tried to convince Langdon that giving up his seat was ill conceived, remarking, "Such a step would have an avaricious appearance, and on the other hand there cannot be a greater evidence of Patriotism than preferring the public good to one's private interest."[28]

Despite these pleas, Langdon happily resigned as representative and took up his new position as agent of prizes. Every time a commissioned privateer brought a prize into New Hampshire and the court condemned it, Langdon received part of the profit. Langdon began to see firsthand the possibilities of making money through privateering; thus, serving as agent only further piqued Langdon's interest in the Revolutionary privateering industry. In a short time, Langdon owned three vessels outright: *Amphitrite, Blosom*, and *Swan*. He was joint owner in three other vessels: *Portsmouth, Langdon*, and *Fair American*. By the end of the war, John Langdon was considered "a rich man," and one can assume privateering served him well.[29]

Robert Morris, the man historians call the financier of the American Revolution, also felt the pull of privateering. Initially against the practice, he thought it seemed ungentlemanly to take property from his business associates in Europe. Morris eventually changed his tune as he witnessed the effects of captures and raids on British shipping and on his own business. In December 1776, Morris wrote to William Bingham, "Having had several Vessells taken from me & otherways lost a great deal of my property by this War, I conceive myself perfectly justifiable in the Eyes of God & Man to seek what I have lost from those that have plundered me."[30]

Morris first invested as a silent partner with William Bingham in the ship *Retaliation*. Captained by George Ord, *Retaliation* brought in thirteen prizes on its first cruise and continued to sail the seas on the lookout for more enemy vessels. Morris was soon singing a different song altogether in his letters to Bingham, explaining, "My Scruples about Privateering are all done away. I have seen such Rapine, Plunder & Destruction ... that I join you in thinking it a Duty to oppose and distress so Merciless an Ennemy." Not all of Morris's ventures were successful—he mistakenly trusted Captain Coctiny de Prejent, who ended up taking his and Bingham's shares and investing them in his own undertakings. Nevertheless, Morris and Bingham did quite well during the Revolution. Morris also outfitted ships through his Secret Committee Network, investing in privateers sailing from Europe, as well as from New Orleans. Clearly, Morris did not agree with Congress that serving as a representative presented a conflict of interest with privateering ventures.[31]

Elias Hasket Derby hailed from a long-standing merchant family of Salem, Massachusetts. His father, Captain Richard Derby, shipped goods throughout the Atlantic, including wine, raisins, soap, handkerchiefs, naval stores, rum, rice, sugar, lumber, and fish. Elias Hasket Derby learned the ways of the trade early in life while keeping his father's books. He also took up commercial enterprises of his own throughout the Caribbean. When the war broke out, Derby owned "no less than seven sail of vessels" and property amounting to $50,000. In the early years of the Revolution, Derby suffered commercial losses that ultimately contributed to his decision to invest in privateer vessels. The first ship Derby outfitted, the sloop *Revenge*, brought in "four Jamaicamen, laden with 733 hogsheads of sugar, besides other cargo." Throughout the war, Derby continued equipping and investing in privateers. While the British navy interrupted the trade of Derby's prewar ventures, the American joined with fellow Salem merchants to continue their seagoing exploits via the arms and efforts of privateers.[32]

The Brown brothers, John Langdon, Robert Morris, and Elias Hasket Derby were part of a monied bloc encompassing numerous families and young entrepreneurial gentlemen looking to cash in on privateering. These included families like the Folsoms and the Salters of Portsmouth, and the Cabots of Beverly, as well as individuals like Hector McNeill, Isaac Sears, Stephen Cleveland, and Edward Norris. Before his infamous treachery, even Benedict Arnold sought an opportunity for himself and his friend to invest in privateers. Arnold wrote Thomas Mumford, "This will be delivered you by Colonel Samuel Griffin, a Gentleman of Character & property, who wishes to be concern'd in a Privateer." "I have engaged to take part of a Vessell if he can find one that will answer his purpose," Arnold explained, "& have told him, I believe you will gladly be concern'd, & will recommend a proper Person to Command her." Arnold might have cut his teeth in the land troops, but he was also well aware of the potential prizes afforded by privateer actions at sea.[33]

Yet not all privateering endeavors were financed by prominent families. Potential partners might be sought among acquaintances or strangers. Richard Ellis queried Governor Richard Caswell of North Carolina, "what part of the Brig," the privateer *Bellona*, "shall I charge you with[?]" "I do not think we can spare you more than 1/8 that will cost you £3000 or very near it," Ellis explained, "but you may have 1/16 or less if you choose it." Joseph Williams inquired of his friend William Coit whether he had "a mind to be Concer[n]d or not . . . in 2 Private[e]rs . . . fixing out of Boston, to Cruize after the Jama ships." Williams informed Coit that 1/16 of the ship's shares was still available, and they could be "equally Concd" in the investment. Jonathan Jackson, a merchant and manufacturer from Massachusetts, outfitted the privateer *Hibernia* along with several other investors, including John O'Brien, Joseph Marguand, Benjamin Jepson, George Searle, and Sarah Toppan, whose shares ranged from 18/48 to 3/48. Another option for pursuing potential investors was to place an advertisement in the local newspaper announcing, "WANTED IMMEDIATELY. A Number of Partners, to be concerned in a Vessel or Vessels, to cruise against our Enemies. . . . The Vessels will have Commissions from a neighbouring *Government*."[34]

Oftentimes, a merchant might be invested in multiple ships with a number of different partners, all in an attempt to gain the greatest profit from privateering operations since there was no guarantee of success. John Broome of Hartford, Connecticut, committed money to at least three vessels in the first half of 1777: the *Fairfield*, the *General Washington*, and the *Adams*. Amos Hubbil and Talmon Bradley were the other co-owners of the brigantine *Fairfield*. Broome's fellow owners of the brigantine *General Washington* included Isaac Sears, Samuel Broome, and Christopher Leffingwell, who hailed from Boston, Wethersfield, and Norwich, respectively. Both John and Samuel Broome were again investors in the sloop *Adams*, but additional owners for this vessel included Andrew Rowland and Jeremiah Platt. John Heard, a distiller from Ipswich, Massachusetts, paid David Pearce on at least two occasions—£181 16s. and £170 8s.—"on account of fixing out his third of an Eighth of the Ship General Starks." Once a venture was fully financed, investors needed to complete a number of tasks: either finding or building a ship, outfitting the vessel for sea, recruiting a crew, and applying for a commission from either the colonial or state government or the Continental Congress. Legally, a ship could not sail until all of these steps were complete.[35]

Investors had many options when choosing a ship for privateering operations. Merchants who owned vessels, like Nicholas and John Brown or Elias Hasket Derby, might choose a ship from their dock to outfit. In order to transform the craft into a privateer, carpenters cut out bulwarks for the cannon, created space in the hull for the magazine, enlarged quarters for the crew, and reinforced the decks. Another option was to purchase a ship. Newspapers often advertised auctions: "To Morrow at Twelve o'Clock Will be Sold . . . Schooner HOPE with her Appurtenances, mounting ten 6 Pounders . . . with all her Warlike Stores, Provisions, &c. as she now lays at Hubbard's Wharf, about 60 Tons burthen. Inventory may be seen in the Hands of RUSSELL & CLAP, Auctioneers." Joshua Huntington inquired of Thomas Mumford, "I wish you to inform me, if you know of a Small Privateer of 8 or So Guns to be Sold att N London or Elsewhere." Huntington explained, "I want to purchase one of that size." He also offered Mumford an opportunity to be concerned in the vessel if he was able to acquire one.[36]

However, with improvements in technology, investors sometimes found it worth their while to commission the building of a new ship with sharper lines and a narrower stern; such a craft would be faster than the bulky merchant ships of earlier years. Additionally, builders could outfit these swifter vessels with any type of rigging. There were a number of possibilities available to financiers and craftsmen, from snows to brigs, from sloops to schooners to brigantines. After choosing, buying, or building a ship, investors looked to outfitting it with all required appurtenances, most importantly powder and cannon.[37]

Before a privateer vessel could leave port, owners needed to ensure their ship was well stocked and well supplied, ready to engage the enemy and cruise for weeks and even months in search of prizes. Proprietors had to consider the number of men in their crew, the size of their cargo hold, and the length of their vessel's voyage when determining how much food and water a venture required. John Broome stored "fifty Barrils Pork & Twenty Barrils Beef, [and] Six Tons Bread" for the crew of eighty men serving aboard the privateer *Adams*. Jonathan Jackson purchased beef, pork, bread, and fish in July 1782 for his privateer *Hibernia*'s voyage. He procured water casks and paid for the "rinsing and cleansing" of old ones. He invested in gallons of West India rum. Jackson also attempted to acquire lemons—probably to keep scurvy at bay—but the "20 boxes . . . proved too bad." Furthermore, he employed a gunner, a boatbuilder, a sailmaker, a blacksmith, a joiner, a carpenter, and a cooper, all in efforts to fully arm and equip his privateer vessel. Jackson made sure the *Hibernia*'s compasses were repaired. He bought tar and turpentine, rigging and rope, tallow, nails, and cordwood.[38]

The smallest detail could not go unnoticed when equipping a privateer vessel. A gauging rod was necessary for ascertaining the capacity of a cask or barrel, and candles were vital to lighting the dark nights for a crew. A medicine chest provided cures for everyday bumps, bruises, and illnesses, but it might also prove invaluable following an engagement. Owners prepared their ships for action by furnishing them with cartridge paper, powder, match rope, flints, lead balls, swivel shot, round and chain shot, blunderbusses, muskets, cutlasses, swords, spears, pistols, and cannon. While owners hastened to complete the outfitting process, they paid wharfage fees and anxiously awaited the day when their vessels would finally set sail.[39]

Once a vessel was secured and being outfitted, sailors, seamen, and merchant mariners were sought to man the decks. Investors often used news-

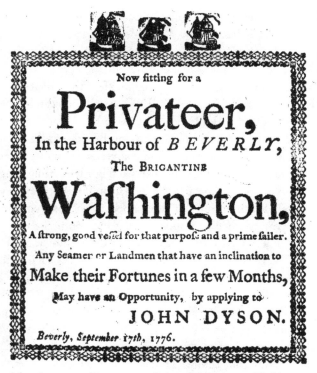

Now fitting for a

Privateer,

In the Harbour of *BEVERLY*,

The BRIGANTINE

Wafhington,

A ftrong, good veffel for that purpofe and a prime failer.

Any Seamer or Landmen that have an inclination to

Make their Fortunes in a few Months,

May have an Opportunity, by applying to

JOHN DYSON.

Beverly, September 17th, 1776.

Advertisement seeking men to sail aboard the privateer *Washington*.
Courtesy of American Antiquarian Society.

paper advertisements to recruit crew members. One such announcement called on "GENTLEMEN Volunteers, who are desirous of serving their Country and at the same Time of making Their Fortunes" to present themselves for the chance to serve on board the "Privateer Brig NANCY." The *Boston Gazette* printed a similar notice inviting "all brave Seamen and Marines, who have an inclination to serve their Country and make their Fortunes." These advertisements sometimes tried to convince would-be crew members of a voyage's potential either by noting that the captain was "a very capital Sailor," or by stating that the ship was "excellently well calculated for Attacks, Defence, and Pursuit." A notice might describe the sailors' opportunity "to make their Fortune with Ease & Pleasure, on Board [a] glorious Sloop." If all else failed, the advertisement might speak to a mariner's patriotism, greed, or love of drink. Once such announcement read as follows: "This therefore is to invite all those Jolly Fellows, who love their Country, and want to make their Fortunes at one Stroke, to repair immediately to the Rendezvous . . . where they will be received with a hearty Welcome by a Number of Brave Fellows there assembled, and treated with that excellent Liquor call'd GROG which is allow'd by all true Seamen, to be the LIQUOR OF LIFE."[40]

Other advertisements cut to the chase quickly: "The private arm'd SHIP, General Sullivan, THOMAS MANNING, Esq; Commander, Now ready for the Sea, will sail on a Ten Weeks Cruize in ten Days. Any Gentlemen Volunteers and others, who incline to enter on Board said Ship, must apply to the Commander at Portsmouth." Some advertisements were more artistic, like one depicting three ships and a stylized border surrounding this announcement: "Now fitting for a Privateer, In the Harbour of Beverly, The BRIGANTINE Washington, A strong, good vessel for that purpose and a prime sailer. Any Seamen or Landmen that have an inclination to Make their Fortunes in a few Months, May have an Opportunity, by applying to JOHN DYSON. Beverly, September 17th, 1776." Notices such as these were often printed several weeks in a row in an effort to garner as much attention and as many seamen as possible.[41]

Sailors and landsmen alike chose to sign up for service aboard privateers. Motivations varied from person to person. Some, such as John Whiting of New London, Connecticut, sought opportunity and money. In a letter from Martinique, Whiting told Thomas Harris, "But when I shall come to America God Only Knows for I have Left the Ship that I Proposed to come Home in." "I am now Going Out in a privateer with Cap[t] Hanton," Whiting explained, "and if I have success I shall be at home Before Spring But I do not proposed coming home Until I Git Some Cash." Whiting sought to literally cash in on the potential prizes captured by privateers. Thomas Painter initially fought on land in a company from Connecticut under Captain James Prentice. After experiencing the war firsthand in the Battle of New York, Painter decided he was "thoroughly sick of a Soldier's life." He decided if he "went into the War again," he would "have . . . [his] furniture conveyed without its being Slung at . . . [his] back." Ultimately, Painter did rejoin the war effort when he "determined to try . . . [his] fortune Privateering." Christopher Vail, originally from Southold, Long Island, also began his service in the land forces. He first fought under Captain John Hulbert of the Third Company of the Third Regiment of the New York Continental Army Line; ultimately, Vail "shipped himself on board the sloop Revenge" in January 1779. Unfortunately, Vail did not note the motivation for his shift in service in his postwar journal.[42]

Manpower was an essential component of successful sea ventures. The crew varied in size depending on the needs and dimensions of the ship. Some vessels sailed with twenty-five men, while others required over one hundred. Sailors Thomas Ruttenberg, Richmond Springer, John Darling, William Page, Edward Ryder, and Lewis Bosworth signed up to cruise for prizes. They fulfilled the respective positions of prize master, carpenter, boatswain, gunner, cook, and cooper aboard the privateer *Independence*. Captain Lemuel Brooks enlisted a crew of fifty on the privateer *Gamecock*, assisted by First Lieutenant John Gordon and Second Lieutenant Thomas Mudon. A letter of agency from the privateer *Terrible Creature* contained ninety-seven names. Though this legal brief revealed who served on the vessel, the text remained silent on the positions, hometowns, motivations, and loyalties of these men. All one can say is that the crew comprised at least those nearly one hundred men serving under Captain Robert Richardson on April 4, 1778, when the document was signed.[43]

Men were ready and able to serve aboard privateers, but the grit and details of their lives are often unknown. In addition, the racial makeup of privateer crews is not always apparent in the historical record. Archival material such as Thomas A. Biddle's cashbook from 1781 reveals that enslaved persons served on board privateers. Margaret Henderson was paid "for her Negro's share of prizes Fame & Betsey." Whether her slave received anything in exchange for his service—part of the prize, additional material incentives, or perhaps even an agreement of freedom—is not accounted for in Biddle's cashbook.[44]

Certainly, enslaved persons served aboard privateers, but for what purpose or at what cost? Articles of agreement for the sloop *Revenge*, signed in Stonington, Connecticut in 1777, listed "Dick Tuttle Negro" as a member of the crew, but did not note his enslaved or free status. One is left to wonder whether Tuttle was forced to sign up for the venture, or whether he volunteered of his own free will. Perhaps the promise of prize money lured Tuttle, or perhaps Tuttle's master signed him up in hopes of securing money to line his own pockets. Privateersman John Palmer noted the loss of an African American man on the vessel during a salvage operation in August 1778, declaring, "One of our Negro fellow Was Drownned." Yet again, the man's status and position aboard the ship are unclear. Privateer vessels were certainly places of racial diversity. The few surviving records provide a small glimpse into this world, but information about the day-to-day interactions among various seamen, the treatment of fellow sailors based on skin color or free status, or the racial divides that might or might not have existed is absent.[45]

The Massachusetts House of Representatives attempted to keep track of men available for service at sea. In December 1775, the house sent charts to local Committees of Safety and Committees of Correspondence for the purpose of recording "a Return of the Number of Men in said Town, who . . . [were] desirous of inlisting, and fit for Marines, or Seamen, on board of armed Vessels, either in the Pay of the Continent, or of this Colony, or of private Adventurers, who . . . [would] fix out said Vessels." Yet even these tallies contained merely numbers and names.[46]

Regardless of the scant information, recruiting efforts for privateers were quite successful, to the point where members of Congress received complaints about the lack of available sailors for Continental ships. William Vernon Sr. informed John Adams that Continental vessels were ready to sail "if it was possible to get Men for them," but he also remarked, "We shall never be able to accomplish [this task], unless some method is taken to prevent desertion, and a stopage of Private ships sailing, until our ships are Man'd." Vernon Sr. further bemoaned the privateers' behavior: "[Their] infamous practice of seduceing our Men to leave the ships, and taking them off at an out Port, with many other base methods, will make it impossible ever to get our ships, ready to sail in Force, or Fleets."[47]

The lure of serving on a privateer versus a Continental naval vessel was clear: better chance of a fruitful voyage and less stringent regulations. Compared to the months and years it often took Continental vessels to set forth from port, privateer vessels were prepared to sail in a matter of weeks, which allowed sailors the chance to earn money and immediately serve the cause. Moreover, there was flexibility in serving aboard a privateer. The time of service varied ranging from a three-month cruise to a five- or six-month cruise. Men such as Thomas Painter and Christopher Vail transitioned between land and sea service. In addition, the base pay for sailors aboard privateers could be twelve to sixteen dollars per month, whereas the navy only paid eight. Coupled with the possibility of prize money and an opportunity to get rich quickly, it is no wonder sailors swarmed onto privateers while leaving the Continental navy desperately seeking to outfit their ships.[48]

Yet the promise of payment was not the only motivating factor for privateers. Some were indeed Patriots, supporters of the call for and cause of independence. Others perhaps sought revenge against the long-standing British practice of impressment, which stripped them of their liberty and deprived them of opportunities to sail aboard other vessels. Some prospective seamen might have known of the horrendous conditions inflicted on prisoners sent to the ships lying just off New York City and joined up to pay back their foes in kind. Privateer crews were assembled of men from vari-

ous backgrounds with equally different motivations, but the one character-
istic they all shared was their desire to serve as a privateer.[49]

Once the crew was assembled, paper work detailing regulations for the
crew's behavior, division of shares, and designated occupations was written
and signed. Articles of agreement among the investors, captain, and crew
laid out specific rules and procedures. These guidelines informed the crew
that they could not leave the ship without written permission from the captain, and that mutiny would not be tolerated. Any guilty parties would be
forced to surrender portions of their prize money, and those caught steal-
ing from the ship would forfeit their earnings to the ship's owners. These
agreed-on measures were often written to protect the investors and their investment. However, a few of the articles sought to compensate and support
the crew. The owners would provide "cannon, Small-Arms, Cutlasses, Sufficient Ammunition, Provisions, a Medicine-Chest, and all other Necessaries"
to ensure the sailors' preparedness and safety. In addition, some provisions
meant that crew members could feel safe in the event of illness or injury: "If
any Person on board should lose a Limb in Action, he shall be entitled to receive one hundred . . . *Dollars* . . . and should any one lose his Life in Action,
his Share or Shares shall continue during the Cruize for the Benefit of his
Friends."[50]

Good behavior and heroic actions in battle were encouraged through the
use of "dead shares" that were "distributed among those whom the Captain
may think most deserving." Bad behavior, on the other hand, would not be
tolerated. If any sailor attempted to "mutiny, or raise any Disturbance on
board, Game, or Steal, or Imbezzel on, or of any prizes, whither at Sea or in
port," one vessel's articles declared, there would be severe ramifications. The
list of behaviors continued, if any sailor chose to "disobey his Officer, prove a
Coward, Desert his Quarters, absent himself" without permission for more
than twelve hours, "[or] exercise any Cruelty or inhumanity in Cold Blood;
he . . . forfeit[ed] his whole Share, or Shares to the Company." "And more
over," the articles continued, the sailor was "liable to Such Corporal punishment as the Committee . . . [thought] fit to inflict." In other words, men
would behave themselves on board the vessel or face the consequences.[51]

Articles of agreement also contained a list of crew members, as mentioned above, either by name or by occupation, and the number of shares accorded to each. Crews usually included a captain, first lieutenant, boatswain,
prize master, surgeon, clerk, cooper, gunner, carpenter, sail master, cook,
captain of marines, and seamen, among others. Crew members received a
particular number of shares based on their position, experience, and social

standing. Captains, usually gentlemen of society, received the greatest number, followed by the first lieutenant and master; seamen and cabin boys usually received the smallest number of shares, even so far as receiving half of one share. In the case of the *Independence*, the captain received eight shares, the first lieutenant five, and the doctor and the second lieutenant six each. The prize masters and the lieutenant of the marines and clerk took three shares each; the chief mate, boatswain, gunner, and carpenter, two and a half each; and the boatswain's mate and the gunner's mate, one and a half each. Other members of the crew received shares of two, one and three-quarters, or one and a half. The "common people" each received one share, while the boys garnered from one-half to three-quarters of a share. Overall, one-half of the total prize belonged to the owners, while the other half was distributed among the crew in the specified shares.[52]

When sailors signed on to a voyage, before leaving port, they often sought agents to handle their prize money and affairs while at sea; seamen "vest[ed] them with every Power to Act" on the sailors' behalf "in this their Character as Agents as the Law impower[ed] them to Act and to do in as full amply & Extensive a manner as . . . [was] Vested in all others Acting under the same Character." Privateersmen expected their agents to look out for incoming prizes and protect their shares. If necessary, agents distributed them to relatives such as Mrs. Perlindrick, who received ninety dollars "for one Quarter of a Share of all Prizes . . . Taken By the Brig America Capt[n] Nicholas Bartlet Commander on the account of [her] husband Richard Perlindrick." In February 1780, Rebecca Snowden "received of Mess[r] Cushing & White Thirty nine pound eighteen shillings on acc[t] [her] husband['s] Prize money capturd by Ship Minerva." Gideon Almy received £145 2s. 9d. from Cushing & White for his son John's service on the same vessel. The receipt noted Gideon Almy "rec[d] [the payment] of virtue of [his] Son's order."[53]

Beriah Brown served as agent for the privateer *General Mifflin*. In June and July 1779, he distributed prize money to Abigail Smith, Hannah Crossing, and Sarah Reynolds, all on behalf of their husbands who served on the vessel. Reynolds and Crossing each received thirty pounds, while Smith received "sixty pounds Eighteen Shillings Lawfull money." The Biddles of Philadelphia, Pennsylvania, a prominent, well-known family, distributed prize money for various privateer ventures. In October 1781, the Biddle cashbook noted a payment to Jacob Kechmle for Mathias Ambruster's "share in prizes Fame & Betsy" totaling six pounds, ten shillings, and three pence. Margaret Henderson, as noted above, collected six pounds, ten shillings, and threepence for "her negro's share" of the same prizes taken by the privateer *Holker*. The Biddles paid Thomas Duff twenty-six pounds, one shilling for "his son's shares in sundry prizes," also taken by the *Holker*. A few months later, John Winter, who served on the *Fair American*, received sixty-five pounds "for his sundry shares in prize Brig^n Ann." Entries throughout the Biddle cashbook note payments made "by Officers and Crew" of specific privateer vessels, whether to the sailors themselves, a parent, child, relative, or other relation.[54]

There were mariners who, in addition to naming an agent, also granted power of attorney before their departure. John Smith named his "trusty friend Mr. John Heard" as his "lawful attorney." The legal directive noted Heard's role "more especially to recieve all sum & sums of money & Effects that may be Coming to me for my Share of all Prizes & Effects that may be taken by the Privateer Fancy ... during the Cruize she now bound on & during any other cruize I may ship for." Sailors risked life and limb for the potential of a prize and the promise of payment if vessels were indeed captured. They needed assurances from agents, owners, and attorneys that their money would be delivered as promised.[55]

Once a sailor embarked on a privateering venture there was no guarantee he would return home to collect his share; appointing an agent or attorney or writing a will ensured the mariner's prize money would reach the right hands if he did not come back. John Shine feared he might not survive his voyage aboard the privateer *Marlborough*. On August 14, 1778, "being in good health of Body and through the Goodness of God of Sound disposing Mind and Memory," Shine made his "last will" settling of his "Estate both Real personal and mixt." Shine "recommended [his] Soul to Go[d]" and then granted his "body to the Earth or Sea to be buried in decent manner." Even privateers made certain to have their affairs in order prior to setting sail.[56]

Yet not all privateers could afford to wait to collect their prize money. Some sailors were strapped for cash prior to embarking on their appointed cruise, while others needed funds before a prize could be libeled in a Court of Admiralty. In these cases, mariners sold their shares to entrepreneurs and investors of a different kind. Some of these men paid a fixed sum to a sailor up front in hopes of securing a greater return on the holdings when the captured ships ultimately came into port and were deemed lawful prizes. John Heard, the same distiller from Ipswich, Massachusetts, noted above, made a practice of buying shares from privateers. Daniel Lakeman sold "one full

Quarter of a Share of all prizes and Effects that may be tacken by the privateer Brigg Called ye Benington" for thirty-three pounds. Heard purchased
from carpenter Abraham Perkins one-half a share, also for the prizes taken
by the *Benington*, for the sum of seventy pounds. Perkins received more than
double the money for twice the interest Lakeman sold to Heard. Perhaps, in
this case, Perkins drove a harder bargain for his portion of a share. Heard di-
versified his portfolio, buying shares from different sailors on various privateer ventures. He acquired one-quarter of a share each from Jonathan Wells,
Thomas Spiller, John Smith, and William Smith, all of whom were shipping out on the privateer *Black Prince* in the summer of 1778. He also bought
stakes in the privateer *Fair Play* in December 1777 and the *Frankling* in April
1781, among others.[57]

Heard might have been a distiller by trade, but in the course of the war
he was also an astute investor in privateer shares. On occasion, he varied his
portfolio further by exchanging or trading claims from one privateer venture
for those in another. Heard "changed" one-quarter of a share in the *General
Arnold* and one-quarter of a share in the *Pallas* "for 1/2 a share in . . . Civil
Usage." He was sure to have several irons in the fire at any one time. Privateering was a risky business. By acquiring stakes in multiple privateer vessels, Heard increased his chances of securing money and returns from a
prize or prizes. Even privateers themselves traded shares. John Wait Junior, a
sailor aboard the *Pilgrim*, did "grant sell and convey to Robert Farley . . . one
Quarter of one full share in all prizes goods & Effects that may be taken
by s^d Ship" in exchange for one-quarter of a share in the ship *Franklin* "on
board of which the s^d Farley . . . Shipped himself." In other words, Wait and
Farley each sailed on a separate vessel but acquired the potential to profit
from the cruise of the other as well. They thus doubled their chance of a return on their privateering efforts.[58]

Though sailors and businessmen made transactions prior to a ship's departure, privateers also sold their shares upon their return to port, sometimes before a prize vessel was libeled in court. In these instances, seafarers
received cash in hand for their efforts far sooner than if they waited for the
next Court of Admiralty session or for the cargo to be sold at auction. Not
surprisingly, John Heard participated in these dealings as well. He paid David Ross £300 for "one quarter of a Share of the Effects Condemned which
came in the Brig Dillon," a vessel "taken by John Lee & crew of . . . prise
Fanny or Fancy." John Shearman bought one sailor's "part & Share of the
Prize Brig^t Brunett Prize to the Genl Mifflin Capt George W^t Babcock

Command for the value of Three Hundred Dollars." Committing money to a known prize and its cargo was still a gamble, but savvy investors would know what those vessels carried in their holds and hoped for high prices at auction.[59]

Privateers were not always the most reliable investment opportunity. Therefore, entrepreneurs such as John Heard, had to take care when purchasing shares from potentially undependable or unknown sailors. In May 1777, Joshua Fisher signed on as surgeon aboard the privateer *Fancy* commanded by Captain John Lee. Fisher entered into an agreement with John Heard, in which the doctor sold one full share to the distiller for sixty pounds. Heard might have recently met Fisher, or perhaps he had other reasons to doubt the surgeon's dedication to the venture, but whatever the cause, the newly minted privateer made further stipulations. Fisher promised that if for some reason he was not "entitled to any Share in ye Prizes aforesaid by reason of" his "not going on said Cruize or by reason of any Default, Neglect, or Misconduct" on his own account, he would "repay ... the sum of sixty pounds." He further pledged to pay for any additional costs Heard might accrue "in consequence of this Deed." A fellow privateer aboard the *Fancy* also wanted to sell shares to John Heard. Samuel Harris presented a note from Captain John Lee that stated, "[The bearer] wantes to sale Part of a Share __ who Ever Purchases any Parte I stan accountable for the said man." Heard ultimately purchased one-third of a share from Harris for fifty-one dollars. Either the word of Captain John Lee stood for something, or Heard was at least willing to take the risk.[60]

Choosing a captain to lead a privateering venture was a crucial decision. The captain could single-handedly determine the success or failure of a cruise. Investors sought men who had seafaring experience and who came highly recommended. Isaac and Thorowgood Smith informed Robert Morris they "had the highest opinion" of Captain Chadwick. They felt assured "not only of his good conduct as a Seaman, but of him as a man to be depended on for his greatfull disposition." Captains were often lured away from other positions, as was the case with Lieutenant James Campbell, who was serving in the provincial militia when he was approached. Campbell informed his fellow officers, "Several gentlemen here are desirous to send me out in a privateer from this place.... I hope to have the Testimony of my Brother officers that I served with Vigilance and attention, since my appointment." The lieutenant assured his comrades that he would not be leaving the land force "but [for] the hopes of being more usefull in another Department." The chance for glory and profit might also have crossed Campbell's mind as he accepted his new position at the helm of the schooner *Enterprize*.[61]

Before weighing anchor and setting sail, investors had to obtain a commission, as described above, either from the colonial government or from the Continental Congress. Investors presented a petition on behalf of their captain, noting his position as "a proper and suitable Person to command" and thus asking the local council "to commission him for that purpose." Part of the process included a signed agreement and payment of a bond. Captain Robert Palmer of Stonington, Connecticut, commanded the sloop *Nancy*, owned by Jabez and Erastus Perkins. The three men signed a bond "in the sum of five Thousand Spanish Milled Dollars." This pledge affirmed the stipulations of the granted commission. Captain Robert Palmer would act according to his instructions and would "not exceed or transgress the Powers and Authorities . . . contained in the said Commission." If Palmer failed to conduct himself and his crew in a befitting manner, he would be held accountable and forced to "make Reparation for all Damages sustained by any Misconduct or unwarrantable Proceedings of Himself or the Officers or Crew of the said Sloop Nancy."[62]

If the investors could not appear in person before the council, they often found a proxy to stand in their stead. Jonathan Titcomb wrote Benjamin Greenleaf, explaining, "We are engaged in fixing out Captain Peter Roberts, the bearer, in a small sloop, for a privateer, and have to ask the favour of you to assist him in procuring a commission. . . . We are all pretty much engaged in privateers, powder vessels, recruits, &c., and cannot . . . come down." Titcomb assured Greenleaf that if he stood by Captain Roberts as a bondsman, Titcomb and the other seven investors "would stand between [the Captain] and harm, as though [their] names, were down instead of [his], in the bond." The Council of Massachusetts issued a commission to Captain Peter Roberts a few days later, noting, "We have thought fit to Commission you for the purpose afores'd & do accordingly by these presents give you the said Peter Roberts full power . . . to sail in the said Vessel on the seas attack take & bring into any Port in this Colony all armed & other Vessels which shall be found making unlawfull invasions attacks or depredations."[63]

Some governments and governors received "so many applications for Commissions for privateers" that they requested more from the Continental Congress. Governor William Livingston implored, "I wish to be furnished with a new Supply as soon as possible." William Greene, governor of Rhode Island, asked Governor Jonathan Trumbull of neighboring Connecticut "for the Loan of Eight" commissions. Privateering was in full swing, but those involved understood that a commission provided the legitimacy and authority necessary for sailors to embark on their journey. They could not proceed without one. Once the investors and captain obtained a commission and posted bond, the ship could make ready to set sail.[64]

The process by which the colonial governments adopted privateering and the colonists themselves actively sought to outfit privateers was the first step taken toward maritime engagement within the greater Atlantic World during the American Revolution. The practice of privateering was a familiar one rooted in long-standing traditions. Maritime towns quickly employed their sailors, laborers, and businessmen in this age-old calling. Merchants modified their vessels for war, investors put money into outfitting ventures, sailors signed on for profit, pride, revenge, patriotism, or a myriad of other factors, entrepreneurs bought and traded shares, and governments signed commissions before the Declaration of Independence was even up for discussion before the Continental Congress. Privateers would bring the conflict to the doorsteps of the British, French, and Spanish. In addition, they would infest the waters of the Caribbean with legally sanctioned vessels seeking prizes, profit, and supplies for the cause. When the Continental Congress decided to commission captains and their ships, they set off a chain reaction felt across the seas and throughout the colonies.

CHAPTER 2

A Privateering We Will Go

A grey fin emerged from the blue-grey waters surrounding the privateer ship *Pilgrim*. Several harpoons sped through the air and found
their target: a large shark. Without delay, a yawl was lowered into
the ocean, and six men hurried off in pursuit of their quarry. There was never
a dull day in the life of a privateer.[1]

A mile out from the ship, the sailors overtook their prey and let loose another harpoon, this one outfitted with a warp to reel in the shark. Yet they
failed to take into account the strength of their target and the length of the
warp. The shark dove for the depths of the sea, taking the harpoon and the
attached line with it. Suddenly, the cord wrapped itself around Mr. Bunker's leg and pulled him overboard. Grasping the side of the boat in an effort to save his life, Mr. Bunker tilted the yawl. Ocean water rushed into the
small vessel. If someone did not act quickly, the yawl would sink, and the
six privateers would meet their deaths at the bottom of the ocean. By some
twist of fate, the line unexpectedly snapped, saving Mr. Bunker. The crew of
six swiftly made their way back to the *Pilgrim*, leaving the shark far behind.
Alas, Mr. Bunker's leg was badly injured, but the rest of his mates reveled in
their unexpected adventure.[2]

The *Pilgrim* and its crew ranged far and wide, crisscrossing the waters
of the Atlantic. Some days were bright and sunny, while others featured
grey clouds filled with rain. The maritime environment could wreak havoc
on a vessel and affect the success or failure of a voyage. Privateers repaired
their ships, fished, and acquired supplies while onshore. They found numer-

ous ways to keep boredom at bay, and they exchanged important information with other privateers and mariners while exploring various ports of call throughout the Atlantic World. Privateers practiced their own rituals and traditions, grappling with the role of religion and the ever-present threat of death at sea. As the ordeal of Mr. Bunker and the shark illustrates, life on the briny blue was unpredictable and dangerous even in the best of circumstances. For sailors serving aboard privateering vessels, a venture could yield fame and fortune, but it might also end in an unpleasant demise beneath the waves.

Sailors aboard these commissioned vessels navigated some of the same waters as the Continental navy and fought the same British foe as the Continental army. Yet privateers' exploits in the Atlantic World—a unique environment with its own set of political, social, and cultural circumstances—created a very different wartime experience. Daily occurrences on the open waters and in foreign ports obliged privateers to make their own rules and regulations. Stopovers during their crossings allowed these sailors to interact with new cultures and peoples while exploring various islands and cities. Upon returning home, however, these same privateers often confronted a public unwilling or unable to understand those Atlantic interactions within the narrow confines of the thirteen colonies amidst revolution. The war privateers experienced was simply too different from the one colonists lived at home. It was a war complicated by interactions with exotic peoples and customs that triggered matters of diplomacy and political maneuvering unfamiliar to many colonists. The story of privateers reflects both a world and a war beyond the typically proscribed boundaries of the American Revolution. Making a career on the ocean was not for the faint of heart, but if one survived to tell the tale, oh, what a story it could be.

❊⬩❁◎◯◎◯❁⬩❊

The first skill necessary for a sailor's success was the acquisition of sea legs. For a number of mariners setting out on privateers, sailing the oceans was a way of life to which they were well accustomed. Even the seasoned sailor, though, might suffer from the rhythms of the whitecaps. John Palmer noted during his cruise in January 1777, "Most all hand See Sick on Board" the *Revenge*. Luckily, after a few days, "all Hand Rather Better." For newcomers, adjusting to ship life could be far more challenging. Solomon Drowne discovered this during his service on the sloop *Hope* of Rhode Island; it was the surgeon's first—and last—time embarking on a privateer. On the ship's first day out to sea, Drowne wrote in his journal, "I begin to be excessively seasick." The illness he experienced was "indeed enough to depress the spirits even of the brave." The following day, Drowne continued feeling "excessive sickness"; on the third day, he was "still lying by." A tempest with a violent gale surrounded the *Hope* on its fourth day out and relieved Solomon Drowne of his ill feelings, as he was more concerned with surviving the storm than relieving the ache in his stomach. Drowne had found his sea legs thanks to the roiling waves.[3]

The weather created its own problems for privateers. The ocean and its environs could be a dangerous and deadly place for inexperienced and experienced sailors alike. Drowne and his mates found themselves buffeted by a raging squall that carried away some of their crane irons and threatened to take the mast as well. Describing the storm as "short and energetic—grand and forcive," Drowne further remarked, "Our ears are assailed by its rude howling through the Cordage—our vessel tossed upon the foaming surges." After the rains subsided, he wrote in awe, "GOD of Nature! who that sees thy greatness on the wide extended Ocean, but must be filled with Adoration; and feel a submission of heart to thy eternal orders."[4]

Storms could cause great damage to a ship. The *Oliver Cromwell* of New London, Connecticut, lost its mainmast, foremast, and mizzenmast as "the Wind Continued verry hard," and all aboard hoped "that it would not Blow harder, but it Continued Harder till After Midnight About one oClock it Seemd to Blow in whirlwinds." Timothy Boardman, the log keeper aboard the *Oliver Cromwell*, described riding out the storm and waiting for a break in the weather so repairs could begin. In the summer of 1778, the *Revenge* of Stonington, Connecticut, was caught in a squall that produced "vary heavy thunder and Sharpe Lighning." Aboard a privateer in late November 1777, Thomas Painter related how the ship was "struck with lightning and one man killed and many more were wounded." "All at once I heard (as I supposed,) one of the guns Discharged," Painter wrote, "while all those who were standing before me . . . seemed to be stunned, so as nearly to fall backward." "The lightning came down the mast, and went directly in the hole," where many crew members had sought shelter from the "palling of the storm." Painter himself was surprised by the presence of lightning, for it was "so late in the season, and a cold stormy day, with rain and snow, and there being no thunder."[5]

Christopher Vail recalled how the sloop *Revenge*, in early 1779, was "knockt about in several gales of wind" that kept the vessel from making any captures. During a cruise on the privateer *Fortune* in April 1781, Zuriel Waterman of Rhode Island noted, "Rainy and high wind from the SE." Only a day out to sea, *Fortune* "had much water in . . . [the] hold; the pump worked very bad," causing the ship to return to shore for repairs. Oftentimes, the weather alone could determine the fate of a voyage.[6]

Raging waters and thrashing storms were only a few of the difficulties the environment offered. A seemingly simple fog could keep a ship from contacting another vessel; such was the case with the *Pilgrim* of Beverly, Massachusetts. Josiah Bartlett described the situation in the craft's logbook: "At day light . . . discovered the Sail to be a large Ship. . . . The weather being very hazy & the Wind blowing a Gale, we could make no particular discoveries. . . . The Severity of the Weather prevented our speaking [to] her." In northern latitudes, the presence of ice in the waters could make navigation difficult and dangerous. The *Pilgrim* "passed a very large Body of Ice, about 2 Miles under . . . [its] lee," on June 10, 1782, off the coast of Newfoundland; "it was judged to be 2 or 3 miles in length & as high as [the] Mast head." On May 26, 1781, Zuriel Waterman and the *Fortune* were sailing off the coast of Isle St. Jean—now known as Prince Edward Island—when "finding the passage very full of ice, thought [it] not safe to proceed"; the crew "altered [the ship's] course in order to sail between the main and Isle St. Jean."[7]

In the winter months as the temperatures dropped, sailors woke up to "about an inch deep" of snow on deck. Even in August, when warm temperatures were expected, John Palmer lamented that it was "coald for the time of year." The sun did shine, though, and there were days sailing on "a smooth sea" with "fresh breezes"; other days were "fair, moderate and pleasant." Nighttime might afford a glimpse at a cloudless, starry sky or "a Very Pleasant moon [and] Shiny Night." Solomon Drowne noted in his journal, "How cheering are the beams of the sun. . . . Those surly billows that erewhile buffeted us to and fro, and would suffer us no peace, are composed as the infant that has bawled itself to rest."[8]

On those brighter days after the storms, when the deck was dry and the sky was clear, sailors went about making necessary repairs to the ship, fixing damage either from the squalls or from encounters with enemy vessels. After one such martial engagement in May 1781, the *Pilgrim* had "all hands Employed, in unbending . . . Wounded Sails, bending others, and repairing rigging." Captain Post of the *Revenge* took advantage of "fine weather" when he called "all hands . . . to Quarter and Exersisd the Canon and Small arms" for an hour. The *Oliver Cromwell* of Beverly, Massachusetts, took advantage of "fair and moderate Winds [and] Hove the Brig upon a Kreen to Cleen &

tallow her Bottom, being very foul." Over the course of two days, the crew of
the privateer *Providence* "hove down, cleaned and graved one side of the vessel . . . [then] hove down, cleaned and graved the other side of the vessel."[9]

Barnacles attached to the hull created problems for privateers. These en-
crusters could multiply quickly, creating a canvas of overlapping shells on
the ship. Crews attempted to remove these nuisances during cleaning so as
to make the craft swifter while cutting through the waters. Sea worms posed
another threat to the vessel by affixing themselves to the ship and eating
their way through the wood. Left unchecked, sea worms could gorge themselves on a vessel and send it back into port permanently.[10]

Sometimes, damage was too great for repairs at sea, and the ship pulled
into the nearest port. Facing a precarious situation, the *Pilgrim* "came to an
Anchor in Man of war Bay in the Island of Tobago, for the purpose of repairing . . . damages." In port at Pointe-à-Pitre, Guadeloupe, on March 22,
1777, "at 6 am all hands" aboard the privateer *Revenge* were set "to Work to
Scraping and Graving the Sloope." They continued until seven o'clock that
evening, when they "finished her Both Sides." Captain Jonathan Haraden of
the *General Pickering* set his crew to work in the first week of February 1779
while anchored in St. Pierre's Bay; "heeled our Vessell & Scrubed her starboard & Boot Top . . . scrubed her Larboard side & Boot top & struck the
Mizen Top Sail Yard & Mast . . . stript our Main Mast and Hoisted it out,"
he recounted. Haraden's carpenter, meanwhile, went onshore to work on
"making a New Mast," which was finally "Hoisted in" on February 8.[11]

In July 1781, the *Pilgrim* pulled into the harbor of Brest, France, where
sailors "hauled the Ship on the Ways, for Coppering." Two days later, the
crew "removed the Ship from the Ways and began to fit her for Sea—50
men were six hours employed in Coppering the Ship, compleatly." Applying copper sheathing to the hull of a ship protected the exterior from various
types of damage, but this expensive option was not available to many privateering vessels. Privateers were often far from their home ports when circumstances left the ship in dire straits. The *Pilgrim* found aid in two different ports of the Atlantic World: Man of War Bay in Tobago, and the harbor
of Brest, France. American ships most likely could not have survived without this foreign assistance—assistance that contributed to the struggle and
thus made the war an Atlantic World conflict. Privateer actions were not
simply taking place along the coast of the American colonies; rather, these
vessels took the action of the war across the Atlantic. The ocean itself was
part of the war.[12]

While the maritime environment wreaked havoc and caused logistical problems for cruises, the deep sea also provided an ample supply of food and sustenance for sailors who might spend weeks or months out on the open water. While sailing near the coast of Ireland, the *Pilgrim* "found . . . [itself] not more than 3 or 4 Miles from the Land, which appeared very hilly and uncultivated. Being quite Calm . . . [they] hove too, and caught several Fish, which were very acceptable." John Palmer and his mates were quite successful during a 1777 cruise on the *Revenge*. They harvested a "large turtle," "18 Codfish," and "a Dolfin" from the sea. Aboard the *Hope*, Solomon Drowne and his fellow mates, caught "a Herring-Hog," which offered "a fine Breakfast, and dinner for the whole crew." The following day, they got "a fishing line under way" and reeled in "a Hake and a few Dog-Fish." Crews also netted "a large quantity of black-Fish" and "plenty of Cod." However, not all attempts at fishing produced positive results; sometimes sailors "threw [their] lines out for Fish, but caught none." During a cruise in June 1781, the *Fortune* "caught [a] great many lobsters" and found "clams very plenty." During the third cruise of the *Oliver Cromwell* of New London, on August 12, 1778, "at Six [in the] Afternoon [the sailors] Caught a Great Turtle which was Kook^d the Next Day for the Entertainment of the Gentlemen of the Fleet." Privateers used—and ate—any opportunity the sea would offer.[13]

The vast waters could not provide all foods and supplies necessary for a cruise, however. Privateer ships were stocked at the beginning of a voyage with victuals including bread, beef, pork, peas, potatoes, flour, molasses, and rum. Live animals were often brought on board as well; one ship had a "half dozen sheep and goats and two coops of fowls and ducks." Depending on the size of a crew, provisions could last days, weeks, or months, but oftentimes the crew needed to find ways to supplement or restock the initial supply. While "anchored under the sand," Zuriel Waterman went ashore with his comrades "to get wood and water [but] found no good watering place." The crew might not have found drinking water, but they discovered "plenty of strawberry vines in blossom." At another point onshore, they "wooded and watered . . . [and] got plenty of gooseberries, there being also strawberries, raspberries, green peas." While replenishing wood and water at Gabarus Bay, men of the *Pilgrim* "upon a Bank near the Shore . . . found Strawberries in their bloom, in the greatest abundance, which were very acceptable, particularly to [the] Sick." Fresh fruit provided an important supplement for sailors' diets; sources of vitamin C were vital for preventing diseases such as scurvy. The *Oliver Cromwell* of Beverly stocked up on "water & wood to proceed" on its cruise while in Bilbao, Spain. During a stopover at St. Pierre's Bay, the *General Pickering* "Rec'd a Bar¹ Pork & a Tierce of Rum . . . 10 Hhdˢ Coffee from the Shore and 2 Hhdˢ of Dry Goods."[14]

Though privateer ships were surrounded by water during their ventures, it was virtually never in a form acceptable to drink. Thus, finding sources of fresh water was crucial. Captain Haraden of the *General Pickering* had "4 Hands on Shore filling Water." The next day, the crew stowed the water in the hold and "brought 31 hhdˢ Water" on board. While ashore in Pointe-à-Pitre, John Palmer reported, "[I took] 4 More With me and Went after Water about 3 miles up the River." For the next two days, Palmer "went after Water again" in an attempt to fully supply the *Revenge*. While anchored close to shore, the *Marlborough* was approached by "5 canoes with fruit. Which [the crew] Bought of them." Sometimes, sailors participated in illegal activities to obtain food. While near land, men from the privateer *Rambler* "at night . . . [went] ashore . . . [to] take geese and hogs from the inhabitants, unknown to the officers." The captain did not condone such actions, but many sailors were happy for a change in fare.[15]

While storms at sea, repairs, fishing, and scavenging required a significant share of their time, sailors often found themselves with free moments aboard ship and during stops in port. While at sea, ships encountered creatures in addition to the barnacles and sea worms that besieged their hulls and the fish mariners caught. Solomon Drowne witnessed "a large number of Whale of the Spermaceti Kind playing round." He noted, "The Father of the Universe has given them the expanded Ocean for the wide Scene of their happiness." The crew of the *Pilgrim* "saw great numbers of Whales in the course of the day, some of them came so near as to strike . . . [the] Ship." John Palmer, too, recorded seeing "a Large Scool of Whailse about three miles" off the *Revenge*.[16]

Zuriel Waterman was impressed with a dolphin, calling it "the beautifullest fish that ever I saw, long and slender with a forked tail, of a beautiful variegated green mixed with blue spots." After witnessing "flying fish skipping over the water," Waterman composed a poem:

> The flying fish now skips o'er the sea
> Pursued by dolphin with speed does flee;
> But sometimes as he rises in the air,
> The birds, they see him and attack him there.
> Danger now attacks him on ev'ry side;
> The fear of both at once, his cares divide.

Not only was Waterman a man of the seas, but it seems he had a knack for poetry.[17]

Entertainment aboard ship was not limited to observing creatures from the sea. During "a pleasant moon-light evening," Solomon Drowne enjoyed the ocean air while "walking the Quarter Deck" to pass the time. A "fair, warm, and pleasant" October day aboard the *Providence* dawned as the men "played whackets upon the quarterdeck, and the hands played hot cockles." A few days later, as evening fell, the "moon almost full shone very bright. The hands danc'd on Main Deck to the fife." While on watch during "a very heavy Squall," John Palmer and his comrades "had a fine Wetting frollick." When foul weather kept the men of the *Fortune* belowdecks, they engaged in an age-old pastime; they "finished every drop of rum aboard."[18]

Sailors found myriad ways to engineer their own entertainments. The arrival of "a pretty bird caught on board: the Carolina red bird," broke up a long day on the *Hope*. Sailors on the *Rambler* watched as a hawk "caught a sparrow that had taken refuge aboard" the ship. Mr. Maly, a mate of Zuriel Waterman during a cruise on the *Hibernia*, was "employed in making [a] cot for [a] dog." There were "4 dogs" on the venture initially, but they "lost one dog overboard" during the cruise.[19]

During an encounter with a fellow American privateer, Josiah Bartlett and Captain Robinson of the *Pilgrim* "dined & spent the afternoon on board the *Scourge*." The following day, Captain Parker and Doctor Spooner of the *Scourge* "dined & spent the afternoon on board [Bartlett's] Ship." Captain Leeds of the *Revenue* dined with Captain Post on board the *Revenge* in August 1778. The crew "kild a pig and Dress'd it" for the occasion. New faces and places offered a much-welcomed change of pace after long days at sea.[20]

When a vessel pulled into port to resupply, undergo repairs, or deliver a prize, sailors also had the opportunity to enjoy visits onshore and the entertainments various towns and cities offered. Josiah Bartlett went ashore in Portsmouth on April 20, 1781, where he "dined with Capt Nicholls ... [and] at Evening attended a Ball. The appearance and behaviour of the Ladies could not fail to give satisfaction, and the general politeness with which ... [they] were treated, impressed" the sailor. Bartlett often made use of his time ashore to visit local amusements, as noted in the log he kept on the *Pilgrim*. While anchored in the port of Brest, France, Bartlett and his mates attended "a Fair which lasted a Week, and where every kind of Merchandise might be purchased." Brest also offered the chance to take in a show; Bartlett "very frequently attended the Plays at the Theater." His opinion of the dramas in Brest was that they "afforded much more amusements

y^n any other of the public diversions. The Scenery, and Dress of the Actors were good, and always adapted to the peices performed, which in general were well chosen." Bartlett continued his patronage of the arts when the *Pilgrim* made a stop in St. Pierre, on the island of Martinique in the Caribbean. He noted in his log, "There are no other public amusements then the plays, which I frequented, with no other advantage then pleasing the Eye with the elegance of Dress, and artificial beauty—too common among the Ladies." Apparently, Bartlett was not nearly as impressed with the theatrical offerings in St. Pierre as he was with those in Brest.[21]

During a stop on the coast of Spain, one crew member from the *Oliver Cromwell* of Beverly "went up to Bilboa Town," where he purchased a "waistcoast [and] Breeches." Sailors often ventured into town to buy personal supplies, such as "trowsers" or various other "Sundry Things." Some men "spent the day very cheerfully in seeing Fashions," while others "walked on Shore & diverted [themselves] in innocent Company & Amusement." When Zuriel Waterman and the crew of the *Fortune* "came to anchor before Narrowshock," they "went ashore and had a dance." John Palmer and some of his fellow sailors went "a Shoar for to See thee Negros Dansing for this Was a Day of frollick With the Negros" in Pointe-à-Pitre. Yet spending too much time anchored or in port could pose potential problems, as Captain James Godfrey of the *Providence* learned during a voyage in the fall of 1779. A majority of the crew, including the "1st lieutenant, master's mate, carpenter, gunner, and captain of marines," disembarked the ship and set off for the shoreline, where they "got very high." The crew then "set the beach afire" whereupon the "captain went ashore to put it out." Captain Godfrey was certainly not pleased, but Waterman noted in his journal that the crew "came off most of them pretty happy."[22]

Visits also provided captains and their crews with information and updates about other vessels and life back home. While exploring the island of Guadeloupe, Zuriel Waterman "got certain intelligence that the *Hannibal*, privateer, was overset in a squall bound from New York to the West Indies." Josiah Bartlett of the *Pilgrim* accompanied his commander, Captain Joseph Robinson, ashore in St. Pierre. There the sailors learned "of the Arival of [their] prize Ship *Suffolk*, at the Island of St Christophers and that Cap^n Carnes had taken upon himself the Agency of her." This was very good news for privateers who anxiously awaited reports of their captured vessels and their sales. Bartlett and Robinson heard word of the Count De Grasse, who sailed from Fort Royal, and of Admiral Rodney of the English fleet, who was near Martinique. Witnesses claimed "the sight of these fleets were . . . the most formidable ever known in these Sea's." Josiah Bartlett also received sad tidings of a personal nature: "the melancholy account of [his] Uncle's death [related] by Captain Darby from Salem in the Ship *Patty.*" Not all news ashore was good news for privateers.[23]

Ships' logbooks often served as travel journals, in addition to their roles as chronicles of the ships' voyages. The journal writer aboard the *Marlborough,* cruising in January 1778, drew sketches of prominent geographic points and areas, including a profile of Cape Verde and a view of Gorea Fort on the island of Gorée, off the coast of Senegal in Africa. Josiah Bartlett of the *Pilgrim* noted lands the ship merely passed by in his log; for example, on May 30, 1781, the *Pilgrim* "at ten AM saw the Land, being SW part of Ireland & exceedingly mountaineous." Later, in July 1782, Bartlett described the harbor of Louisbourg, which showed "the marks of ancient war; Block Houses, Barracks, the reliques of Fortifications, and the landing places of Generals Amherst & Wolf on their expedition."[24]

Bartlett likewise kept detailed accounts of the cities and towns he actually visited, commenting on a town's size, location, inhabitants, and housing, as well as various other aspects of city life. The first stop across the Atlantic for the *Pilgrim* was the harbor of Brest, France, which, according to Bartlett, was "very justly called one of the Best in the World." The mariner described how "the Country in general [was] level, [and] fertile, and the plantations regularly laid out." The French military presence impressed him, and he pointed out, "Every branch of Marine Business is executed with the greatest dispatch, four or five Thousand Slaves are constantly employed in the dock yards." Bartlett also found the town well planned, with paved streets of an agreeable width and houses that stood four or five stories tall. However, Bartlett was not impressed with the French's "neglect of the Cleanliness in their Houses."[25]

Six months later, while sailing on a second cruise aboard the *Pilgrim,* Josiah Bartlett offered his opinion regarding the island of Tobago, which was quite different from the port of Brest. When first entering Man of War Bay, Bartlett recorded this initial impression: "The entrance of the Harbour affords nothing but barrenness and dessolation." Upon further inspection, Bartlett noted the presence "near the shore [of] five or six Hutts, and a tract of clear'd Land," which he discovered was in fact "a plantation." While exploring the island the next day, Bartlett climbed "an exceeding high mountain" to gain a better view of the countryside. Though the majority of the island was "totally uninhabitted, [and] consequently uncultivated," a few plantations were visible.[26]

While visiting one such plantation, Bartlett met the wife of the planter. The mariner described the woman as a "a likely Negro girl" who treated him with "every mark of civility and . . . entertained [him] in a manner that discovered her associate not to be unacquainted with the manners & Customs of the polite world." In addition, Bartlett learned that the plantations' slaves, whose "great labour & nakedness, could not fail to excite sensations of pity in a breast unaccustomed to Cruelty," inhabited the huts he had seen from the ship. Making his way back to the vessel, he described the mainstays of the island: cotton wool, sugarcane, and coffee. Noting that "vegetables may be procured plentifully," Bartlett also seized an opportunity to gather some food; he "picked a quanty of the finest Limes [he] ever saw." The *Pilgrim* made sail the following day, January 3, 1782.[27]

Writing from the deck of the ship in March 1782, Bartlett described Tortola as "greatly cultivated & in a very flourishing state." Reminiscent of Tobago, Tortola also had a number of plantations worked by slaves. Bartlett described the town as "compact, but small; its situation low, & the Air consquently confined by Mountains adjacent, which were exceeding high." The harbor was also small, but it seemed able to serve its purpose and offered shelter from stormy seas. Bartlett was quick to point out, however, that his observations certainly were not "perfect." Despite his concern, the sailor's descriptions in his logbook are significant in terms of the information they provide and the picture they impart of the islands that American privateers sailing in the Atlantic World visited and encountered.[28]

Bartlett continued noting his impressions of various islands and towns as the *Pilgrim* made its way through the Caribbean. In May 1782, while visiting St. Pierre, Martinique, he observed that the town was approximately two miles long and lay at the foot of a mountain chain. Unfortunately, in Bartlett's eyes, the chain "naturally retard[ed] a circulation of free air, and render[ed the town] entirely subject to the intense heat of the climate." In his opinion, the town was well designed with intersecting streets. A stream flowed through the city's center and provided "cleanliness," which was of high importance in Bartlett's mind. The housing in St. Pierre was compact, and he opined, "Convenience seems to have been considered before elegance"; the sailor was not much impressed. The people themselves were "numerous, industrious, and of a variety of complexions," but Bartlett had little chance for interaction as their language was "unintelegible."[29]

A visit to the town of Basseterre proved far more enjoyable for Bartlett, as it was "much more pleasantly situated then St Pierre, by reason of a free circulation of fresh air." While the housing situation was less crowded and pleased Bartlett because it was "much more elegantly furnished," the streets of the city were "so exceedingly dusty" that it "render[ed] walking very disagreable." Bartlett did not stay long in Basseterre, so he was unable to make his usual plethora of observations. However, he did speculate that "from the reception [he and his fellow sailors] met with, & the treatment [they] received . . . a month might have passed agreably" in the town. Bartlett's fondness for Basseterre over St. Pierre might also have stemmed from the fact that the inhabitants of the former reminded him of his home and spoke a language that was "inteligible" compared to that of St. Pierre. Regardless, the log keeper and the *Pilgrim* were back on the water the next day.[30]

Josiah Bartlett of the *Pilgrim* was not the only privateer who offered remarks and observations in his logbook. Zuriel Waterman of Rhode Island wrote accounts of a number of privateer ventures, though none was quite as detailed as Bartlett's. In November 1779, while sailing on a cruise with the vessel *Providence*, Waterman noted the appearance of Foxborough Isle, off the coast of New Jersey. "It has but one wretched house upon it," he stated, "being mostly a marsh except a small spot of rising ground where the house stands." He was far from fascinated with the island, but he noted its location near Clamtown and Little Egg Harbor, and recorded the names of the inhabitants of the home, Moses Mullener and his family.[31]

While aboard the privateer *Hibernia* nearly two years later, Waterman found himself on the island of Guadeloupe. Though fire (or perhaps a hurricane) had recently destroyed part of the town, he found his way to the hospital, where "the sick were exceeding well treated." As the ship's surgeon, Waterman might naturally have been curious about the treatments and procedures doctors in the West Indies used. He noted that the structure of the hospital building was "fine" and "large . . . situated on a hill," adding, "It is long and has 2 wings." Waterman was probably not nearly as impressed with the behavior of the French doctors he encountered. One became intoxicated, and while he was being taken ashore by two African Americans, the doctor "flogged them all the way with his fist." The French physician was in such a rage that he fell into the water not once but twice, and he was finally "taken out almost drowned." Waterman did not record in his journal what became of his fellow medic.[32]

Following his foray on Guadeloupe, Waterman visited the island of Martinique—that same island Josiah Bartlett of the *Pilgrim* frequented. Waterman's perceptions of the island were similar to Bartlett's in that he noted the presence of mountains, describing them as "very ragged and broken with fine rills of water running into the sea." The surgeon commented on the cultivated land dotted with African American huts. The island also contained "some windmills to grind cane [and] some cannon . . . planted along shore." The next day, February 6, 1781, dawned pleasantly and afforded Waterman the opportunity to go ashore and explore the island. The doctor noted "the fields of coffee, orange groves, [and] tamarind trees" as he surmounted a steep hill to gain a better view. Waterman's observations complement and expand upon those Josiah Bartlett kept in his journal; both men's writings advance the horizons of privateers and explain the experiences of sailors while onshore.[33]

The log of the *Marlborough* and the journals kept by Josiah Bartlett and Zuriel Waterman aboard their respective voyages paint a picture of the Atlantic World beyond the shores of the American colonies. Part of the logbook Timothy Boardman maintained while sailing on the *Oliver Cromwell* of New London, Connecticut, provides a rendering of life much closer to home for sailors, though sometimes just as foreign. The final section of Boardman's narrative is entitled "Remarks of Our Gunner on Charlestown, in S.C." The gunner, most likely a sailor from New England, shared strong opinions about the southern coastal town. While the sailor appreciated the location of the city, which was "pleasantly Situated on Ashley River on verry low Land," and complimented the construction of the nearby buildings as "extreamly well Built," he found a great deal lacking in Charleston society as a whole.[34]

The gunner began by expressing his discomfort with the practice of slavery. He took issue with the system of ripping people from their homelands and transporting them to a strange place without teaching them religion or allowing them their freedom. The idea that an "enlighten[d] People, a People Professing Christianity Should treat any of God's creatures in Such a Manner" disgusted the gunner. The next topic on the mariner's agenda was that of attending church; according to his remarks, hardly anyone ever did so. Rather, the privateer noted that "horse Racing, Frolicking, Rioting, Gaming of all Kinds Open Markets, and Traffick" were the "Chief Business" of Sundays—a wholly unacceptable practice in his eyes.[35]

The gunner further took Charlestonians to task for their laissez-faire attitude toward marriage and the practice of taking multiple women—and female slaves—to bed. He fumed at length about decorum and the role of proper attire when men and women interacted. The lack of "decent Dress" and the appearance of slaves "of both Sexes . . . in Such Dishabitable [apparel] as to be oblige[d] to Display those Parts which ought to be Concealed" greatly vexed the sailor.[36]

His criticisms of Charleston did not end there. The gunner noted that, in addition to the amusements listed earlier, "black Gammon, Shuffle Board ... that Noble Game of Roleing two Bullets on the Sandy Ground ... [and] Whoreing and Drinking" were all vices found in plenty in South Carolina. He also expressed dislike for South Carolinians' food and warned that a man from Carolina might be your friend one moment, but "then for a Shilling would Cut Your Throat." The overall picture the seaman painted was certainly not a flattering one.[37]

Toward the end of his remarks, however, the gunner turned his attention to more positive aspects of the city, albeit with a few caveats. He noted that there were "gentlmen of Charracter ... who Ritchly Deserve[d] the Name" living in Charleston, though they were few and far between. The gunner excused the absence of such men with the explanation that the present conflict had caused many of them to remove from the city; thus the town was "much alterd from what it was before." Nevertheless, Charleston possessed well-built public buildings, fine churches—though they were not "the Most elegant [the gunner] ever Saw"—and well-planned and well-laid streets, even though they were "verry Sandy." The presence of insects, particularly "musketoes," greatly bothered him and made a long stay in the city rather unpleasant. In the end, even the compliments the privateer paid were not a rousing endorsement for Charleston.[38]

The gunner concluded his account with another condemnation of slavery. He scolded the white population for their laziness and love of luxury and sport. Discarding the often-used excuse that white people could not "endure the heat of the climate," the sailor argued that if whites applied time spent at leisurely activities to a "moderate Days work," they could accomplish a great deal indeed. The gunner was convinced that white people in and around Charleston had adopted "foolish wicked and Absurd Notions" to justify slavery and their own inexcusable habits. He ended with a fervent hope that as America fought to "preserve thy Own Freedom ... [the new country should] be Sure to let Slavery of all kinds ever be Banish[d] from thy habbittations." Little did he know that New England troops in a future conflict—the American Civil War—would also view their southern brethren in similar fashion. Though the sailor admitted he "only [made] this Obs[n] for [his] own amusement never Intending" it would be read "but by particular friends" and therefore omitted "any niceities of Expressions," the remarks did find their way into the logbook of Timothy Boardman. These remarks provide an important portrait of how one privateer viewed men and society in a fellow colony. Clearly, the gunner found many of the Charlestonians' practices strange and, in his particular view, unacceptable for and unbecoming of a gentlemanly society.[39]

The distinct travel sections of these logbooks illustrate how and where sailors interacted with various residents of the Atlantic World. The cultural exchanges that took place began on a micro level with individual privateers. Over time, as more privateers participated in the war and experienced the Atlantic World, these exchanges expanded and overlapped, constituting a unique experience unmatched by wartime activities or any other Patriot forces' interactions. Fleshing out this typically overlooked privateer experience continues expanding the American Revolution beyond the borders of the colonies themselves. While these mariners' exploits in France, Ireland, Martinique, Guadeloupe, Tobago, and Tortola were vastly different from those of other American combatants and the Continental Congress in Philadelphia, they were no less valuable to the overall outcome of the conflict. Nor are they any less legitimate to historical understandings of the war today. Stepping foot on the shores of European and Caribbean nations and islands, privateers engaged in much more than simple sea battles and captures of prizes; they experienced the American Revolution as part of the Atlantic World.[40]

Once a ship came into port, captains often allowed their crews to disembark and tour the nearby towns, which, as the travel logs indicate, a number of seamen freely did. However, this freedom to explore came with risks, as sailors might engage in unacceptable behavior or, perhaps worse, they might desert the venture and never return. Before the cruise of the privateer *Providence* even really got underway in September 1779, one "Stephen L___ ran away" from a boat going ashore for milk. The captain of the marines and one of the prize masters pursued the young man but were unable to catch him. Zuriel Waterman noted in his diary that Stephen had entered the privateer service under the assumption of being "a good seaman," but when he refused to climb the rigging, the newly minted sailor "acknowledged he was [in fact] no seaman." Thus, it may not be surprising that he turned tail and ran before the vessel ever left port, leaving behind "3/4 of a share." A month later, again aboard the *Providence*, five men "stole off undiscovered" while the ship was anchored. One sailor was so desperate to escape he "went off without shoes or stockings on, leaving 2 pair of good stockings and 1 pair of shoes, etc., in his pack." The officers of the *Hibernia* had to use force to keep their men on board when two sailors attempted to go ashore. The duo brandished pistols, but the officers maintained the peace, resulting in "broken shins, one forefinger, a jacket [torn], and one pistol stock broken."[41]

Illegal actions and behaviors could not be tolerated, for if the captain and his officers showed weakness in enforcement, the crew might refuse to work, abandon their duties, or even mutiny. While standing watch aboard the *Revenge* on the morning of April 8, 1777, John Palmer "heard Sumbody hallow as tho they Was a Drownding." Quickly, the crew hauled up a fellow sailor who "had Stoling Som Things and Went to Rhun a Way." The would-be thief was placed "in irons" until later that day, when he was "whipt Nineteen Lashes [with] the Cat of Ninetails on his Naked hide."[42]

Swift punishment was called for when sailors disobeyed. John Kelly and Joseph Stuart learned this lesson at the hands of Lieutenant Harris aboard the *Providence*. Stuart refused to work one day because he claimed he was injured with boils. Harris, not believing the sailor, "thrashed him around pretty severely" with a hunting whip. The lieutenant then went after Kelly, who was hiding from the officer. Harris struck Kelly and "repeated his strokes to make him rise, but K[elly] stood it out for some time; after 20 strokes or thereabouts, H[arris] left off." The diary does not divulge what became of Kelly and Stuart after this incident, but the ship proceeded on its cruise. The captain of the Marlborough sent the boatswain to another vessel, for he "behaved So Bad ... Abusing the Doctor & Officers on Board." Sailors might face punishment for accidental actions as well; for instance, a man named Andrews "was cobb'd for puking on deck where the meat was a cooking in the lee suppers."[43]

The implementation of rules aboard ship served a dual purpose. First, these regulations ensured the captain and his officers could maintain control of the crew. Unlike the Continental navy, which drew up specific guidelines that any ship in service had to follow, privateers were privately owned and operated ventures. There was no privateer guidebook that each ship followed; every vessel functioned under its own flag. Hence, a crew needed to know and understand the procedures and punishments of their craft. The second purpose of these rules and regulations was to find and impose order on an inherently disorderly situation. Far from any civil authority or from the owners of the ships or the financiers of the ventures, privateers were at the mercy of their circumstances. In particular, captains aboard privateers were in a unique situation unto themselves. Operating in an isolated environment—on board a solitary vessel and in the middle of an ocean oftentimes—a ship's captain had no recourse or support if he failed to subdue his crew. A captain facing mutiny could not appeal to Washington or the Continental Congress for aid. He had to take swift action to maintain control of the sailors under his command lest he lose the endeavor and the ship.

Without a code to follow, ventures could quickly dissolve into mutiny and chaos. A captain had to be careful in case his crew decided to turn against him. The sailors aboard the privateer *Chace* wanted the opportunity "to go ashore to plunder the inhabitants" of Nova Scotia, but the captain refused and "hoisted the boat aboard" to prevent their going. The crew "threatened to carry the brigt. in another port," upon hearing which the captain "put them in irons." "All hands" of the *Revenge* in April 1777 refused to work "till they Was allowd Some money for their Shears," presumably to spend ashore. The lieutenant gave "his Word that [the sailors] Should have Som money Before [they] Saild." This promise placated the crew, and they returned to their duties. The lieutenant did indeed make good on his vow; the captain distributed two dollars to every man a few days later. Dangerous situations such as threats of mutiny, insubordination, and acts of disorderly conduct had to be addressed and contained.[44]

Desertion, laziness, and mutiny were only a few circumstances that could endanger the strength of a crew. Disease, injury, and death also posed serious risks to sailors aboard privateers. Smallpox was a genuine threat during the American Revolution. George Washington inoculated his troops in 1777 and 1778; he realized the hazards of marching and fighting with susceptible soldiers. Captains of privateer vessels also recognized the risks. Captain William Cole, of the *Oliver Cromwell* of Beverly, decided to inoculate his entire crew after smallpox broke out and "several [of his men were] buried in a Day." The decision to purposefully infect all the crewmen most likely stemmed from the knowledge that once the live virus was inserted beneath a mariner's skin, he actually had the disease and was able to communicate it to others. Otherwise, the infected sailor would have to be quarantined—a feat quite difficult on a ship in the middle of the ocean where crew members resided in such close quarters.[45]

The keeper of the journal aboard the *Oliver Cromwell* was inoculated by a doctor from another vessel, the *Civil Usage*, after which "at Night [he] took a Mercurial Pill." For the next few days, inoculations continued. On August 26, 1777, "five more . . . People were innoculated" aboard the vessel. The writer of the *Oliver Cromwell*'s log noted that smallpox affected not only his body but also his mind. He had "melancholly Apprehensions respecting the Small-Pox," but he tried to "commit [himself] & case to the Disposal of a Divine Providence."[46]

Captain Joseph Conkling of the *Revenge* made a similar decision regarding inoculation. In mid-May 1778, Conkling stated, "All hands that had Never had the Small Pocks Was a Nockalatid Which Was a Bout twenty."

The following day, they were "as Well as [could] Be Expected." Later that same week, those infected began to "complain with Soare arms." On May 30, John Palmer noted in his log that the patients' symptoms were worsening: "The Small Pocks People Be Gin forto Gro Sick With Pains in theire head and Back." When the ship came to anchor the following day, Conkling brought them ashore to a house he had secured for their recuperation. A few days later, the doctor "went a Shoar for to Go and See the Small Pocks men."[47]

The inoculation procedure involved placing a live variola virus in an incision on the hand or arm. Following this procedure, the patient typically broke out in pustules, though the number was relatively small compared to those on patients who broke out naturally. Aboard the *Oliver Cromwell*, the log keeper experienced "pain in [his] Head & Limbs, with alternate Heats & Colds," followed by "a restless Night" with little sleep. He continued to take doses of "calomel," or mercury, to help with the effects. The writer also aided his fellow inoculated crew members. He gave "2 doses Physick to 2 others & an Emet to another." Meanwhile, six days after the inoculation procedure, the log keeper's symptoms worsened, as he felt "alternate Heats & Colds Head-ache, Eyeballs sore & ach &c & a great Sinking & Lassitude."[48]

The mark of smallpox soon showed itself. While the writer fluctuated between freezing cold and boiling hot, the doctor "discovered a Pock on [his] cheek." Over the next few days, the pox continued to erupt all over the sailor until he had "now about 100 Pock, very kind." He stopped taking medicine and instead "exercise[d] as much as" he could "without heating [him]self & live[d] low." The journalist might be considered lucky as he only had a few more pocks break out; he noted how they "fill[ed] fast & well," and soon his "Pock [began] to turn."[49] Fellow mariners who suffered from a natural outbreak were "removed on shore" so as not to endanger the rest of the crew. John Palmer recorded that when the first lieutenant aboard the *Revenge* in April 1777 "brock out with Sm[all] Pock," the crew "made all Sail" toward the nearest harbor. First thing the next morning, the captain went ashore "for to Git a Place to Leave [the] Leutennant." A natural outbreak often resulted in far more acute symptoms and potentially death, whereas the inoculation procedure usually caused a less severe form of the pox. Timothy Boardman recorded in his journal that another privateer ship, the *Defence*, "had Five Men Broke out with the Small Pox" on April 7, 1778. The following day, "they [the ship and its crew] Lost a Man wth the Small Pox." Joseph Stickney of the *General Pickering* "died of the Small Pox at the Hospital" on the evening of February 20, 1779, while the ship was anchored in a nearby bay. On board the *Marlborough*, smallpox also made an appearance, with "the Innoculated persons Breaking Out [and] Others Complaing of the Symtoms." Smallpox could potentially decimate a crew if not dealt with swiftly and responsibly.[50]

Smallpox was but one of the medical pitfalls on privateering vessels. Sailors and surgeons dealt with circumstances varying from a headache or cold to the loss of limb or life. John Palmer of the *Revenge* recalled, "[I] cut my hand With thee Drawingnife Very Bad," though he recorded no treatment for the injury. Aboard the same vessel, one crew member was "takin With Convulsion fitts Very Bad," though luckily was "rather Better" the next day. As the surgeon on several cruises, Zuriel Waterman was charged with obtaining vital medical supplies for the ship. Before setting sail on the *Argo* in 1780, Waterman "went to the G. Hospital to get medicines for the sloop." While serving aboard the *Hibernia* in February 1781, Waterman was called aboard another ship to bleed the captain, though he did not note the reason for the procedure in his journal. Even Waterman found himself under the weather at times; one day he was "taken violently ill . . . with bad pain in [his] bones [and a] headack." Captain Christopher Brown of the *Marlborough* was "taken Ill of a Fever" during the ship's cruise near the coast of Africa in 1778.[51]

Dr. Solomon Drowne of the ship *Hope* also offered his services to fellow vessels, since not every privateer ship carried a surgeon aboard. He was called to a snow by the commander, Captain Small, "to do something for his Rheumatic Knee, and see a very sick boy." Drowne offered a prescription and gave directions to the captain for overseeing his illness and that of the young man before returning to his sloop. Treatment could be as simple as giving "2 Men Physick" if they were feeling ill. Following a "squally" storm with "Strong Gales & rough Sea," the log keeper of the *Oliver Cromwell* of Beverly "dress'd several wounds" on his crew, most likely obtained while trying to keep the ship afloat during the deluge. Two weeks later, several members of the crew were "annointed for the Itch. Several were Sick & took Emet[s] and Cath[s]. One [was] wounded in the Wrist by a Knife & Several Boils."[52]

Yet a surgeon was not always successful in treating his patients. Sometimes—oftentimes—injuries proved fatal. While foraging onshore, Joseph Prentis of the privateer *Wasp* was shot and killed; his crew "buried Prentis on an Island in Pennant bay." When Hezekiah Burnham was "taken sick" aboard a sloop, several sailors brought him ashore to be looked after in Port Morant, Jamaica. Burnham died that evening, and fellow sailor Gideon Olmsted "gave £3 for a coffin." A thoughtful American man "gave a suit to dress the corpse and decently buried him," while Olmsted gave "a pair of silk gloves" to the "very kind woman" who had looked after Burnham.[53]

Burial in the ground was not the norm, however; most deaths occurred in the middle of the ocean and required a burial at sea. The rite consisted of the sailor being "sewed up in his hammock and sunk." Early in May 1778 aboard the *Revenge*, "Master Wick [was] Very Poorly indeed and Several others . . . all most all the People Sick." John Palmer indicated in the log-book that Master Wick's condition continued to deteriorate, stating, "[He] Groase Weeke fast." A few hours later, Wick was dead, "and at 5 in the af-ter Noon [the crew] Buried him," most likely in a sea burial. Luckily, the re-mainder of the crew returned to health.[54]

Ritual, tradition, superstition, and religion each played a role in the sail-or's everyday life. Burial at sea not only made sense pragmatically—the smell of a corpse in the hold plus the potential spread of disease were certainly factors recommending it—but there was also the idea that a sailor who had spent his life upon the oceans would want to meet his end there. Earning the privilege of being called a true seaman was a rite of passage. A num-ber of privateering logbooks described the ceremony of shaving and duck-ing performed when crossing the Tropic of Cancer. On Friday, December 21, 1781, the privateer ship *Pilgrim* "passed the line of the Tropic of Cancer." The occasion was met with "much diversion for [the] Ships C° though at-tended with a very disagreable ceremony to such as never crossed it before." Josiah Bartlett, the writer of the log, did not elaborate on this unpleasant observance. Timothy Boardman, sailing aboard the *Oliver Cromwell* of New London, described the rite thus: "Cros^d the Tropick Shav^d & Duck About 60 Men." John Palmer of the *Revenge* noted that when the ship "croast the Tropick Line [he and his fellow sailors] Shavd all Raw hands."[55]

Zuriel Waterman, traveling on the *Hibernia* in 1781, provided a more de-tailed account of the ritual. When the weather was nice enough, Waterman had "two handspikes lashed horizontal and parallel; [he] sat on the lower, the upper one being against [his] breast . . . was lashed to them, hoisted up to the weather foreyardarm, and giving three cheers, [the crew] let [him] go by the run in the sea, doing thus 3 times." Waterman had the opportu-nity to buy his way out of the ritual, but he "refus[ed] to pay anything more" and thus went through with the ceremony. The sailors aboard the *Marlbor-ough* were also offered a buyout option when "two of the men dressd in Tar-paulins Come to Demand the Bottle and pourd when All those that never Crossd it had to pay." The custom of shaving and ducking—shaving first-

time crossers' heads and ducking them into the ocean—was a common practice among seagoing vessels in the eighteenth century. Privateers, though not
formal or official combatants and vessels like members of the Continental
navy or British ships of the line, still participated in and recognized these rituals of the sea.[56]

Superstition and religion may seem an odd pair of belief systems today,
but sailors aboard privateers recognized and respected both of them. For example, prior to the beginning of a voyage, seafarers might place a silver coin
under the mainmast in hopes of a successful voyage and a plethora of prizes.
A crew might whistle in unison to conjure a favorable wind, but they had to
take care, for whistling when the ship had the advantage could prove disas-
trous. The *Pilgrim* returned to port in July 1782, only to discover that most
of the prizes taken had not yet arrived, leaving the crew "murmuring at the
frowns of Fortune." While Revolutionary seamen believed in these perhaps
fanciful notions of producing good luck and fair winds, they also frequently
called on a higher being in their times of need and recognized holy days
and practices. Zuriel Waterman remarked in his journal, "Ash Wednesday
28 [the] First day of Lent." Solomon Drowne tried to retain a semblance
of his religious life aboard the sloop *Hope*; he noted in his journal, "It being Sunday, try the efficacy of a clean shirt, in order to be something like
folks ashore." When a violent gale threatened the *Hope*, Drowne stated, "A
becoming fortitude in general predominates on board, though horror stalks
around. —They who go down to the sea in ships, do indeed see the wonders
of the LORD in the deep."[57]

The crew of the sloop *Peggy* might not have followed religious rituals
quite as closely. When stopped by the Committee of the Inquisition in February 1779, the vessel received "several Injunctions with respect to the observance of certain Ecclesiastical Regulations." Yet the log keeper on board
did not fail to give praise to a Supreme Being just two days later when the
ship pulled into port: "Secur'd the Hatchways &c. and quit the Vessell __
Thank God!" While cruising aboard the *Fortune*, Zuriel Waterman had a
near-death experience. He was returning to the ship from shore when a flat-
bottomed boat he was in overturned. Waterman was in the cold water for
fifteen minutes before being pulled out; he later wrote, "Thus by the great
mercy of God I was saved. . . . May I never forget this signal favor of heaven,
but always remember it with gratitude and trust in Divine Providence." In
April 1777, the crew of the *Revenge* turned the corner after an initial bout of
seasickness, and John Palmer exulted in his log, "All hands Harty and Well
thank God." When Palmer came home in September 1778 after his third

cruise aboard the privateer, he closed his journal, "At 2 Returnd home Safe thanks Be to God for all his marsis."[58]

Some privateers readily took the opportunity to attend church when in port. While anchored in Guadeloupe, Zuriel Waterman "early in the morning went to church with Dr. Rawson." Waterman was struck by the elegance of the church, observing, "There was a very beautiful altar with a large golden cross on the table ... supported with angels with beautiful carved work around it." He also described a carved alabaster statue of the Virgin Mary holding the baby Jesus in her arms. Five other individuals came into the church while Waterman and Rawson examined the structure. These churchgoers "went to the marble basin of holy water, dipped their fingers in, and crossed themselves on the forehead and breast." Waterman and Rawson followed suit. The two doctors then visited a second church, where the parishioners "were singing ... As soon as they stopped, they all fell on their knees to prayer." At the end of the service, "a small bell rung for about 1 1/2 minutes, during which time they were all on their knees at prayer." In addition to attending church, Waterman noted the observance of holy days: "Sunday last being Shrove Sunday, that and yesterday and today are three great holy days with the inhabitants [of Guadeloupe]; every night they have a dance on the beach with music, etc." While privateers could be out at sea for weeks or months, many maintained a semblance of shore life and practiced their faiths and beliefs to the best of their abilities.[59]

For sailors who survived the perils of weather, disease, and injury and "earned their stripes" through various ceremonies and rituals, the open sea offered vast opportunities. The main goal of privateering ventures consisted of capturing prizes and returning them to port successfully. However, in the midst of trying to chase and engage other ships, privateer vessels oftentimes found themselves face-to-face with friendly vessels rather than the enemy. On the morning of June 3, 1781, the *Pilgrim* "saw a Sail to leward, & gave chace." Upon closer examination, the crew judged the vessel to be armed. They continued in hot pursuit, and "after a very severe Chace," the *Pilgrim's* sailors made contact with their quarry. The vessel turned out to be the *Essex* from Salem, "no prize" for the privateer. Instead, the two ships continued in company. The following morning, they "tried the Ships in Sailing," and the *Pilgrim* "beat the *Essex* greatly." A few days later, the *Pilgrim* again gave chase after a spotted sail, but once more the vessel turned out to be friendly: "the Ship *Defence*, Capt Edmunds, belonging to Beverly, from Bilboa on a Cruize." The *Defence* joined the *Pilgrim* and the *Essex* in sailing together.[60]

Encounters between non-enemy vessels did not always end well, however. The meeting of the *Pilgrim* and the *Mohawk* serves as a case in point. The two ships "ran aboard each other, by which accident [the *Pilgrim*] carried away [its] figure Head & received some other injuries." Both crews argued over who was at fault, for their seamanship was at stake and "each party [was] naturally urgent to vindicate . . . [its] own conduct." Josiah Bartlett determined, "Both Captains were aiming to take the same position should we not have proved friend to each other." Thus, he further concluded that both captains were equally guilty. Yet there was no way to determine the status of friendship until it was too late, and in this case, the damage was done. Such were the perils of taking up the chase and engaging another vessel.[61]

Examining the process of the chase makes these encounters between confederate vessels understandable. The lookout spotted a sail, but there was no indication on the sail of whether the vessel was friend or foe. Thus, the ships commenced a chase. Once the craft were in close proximity, they each raised their colors, but this was not always foolproof. Some ships raised false colors to deceive their pursuers. In the end, it was not until the vessels could speak with one another that a determination could be made about the status of the pursued ship. When a conclusion was reached, if the vessel indeed proved to be friendly, a ship might give a signal. For instance, the *Oliver Cromwell* of Beverly at "early A.M. Saw a Sail & stood for her. At 9 d° came up, judged her to be Capt. Lee of Marblehead, a Privateer Brig, [and] fired 2 Guns to Leward in Token of Friendship." After the sailors on the *Oliver Cromwell* spoke with Captain Lee, the two vessels "agreed to keep Compan[y] . . . & Cruize in Consort Several Days." In August 1778, the sailors of the *Revenge* first "fell in With . . . the Sloop Beaver," then added the *Revenue* to their cohort as they sailed "in Company." The privateer *Tyrannicide* of Boston met the frigate *Warren* in open waters and "agreed to go as Consorts together and cruise off Newfoundland." Cruising together offered protection and perhaps a greater chance at taking a prize.[62]

When a fellow ship turned out to be friendly, vessels often convened in open water to exchange knowledge of enemy movements, information, supplies, and even passengers. While cruising off the coast of the New England colonies in November 1779, the *Providence* learned from the *Comet* "that the English had evacuated Newport, Rhode Island . . . after blowing up the courthouse, granary, lighthouses, and their fortification on Tonomy Hill." This was important intelligence for privateers cruising in British-patrolled waters. When the *Fortune* met up with the *Revenge* on May 23, 1781, the latter informed the former that "the *Rambler* had taken a Bermudian brig loaded with salt," proof that the waters of the Caribbean yielded fruitful captures. After passing the coast of Antigua, the *Pilgrim* gave chase to a brig, which the captain and crew soon found sailed from Brest, France, to Guadeloupe. The brig informed its pursuers that four days earlier it "parted with a Fleet of 7 sail of Battle Ships & a large number of Troops, bound to Martinico." The *Marlborough* obtained from the captain of the *Sally* the position of "a Snow belonging to London Under french Colours & Some Other Vessels & a rich factory," while the *Oliver Cromwell* of New London gathered that "the Jamaica Fleet ... Pass^d the Havanna ten Days Back."[63]

Friendly vessels also carried news of events closer to home. The *Vengeance* of Salem, Massachusetts, shared with the *Revenge* of Stonington, Connecticut, in late August 1778 "that the Island of Newport Was Not Given up when [the ship] Saild" eleven days earlier. Rather, the *Vengeance* reported the Americans "landid 7000 men on theare and Remain in 3 mild of the Enem[y] When he Left." The information and gossip network among privateers could be invaluable. In the absence of modern-day technology to inform vessels of enemy movements, the sharing of information between ships was one of the only ways to gain intelligence and prepare for various confrontations.[64]

Encounters afforded the opportunity for more than just the transfer of information—other valuable commodities also changed hands. When the *Fortune* and the *Comet* met in May 1781, the former gave "lb. 20 bread, lb. 40 beef, and 1/2 gal. rum" to the latter to help the *Comet* on its homeward journey. Yet when the *Rambler* encountered a schooner off the coast of Nova Scotia and "requested water and bread," the captain of the former only gave "after some delay ... about 3 pints water and 3 biscuits per man and nothing more." In this case, a friendly vessel was not particularly helpful. The *Pilgrim* participated in an exchange of passengers in May 1782 when its sailors came upon a sloop from Bermuda to Antigua. Aboard the vessel was a passenger "by the name of Bonetheau ... [who] represented to have fled from Charlestown S° Carolina, to escape the cruelty of the Enemy." The *Pilgrim* took Bonetheau aboard. When the ship encountered a schooner "bound to George-town," Mr. Bonetheau was put "on board her by his own request."[65]

In early 1781, Zuriel Waterman served as surgeon aboard the ship *Fortune*. Toward the end of the vessel's cruise, she encountered the *Rambler*, commanded by Captain Fuller. The captain requested Waterman's presence on the ship, most likely because he lacked a doctor on board. With "the captain and all the officers [of the *Fortune*] consenting, [Waterman] accordingly went in the *Rambler*, leaving the *Fortune* about 11 A.M., having been aboard 79 days, 4 . . . hands leaving at the same time." Thus, privateer vessels also served as places of exchange on certain occasions.[66]

Sailors aboard privateers experienced a great deal during their time at sea. From completing daily chores to dealing with the weather, from staving off boredom to exploring various ports and cities of the Atlantic World, these men experienced a vastly different American Revolution. Their services allowed them to encounter, live through, and understand the war from a broader perspective. As well-traveled, even cosmopolitan men, these sailors witnessed firsthand how forces in and of the Atlantic World shaped the Revolution and, indeed, their own everyday lives—from the call to outfit privateers to recruitment, preparing for cruises, and the voyages themselves—all of which war changed and challenged. From Brest, France, to St. Pierre, Martinique, from Sierra Leone, Africa, to Halifax, Nova Scotia, privateers crisscrossed the Atlantic, encountering friendly and allied vessels along the way. As such, the events chronicled in chapter 1 and those recorded in the logbooks, diaries, and journals featured in this chapter may seem pedestrian by the standards of the sailors themselves, but in truth they are actually quite illuminating. They drastically expand the cultural and political reaches of the Revolution, all while encompassing a far greater tract of land—and sea—than the standard thirteen colonies.

Nevertheless, not all encounters were peaceful and pleasant. As chapter 3 will reveal, these same sources also record what happened when privateer ships approached a vessel that proved to be hostile—an enemy ship of the British Empire.

CHAPTER 3

When Cannon Balls Do Fly

*I*n the midst of the Caribbean Sea, five vessels convened under a spring sky. American privateers in pursuit of prizes, goods, ammunition, and glory, these crews temporarily created a fleet and set their collective sights on the nearby island of Tortola. Armed with six- and nine-pounders, hundreds of men, and inviting reports that the town was barely protected, the privateers drew up a plan of attack. Two hundred men would land on the island and take the town, while the ships provided firepower from their cannon. By the time anyone in Tortola realized what was happening, it would be too late. On the evening of March 4, 1782, the ships set sail for their destination.

Hindered by a night bereft of moonlight, the privateers passed the nearby island. As morning broke, the realization dawned that the small fleet had missed its target by three miles. Determined to attain victory, the captains held yet another conference and decided, having lost the element of surprise, to demand the surrender of the town. Yet luck was not on the privateers' side. Two of the vessels, the *Brutus* and the *Halker*, displayed distress signals, and the *Franklin* and the *Pilgrim* sailed to their relief.

Sailing among the islands, the *Pilgrim* spotted several vessels flying English colors. The *Porus*, the flagship of the expedition, engaged with two such craft, receiving damage to its hull and rigging in the process. To the relief of the crew, no man was injured during the cannonade. The venture had failed, though; Tortola was safe. The five privateers disbanded their makeshift fleet, and each sailed off empty-handed into the sunset. A new day would dawn with new enemies to hunt and new prizes for the taking.

The main objective of a privateering venture was to successfully capture enemy ships, take them as prizes, and send the vessels back to port where they and their cargoes would be sold for profit. This sequence of events sounds simple enough, but the task of chasing, capturing, and maintaining control of an adversary's ship was a challenging, perilous endeavor. While many engagements resulted in the successful capture of a prize, privateers also faced the possibility of being captured themselves, taken prisoner by enemy forces. Privateers held out little hope of a prisoner exchange; they were rarely assessed for such action because Great Britain labeled them as pirates—a foe unworthy and undeserving of such consideration.

Privateers operated outside of this purview at times, as the foiled plan for the capture of Tortola highlights. Captains and crews had the freedom to take action that did not adhere to the primary objective. Tortola was not a hostile ship, but rather an enemy town filled with potential loot. Far from the Continental Congress and its policies and procedures, these vessels and sailors found themselves in unfamiliar territory, often making decisions in their individual best interest rather than that of the struggling American nation. They inhabited a maritime realm wherein American citizens were not always recognized or accepted. Privateers' actions would ultimately affect not only their immediate circumstances, but also the establishment of relationships and bonds with foreign powers, friendly and belligerent. While privateers were tasked with engaging the enemy, the enemy could be elusive and unknown. At the least, captains might argue that a seized target was the enemy when in reality it was not.[1]

Gustavus Conyngham, one such privateer captain, plied the waters of the Atlantic World searching for prizes in the years 1777–1778. Hell-bent on harassing and capturing as many vessels as possible, Conyngham commanded several cruises in the waters surrounding Ireland and Britain, off the coasts of France and Spain, and farther south in the warmer waters of the Caribbean. Taken as a collective case study, his voyages and experiences—with their battles, diplomatic entanglements, and even periods spent as a prisoner of war—illuminate the full breadth of what it meant to sail as a privateer. Renditions of Conyngham's adventures are perhaps more complete and better documented than those of his many contemporaries. But at their core, as will soon become clear, these accounts are generally representative of how myriad privateers transported a war for the fate of the colonies to the very doorsteps of Europe, the Caribbean, and the Atlantic World at large.[2]

In the fall of 1775, the *Charming Peggy* weighed anchor and left Philadelphia for European waters under the captaincy of Gustavus Conyngham. Conyngham hailed from an Irish family who had immigrated to the colony of Pennsylvania when he was a young boy. Connected to the trading house of Conyngham & Nesbit through his cousin Redmond Conyngham, Gustavus Conyngham took to the sea at a young age and honed his craft under the tutelage of Captain Henderson in the Antigua trade. After working his way up through the ranks—and marrying Anne Hockley in 1773—Conyngham found himself master of the *Charming Peggy*; he was charged with procuring supplies such as "salt-peter, arms, medecins [*sic*] & every thing Necessary for War well known the Great need & scarcity the little Supply" Patriot forces had. This particular voyage failed to complete its mission. While in the English Channel, the *Charming Peggy* encountered a British cruiser and was boarded by a prize crew. Conyngham regained control of the ship and slipped away in a dense fog, only to be detained near Texel Island, Holland. British authorities in port complained to the Dutch government and, hence, stopped the Dutch from loading any military supplies on board the vessel. Lack of options forced Conyngham to sell his ship and find another way home.[3]

During the next year, Conyngham searched for another vessel. He was not yet ready to give up or give in. Meanwhile, in the colonies, Washington and his troops engaged in the New York and New Jersey campaign, ending with victories at the Battles of Trenton and Princeton. This series of events led to Conyngham's presence in Europe and his meeting with Benjamin Franklin in 1777—an encounter that led directly to his cruises in the Atlantic.

Newly arrived in France, Benjamin Franklin served as one of the American commissioners, alongside Silas Deane and Arthur Lee. Conyngham and Franklin met in Paris, where the seafarer asked the doctor for the opportunity to serve as captain aboard an American vessel. Franklin penned a commission for Conyngham, dated March 1, 1777, and sent him to Dunkirk to meet William Hodge. In England, Hodge purchased the English-built *Admiral Pocock* under false identities, so the vessel could neither be traced back to him nor be connected to American interests. John Beach, who would ultimately serve as first lieutenant on the cruise, brought the vessel to Dunkirk, where it was outfitted and renamed the *Surprize*. On May 2, 1777, Conyngham took command off the coast of France so as not to arouse the ire of the British or the French. The captain secretly boarded the vessel under cover of darkness with guns, ammunition, and additional crew members. The *Surprize* was ready for privateering ventures at sea.

Cruising the waters of the Atlantic provided numerous opportunities for privateers to chase and capture British vessels, particularly packets—ships that carried official mail. Conyngham and his crew were successful their first day in the English Channel; the *Surprize* "took the harwick packett & Brig Joseph on 3d and 4th May 1777." The packet, a vessel named the *Prince of Orange*, was carrying mail from Harwich to Hellevoetsluis in Holland. Communications such as these could provide invaluable information to privateer captains and the American commissioners in Paris. Alas for Conyngham, the dispatches from the *Prince of Orange* were thrown overboard before they could be read.[4]

In June 1781, a sailor aboard the *Pilgrim* of Beverly, Massachusetts, wrote in the ship's log, "Saw a Brigg close on board us, we fired several times at her while striving to escape us." When the *Pilgrim* finally pulled aside the sloop of war *Snake*, the American privateers learned the vessel was "sailing from St Kitts to Europe wth dispatches from Sr Geo B Rodney." The captain of the *Snake* "destroyed them [the documents] when he struck his Colours." A month later, the *Pilgrim* encountered "His Majestys Packet Brigg^{tn} *Comet*" journeying from Jamaica to London. Once again, the *Pilgrim* lost out on communications, the "dispatches [having been] destroyed" when the crew boarded the ship. The third encounter with a packet proved more fruitful for the *Pilgrim* on January 28, 1782, when the vessel "toward Evening saw a Sail to Windward, [and] Gave chace." After boarding the pursued ship, "the *Prince William Henry*, a packet from Falmouth, with dispatches for the West India Isl^{ds}," the crew of the *Pilgrim* found the mail had been destroyed, but they "saved sundry public papers which were sent into port."[5]

Nearby ports served an important function for Continental and privateer ventures in foreign waters. A secure, friendly, easily accessible port was necessary for prize taking and for making sale transactions. John Adams wrote to James Warren on March 31, 1777, "We have this day received Letters from Europe, of an interesting Nature . . . that all the Ports of France and Spain and Italy and all the Ports in the Mediterranean, excepting Portugal, are open to our Privateers and Merchant Ships." Adams correctly stated that France and Spain wanted—covertly—to aid in the war effort by outfitting, repairing, and harboring privateers in select ports. However, the administrations of both France and Spain had to tread carefully, as neither was prepared in early 1777 to declare outright war against Great Britain. Hence, when Gustavus Conyngham openly sent his prizes the *Prince of Orange* and the *Joseph* into Dunkirk, he violated the code of secrecy and caused an international incident.[6]

Correspondence flew across the English Channel in reaction to Conyngham's audacious actions. The incident elicited "a great noise" in Paris; one British agent in the city wrote to the British Foreign Office, "Officers of packets ought to have strict orders to sink the mail immediately on the approach of any vessell that carries the Appearance of a Rebel privateer." Lord Stormont, David Murray, second Earl of Mansfield, the British ambassador to France, met with Charles Gravier, Comte de Vergennes, King Louis XVI's minister of foreign affairs, about the incident. Stormont noted in a letter to Lord Weymouth that he asked the comte "to have an order sent by Express to Stop and Examine the Pirate and set at Liberty the Prizes He had taken."[7]

The French minister responded with swift action; under the Treaty of Utrecht of 1713, France could not shelter British enemy privateers in its harbors. Vergennes wrote the Marquis de Noailles, the French ambassador at the Court of St. James, "There is a great distinction to be drawn between simply admitting, in case of need, and for the moment, a privateer with her prize, and permitting that same privateer to lie, so to speak, in ambush in a neutral port: this latter case is precisely that of Mr. Cunningham." France could—and would—aid American privateers in secrecy. But at this time, the French government could not tolerate a blatant violation of understood protocol such as Conyngham had perpetrated. Conyngham and his crew were imprisoned, the *Surprize* confiscated, and the *Prince of Orange* and the *Joseph* released to their owners.[8]

The captain's imprisonment did not last long, however, due to the efforts of Deane and Franklin. In two short months, Gustavus Conyngham found himself on board another ship, the *Revenge*, once again cruising the Atlantic. Conyngham received instructions from the commissioners to sail directly to America to deliver "the dispatches instrusted to . . . [his] Care," but his orders included a caveat. "If attackd first by our Enemies," the commissioners told him, "the circumstances of the case will extenuate in favor of your conduct, either in making prizes for your own preservation, or in making reprisal for damages sustaind." As a privateer captain, Conyngham possessed significant autonomy. Isolated and alone in foreign waters, privateer commanders made split-second decisions without consulting anyone else. As Conyngham learned while captain of the *Surprize*, these decisions could instantly cause an international incident.[9]

AUGUSTATUS KUNINGAM

Captain Gustavus Conyngham, American privateer.
Courtesy of the Naval History and Heritage Command, Washington, D.C.

The *Revenge* had a crew "composed of all the most desperate fellows which could be procured in so blessed a port as Dunkirk," including "sixteen . . . Frenchmen." Well before the French officially joined the war and sent troops to aid the colonies, privateers of different nationalities worked and fought together. The company of a privateer vessel, particularly one sailing from a foreign port, often included sailors from a variety of nations. The *Revenge*'s distinct crew did not particularly care for the commissioners' commands. They wanted to engage British merchant vessels and take prizes; Conyngham obliged. The ship left Dunkirk and sailed into the North Sea, where the mariners "made several prizes in the German Ocean, N. Seas, Irish Channel & Western Ocean."[10]

Conyngham and the *Revenge* were not alone in the waters of the Atlantic World during the course of the war. American privateers set sail from various ports to engage the enemy and attack British shipping with one eye on prize money and the other, perhaps, on patriotic purposes. Sailing off the coast of Africa in the early months of 1778, the *Marlborough* of Rhode Island "saw a Sail. Bearing SBE . . . [the ship] hawld [its] wind and Stood for her." Shortly thereafter, the sloop pulled alongside the privateer, and "the Captain Sent Mr Cleveland and one man to take possesion of her." The *Marlborough* secured the prize vessel as well as its hold of "cloth guns [and] tobacco." Five days later, "without a Gun being fird on either Side," the *Marlborough* captured the brig *Pearl*, a letter of marque from Liverpool. The ship's cargo yielded camwood, ivory, rice, and gum.[11]

Sailing from the port of Salem, Massachusetts, in 1781, the *Pilgrim* took "the Brig^n *Three Friends*, Capt. Beckwith, from Cork, bound to New York & loaded with Provisions," during its first week at sea. The *Pilgrim* had great success in May 1781 when it took "the Brigg *Albion* . . . from Jamaica, bound to London laden with Sugars Rum &c.," followed by "the Sloop *Stagg* . . . with Salt & Beer, from pool Bound to Newfoundland," and the brig *Ann*, "with Salt & provisions," also bound for Newfoundland. Sailing aboard the privateer *Chace* on December 3, 1781, Zuriel Waterman noted in his journal the capture of a brigantine "from Antigua bound to Halifax . . . [carrying] about 40 hhds. rum cargo." The *Revenge* of Stonington, Connecticut—not to be confused with the vessel of the same name under Conyngham—"spoke" with a vessel "at Sunrise" on March 16, 1777. It proved to be a "schooner from Halifax Bound to Dominica Laden with Fish and Lumber." The crew immediately roused the captain and mate and boarded the schooner. The *Revenge* easily took its prize, which left "all hands in Good Spearits."[12]

Luck oftentimes played a role in the capture of a vessel. Such was the case with a brig taken by the *Pilgrim* in June 1781. The *Pilgrim* had avoided a fleet of ships "standing to the Westward," not wanting its sailors to find themselves outgunned and outnumbered. One vessel, however, a brig under Captain Vaughn, "was returning to the nearest port having sprung a leak." The crew boarded it, and it was sent to "the nearest Spanish port, in charge of a prize Master." The *Oliver Cromwell* of Beverly, Massachusetts, also used Spanish ports for its prizes. On July 31, 1777, the privateer spotted a sail and gave chase. After giving "her a Gun," the crew overtook "a small Sloop called the 3 Sisters . . . Loaded with Butter, and Sheep Guts." Making berth from Cork and bound to Lisbon, the prize was sent to the port of Bilbao under the direction of Mr. Horton, most likely a prize master.[13]

Traveling in company with the *Revenue* in the spring of 1777, the *Revenge* of Connecticut "maide sail" after spotting a vessel bearing west by southwest. Though their quarry was a "grate Ways of[f]," the privateers "gave her a Gun" until they were finally able to speak to it. Their prize was a vessel named the *Lovely Lass* sailing from London to New York. The crews spent the following day "imploy'd in Taking things out of the Prise and Bringing them on Board the Privateers." When the transfer of items was completed, the privateers "dischargd her [and] Shee made Sail," at which point they "bid the Lovely Lass adue." The two privateers were once again in pursuit of a potential prize several weeks later. The *Revenge* took the lead, giving it "several Bow Guns," followed by "4 Broadside[s]." "Now all most in small arm shot," the sailors on the *Revenge* prepared for another broadside when their target "hawld Down her insine." Crew from the privateer boarded the vessel, "a Snow from Mountserat Bound to London," whose cargo consisted of "shoogar and Cotton Wool." Both the *Revenge* and the *Revenue* "put a Prizemaster and 7 more men on Board."[14]

Dr. Solomon Drowne, serving aboard the *Hope* of Providence, Rhode Island, described his discomfort with chasing and taking prizes: "There seems something awful in the preparation for an attack, and the immediate prospect of an action." Yet the crew of the *Hope* was pleased with their bounty, as Drowne "hear[d] the Huzza on deck in consequence of her striking." The *Hope* took prize of a snow sailing from Kingston, Jamaica, to New York. The vast cargo haul included "149 Puncheons, 23 Hogsheads, 3 Quarter Casks and 9 Barrels of Rum, and 20 Hogsheads Muscovado Sugar"—quite good for a day's work at sea.[15]

There were days that proved much less fruitful for American privateers. Despite their many successful encounters and prizes taken, vessels engaged

in numerous chases and exchanges that came to naught. A few days after its successful capture of the snow, "a sail [was] cried" aboard the *Hope*.
The privateer vessel pursued what appeared to be a brig, and the chase continued "till night prevent[ed] [further action]." Timothy Boardman, sailing
aboard the *Oliver Cromwell* of New London, Connecticut, noted three days
in a row where the ship "saw a Sail [and] Gave Chace" without success. A
month later, the *Oliver Cromwell* spied "a Large Jamaica Puncheon Floating." The privateer sent a ship in pursuit of the craft "but Could not Get it."
The crew was disappointed, for they "Suppos^d it was full of Rum." One evening in April 1777, the *Revenge* spied a sail, so the privateer "hove about and
Stood after her." Ultimately, John Palmer recorded, "[The sailors] concluded
it Best Not to Speek With her to Night." The next morning, the privateer
discovered the ship was no prize, but a neutral vessel bound from France to
Hispaniola. On another cruise in May 1778, the *Revenge* spied a "sloop to the
Westward" of the craft. The privateer set out after it, but ultimately "gave up
Chase for Shee out Saild" them.[16]

Zuriel Waterman, sailing aboard the privateer *Providence* of Providence,
Rhode Island, recorded the twenty-four-hour pursuit of a vessel on October
31, 1779. He wrote, "A little before sunrise [we] saw a sail bearing S easterly
from us; [we put] out oars and rowed" in the hunt. As the distance between
the two vessels shrank, the *Providence* set out its boat. A dense fog settled
over the scene, and the small craft was lost to sight until "at 1 P.M. the boat
came back; they [the pursuing sailors] got within 1 mile of her [the potential prize] when the fog came up very thick, so they lost sight of her." The
fog cleared an hour later, and the *Providence* took up the chase again, lowering the small boat back into the water. Waterman recounted the *Providence*'s
actions as evening fell: "[The crew] fired several guns and showed lights at
masthead by turns all night as signal for our boat, but saw nothing of her."
The sun rose over the water, but the small boat was still nowhere to be seen.
As the morning hours faded, the vessel returned to the *Providence*, and those
aboard it reported that "they got very nigh the brig last night so as to hear
the people talk, cut wood, and a dog bark; they judged her to be a British
brig; they prepared to board her when a thick fog came on, and they immediately lost sight of her." After twenty-four hours at the chase, the *Providence* came up empty-handed; such was the luck, or lack thereof, of a privateer venture.[17]

Encounters between privateers and their prey could result in nonviolent
actions such as those discussed above, but there were also instances of battles at sea. These violent clashes of ship against ship, sailor against sailor de-

termined the ultimate fate of a vessel, its crew, and its cruise. On the morning of August 31, 1778, the *Oliver Cromwell* of Connecticut spied a brig in the distance. The privateer "gave her Chace" and raised its colors; in turn, the brig "hoisted English Colours," and the *Oliver Cromwell* "gave her one gun which made them come Tumbling Down." Earlier that year, the *Oliver Cromwell* had engaged in a fierce battle with the *Admiral Kepple*. Initially flying French colors to deceive the American privateer, the *Admiral Kepple* proved a British ship. Timothy Boardman described the scene in his logbook: "We Gave her a Bow Gun She Soon Returned us a Stern Chaise & then a Broad Side of Grape and Round Shot." Aware of his ship's size and position, the captain of the *Oliver Cromwell* gave "orders Not to fire till . . . [the sailors could] See the white of their Eyes." In the ensuing battle, the *Admiral Kepple* fired another broadside, while the *Oliver Cromwell* "hel^d Tuff & Tuff for About 2 Glasses." In the end, the American privateer emerged the victor, but at a cost—"one Kill^d & Six wounded one Mortally Who Soon Died," in addition to the ship being "hull^d 9 Times with Six Pound Shott Three of which Went through [the] Birth."[18]

On May 26, 1780, Philip Freneau aboard the *Aurora* of Philadelphia, Pennsylvania, found himself in the midst of an all-out battle. A British frigate accompanied by two prizes bore down on the *Aurora* and "began bringing her cannon to bear" on the vessel. A hail of cannon fire broke out among the ships. The privateer crew of the *Aurora* realized they were outnumbered, but there was no chance of escape. The British frigate took aim at the American vessel and found its mark; "one shot went betwixt wind and water, which made the ship leak amazingly, making twenty-four inches in thirty minutes." The four-pounders of the *Aurora* were ineffective, so the privateers loaded and fired the nine-pounders. Yet this was not enough. The frigate sent a twelve-pound shot that hit "a parcel of oars lashed upon the starboard quarter, broke them all in two, and continuing its destructive course struck Captain Laboyteaux in the right thigh, which smashed it to atoms, tearing part of his belly open at the same time with the splinters from the oars." The British frigate prepared for a broadside, and after over an hour of fighting, it took the *Aurora* as a prize. Captain Laboyteaux died later that evening.[19]

Clashes between vessels could last for hours or end in mere moments. After fifty-five minutes of fighting on the evening of May 2, 1781, the *Pilgrim* took "the Brigg *Alfred* from Liverpool bound to New York, loaded with prov^s Dry Goods &c. mounting 14 Six pounders and commanded by Capt Collinson." The American privateer "received no great damage," while the prize "had her mast and rigging exceeding injured." A few months later, in

September, the *Pilgrim* chased, caught up with, and engaged the *Peggy*. Josiah Bartlett recorded the incident in the ship's logbook: "Having fired one full Broadside at us, [the *Pilgrim*] returned the Compliment, being close on board her, and [the *Peggy*] Struck her Colours." Sailing from Nevis to Halifax, the prize contained rum and sugar. The vessel also carried "several Gentlemen & passengers, and a Mrs Rogers, and 2 agreable Young Ladies her Dau^s."[20]

Only a few weeks out on a cruise aboard the *Revenge* of Connecticut, John Palmer described an exchange of fire between the privateer sloop and "a Ship Mounted 14 Guns." As the *Revenge* shifted position in the midst of the engagement, "theare came up a Squall of Wind and Reign" that parted the ship from its target, ending the battle before it had truly begun. Weeks later, the *Revenge* drew "very fast" toward a spotted sail. Upon closer inspection—drawing within range of "musket Shot"—the privateer "quick found her Superior force to [it]." Once the aggressor, the *Revenge* quickly became the target as the vessel gave chase and "fird Several Shot." The third shot, John Palmer described in his journal, "fird away one of our Lonyards and Struck our Starbord bow Gun." After sustaining still further damage, the *Revenge* "made all Sail for to Git Cleare of hur."[21]

In another instance, the *Revenge* attempted to take a vessel by firing "a broad side of Grape Shot." When the vessel maneuvered, the privateer countered and "kept fireing on her Several Broad Sides." Alas, the *Revenge* "could Not catch her Nor fire a Way her Masts so [it] Chased her till 2PM then hove about." In the early months of 1781, while serving aboard the privateer *Hibernia* anchored at port in Guadeloupe, Zuriel Waterman witnessed the arrival of the *Holker* and its prize, "a cutter of sixteen guns which she took after three hours of engagement." The following day, Waterman heard that the *Randolph* "engaged 2 English privateers and got badly mauled and lost many men, just escaping them," and had recently arrived in Fort Royal Harbor.[22]

At a distance, privateer vessels used false colors and flags to deceive enemy vessels prior to engagement. Both sides' use of this deception at sea allowed the pursuer to move closer to its target. Gideon Olmsted recalled such an action during his time aboard the *Polly* in July 1778. Sailing under French colors, the *Polly* encountered the *Ostrich* off the east side of Jamaica. When the *Ostrich* "fired a shot" at the privateer, the crew "hauled down [their] French colors." The captain of the *Ostrich* demanded the *Polly* "bring to or he would fire into" the vessel. With that ultimatum, the *Polly* "hoisted . . . Continental colors at [the] main top gallant head and" proceeded to fire "a broadside into her [the *Ostrich*]." The battle had begun.[23]

The two vessels exchanged broadsides, and the crew of the *Ostrich* boarded the *Polly* "by running her bowsprit on [the privateer's] quarterdeck." According to Olmsted, all but seven men on the deck fled from their positions, but those who remained "were determined to die before [they] would give up." The men from the *Ostrich* attacked "with their spears and tomahawks." Subsequently, the two ships were grappled together while both sides "fought with small arms, blunderbusses, hand grenades, fire flasks, spears and tomahawks, and coehorns . . . then fell off from one another and then played with cannon and small arms." The action continued for several hours until the *Ostrich* "hauled down her British colors." Victory seemed at hand for the *Polly*, until out of the distance an "8 gun brig came up under British colors . . . they both engaged" the American vessel. The brig, *Lowestoffe's Prize*, turned the tide in Britain's favor; the *Polly* was lost and taken as a prize.[24]

While in pursuit of a vessel in the summer of 1777, the *Revenge* of Connecticut showed "English Colors" in an attempt to deceive its quarry. When the sailors on the privateer "haild her," they found this ship to be a worthwhile prize: a brig on course to Newfoundland from Dominica with rum in its cargo hold. The *Oliver Cromwell* of Beverly, Massachusetts, engaged two vessels on August 6, 1777. The enemy vessels fired first, but the *Oliver Cromwell* "took no Notice of [them] till [they] came nigh enough to give her 2 Broad Sides." The firepower of the American privateer quickly forced the first vessel to "beg" off and "desist [the *Oliver Cromwell's*] Fire on her." Without the ability to flee, vessels damaged in battle had two choices: fight to the death or surrender. Land troops might be able to retreat over terrain or water, for the coast was always near. For privateers in the midst of the ocean, running—or rather, swimming—for safety was not an option.[25]

The captain of the *Oliver Cromwell* then turned his attention to the second enemy vessel; the privateer "charged the other with an incessant Fire for almost 3 Glasses" until that vessel, too, decided to disengage. Alas, night was swiftly falling on the three ships. With the threat "of the Man of War which had been in Chace all Day, & was now reasonably expected to be near up," the officers of the *Oliver Cromwell* decided to give up the assault. An unknown writer kept a journal during the venture and noted the efforts of the crew: "Capt Coles (to his eternal Honour be it remembered) with all the other Officers behaved with the greatest Magnanimity & Bravery possible." The log keeper offered further commendations, stating, "The Seamen & Marines . . . with remarkable Unanimity, good Order, & Heroism seemed to vie with each other, which should excel in their several Departments." Indeed, the journal even contains an incomplete poem in honor of the battle:

Then must our parent State Confess
That we their freeborn Sons excel
In Courage, & true Excellence
Our British Foes, tho they act well
Coles, with his brave Officers
His Men both martial
bold & brave.[26]

Engagements occurred not only at sea but also on the beach, as privateers ranged along the shorelines of the Atlantic. Privateers fought land engagements, however small, on foreign soil. Sailing off the west coast of Africa in February 1778, the *Marlborough* "mand 2 Schooners and the Barge with About 50 men Well Armd to go on Shore." The shore party landed safely and placed sentinels on guard duty. Under heavy fire from local African residents, the crew kept up "a Constant fire from the 2 Schooners & Small arms on Shore." The privateers came away with "cases of Ginn pipes of ginn Powder arms and Dry goods of Various kinds." King Tom, a local resident, eventually negotiated a truce with Captain Babcock of the *Marlborough*. The result of the attack "was Killd on Shore 1 Black & 1 french Boy, By the Centinels and Som wounded."[27]

The following day, Captain Babcock went ashore and made an announcement. He declared that "if [the residents] would Surrender all English property in their hands he would treat them with honour. & Leave their Craft, and Buildings Unmolested, but if not—he Should Burn, Sink. & Destroy Wherever he was resisted." Two traders from Rhode Island approached Babcock "begging to Save their House & Effects (the Captain assurd them he woud)." A nearby town learned the truth of this promise. Babcock "sent Capt Brown on Shore with 15 Men Well Arm'd in Order to Bring another Load of Wood & to Burn the Town Stores &c agreable to the Captains Orders & Instructions—as it was English property. and As they wou'd not Capitulate . . . Upon Honourable Terms." Soon afterward, "the Buildings were all in flames."[28]

In the height of a melee, privateers fought not only for the enemy vessel, cargo, or goods, but for their lives as well. While engagements brought the opportunity for prize and profit, conflict also meant the chance of injury and death. After its encounter with the two British vessels, the *Oliver Cromwell* took stock of its crew. The unknown author of the ship's journal wrote, "Through the marvellous Goodness of God not one Life was lost on our Side." However, the first lieutenant did not escape unscathed; the officer

"was wounded by a Cannon Shott in both his thighs, just above the Knees."
Several other crew members were also "very slightly wounded."[29]

Gideon Olmsted noted after the *Polly's* engagement with the *Ostrich* and
Lowestoffe's Prize that the ship's company "had 100 men including officers
and boys when the engagement begun." He then added, "We had better
than half killed and wounded." In the midst of battle, Captain Proshon of
the *Polly* sought out Olmsted at the wheel; the latter man had taken up the
position after three others were killed. As the captain stood by Olmsted, "in
the height of his glory a cannon ball struck off the top of his [Proshon's]
head." Some of the wounded were carried aboard *Lowestoffe's Prize*; Olmsted himself "was slightly wounded by the force of a cannon ball, [and had]
one arm and one thigh which swelled much." Olmsted commended the efforts of his mate John Buckland, who "was slightly wounded on both legs,"
recalling, "While he was afighting upon the quarterdeck a fire flask fell so
nigh him that burnt one, the other, leg very bad." After an encounter with
the *Isabella*—a sloop sailing "from Baltimore in Maryland . . . to Lorient in
France"—Zuriel Waterman, the surgeon on the *Providence*, treated "one of
her [the *Isabella's*] hands [who] came aboard to have his hand dressed which
was mashed." In pursuit of a canoe off the shores of Isle de Loss in Africa,
Lieutenant Eldred of the *Marlborough* was injured when "several Cartridge
Boxes" caught fire and "burnt Lieuᵗ: Eldred. Legg & Schorch'd 1 Man."[30]

Making moves to specifically avoid a battle or conflict with a superior
vessel might save lives during a cruise. In September 1778, the crew of the
Revenge found themselves caught in a chase with a "Brittish frigate" which
"drawd" near the ship "very fast." Fearing they might be taken and attempting to escape unscathed, the privateers "concluded for to Lightning [their]
Vessels By Starting Sum Water and Heaving over three Cannon." Though
the *Revenge* gained speed, the frigate continued its chase. The privateer
"hove over two more Cannon" and five hogsheads of water. While the crew
fully expected "to Git taken," as fate would have it another ship appeared in
the distance, and the British frigate "hawld hur Wind after the other Ship."
Two days later, the *Revenge* dropped anchor in New London Harbor: home
safe and sound.[31]

Despite the risks to life and limb, American privateers chased and engaged enemy vessels in hopes of securing a prize. When the *Oliver Cromwell* of Connecticut took the *Admiral Kepple*, the prize contained "one Chist
of Holland a Quantity of Hatts & Shoes Cheeses Porter & Some Crockery
Ware Small Arms Pistols Hangers two Brass Barrel Blunderbusses [and] a
Quantity of Riggen & C." Material goods from a prize might be used on

board the privateer vessel, such as the "4 Carriage Guns Caring 6 Pound Shot" that were "hoisted in and mounted" on the *Marlborough* from the captured *Fancy*. After the *Oliver Cromwell* of Beverly, Massachusetts, took three brigs in one day, the crew hauled in holds "loaden with Fish Several Bales of Goods, some China ware, & other Valuables," plus another "fine Prize [of] 103 bales of Goods."[32]

Goods found aboard prizes, as well as the vessel itself, could be sold in port for pure profit. Captain William Cole of the *Oliver Cromwell* ordered Mr. Thrash to take command of a recently captured prize filled with fruit. Cole told Thrash "to Sell the Fruit (if much damaged)" in the port of Bilbao, Spain, "& fo[r]ward the Vessell with a Cargo to Salem." If the fruit was "fit to proceed," Thrash should keep the cargo intact "& proceed di[rectly] to Salem." The *Hibernia* sent one of its prize vessels to Fort Royal, and it was "sold there for the use of the [French] Royal Navy." African Americans taken with the prize were also sent "ashore to sell."[33]

If the potential revenue from a prize's hold did not seem particularly high, a captain might choose to ransom a ship. During his ventures in the North Sea, Gustavus Conyngham took the British brig *Patty* and ransomed it for £630. The privateer *Chace* captured a shallop in December 1781 and ransomed it for "700 dollars." Oftentimes, the captain of a privateer sent a prize master and a small crew aboard a prize. This crew was charged with maintaining control of the vessel and taking it into port, where it would be condemned at court and sold. The captain of the *Rambler* "dispatched Mr. A. Crawley and ____ Parker in the prize schooner for Newburyport." Three other men were sent in the prize *Katy* with "orders to go to Dover."[34]

Crews feared for the safety of their prizes. If a captured ship was lost or retaken, there was no recourse and, as a result, no prize money for the privateers. A prize needed to make it to a safe port and into trusted hands; otherwise, the efforts of the crew amounted to nothing. The *New-York Gazette* reported the loss of one of Captain Gustavus Conyngham's prizes, the brig *Venus*. According to the article, the *Venus* was initially "bound form Greenland to Liverpool, with some Blubber and Whale-bone, when taken, on the 3^d of August, by a Cutter Privateer, called the Revenge, of 14 Pounders, fitted out and manned at Dunkirk and commanded by Gustavus Cunningham of Philadelphia." The ship was retaken on October 4 by "Capt. Daniel Campbell, in the Revenge Privateer." While sailing alongside the *Pilgrim* in June 1781, the *Essex*, under Captain Cathcart from Salem, Massachusetts, spoke with the *Good Intent*, "a Transport from Jamaica bound to Europe." An American cruiser, the *Rambler*, had boarded the *Good Intent* ten days prior "and stripped her of everything, except Sick Soldiers & Women." With nothing left aboard the *Good Intent* worth taking, the *Essex* decided to move on and released the ship. The *Rambler's* prize still had a chance to make a successful journey into port, albeit with an empty hold.[35]

The following spring, the *Pilgrim* "saw a Sail a head and gave chace, at 7 [the privateer] fired 2 Shott at her, & she hove too." The *Pilgrim* discovered the ship was the sloop *Sally*, "a prize to His Britannic Majesty's Ship *Garland*, when taken from New Haven bound to Havannah." Subsequently, the crew of the *Pilgrim* took control of the *Sally* as its own prize and placed Mr. Nothey on board as prize master bound for Salem, Massachusetts. The crew of the HMS *Garland* had no idea their recently acquired prize no longer belonged to them; the vessel was now prize to the *Pilgrim*.[36]

In the morning hours of September 30, 1781, the privateer *Chace* of Salem, Massachusetts, spotted a ship "within shore" distance. The *Chace* pursued the vessel and "engage[d] her . . . she could bring no guns to bear upon" the privateer. Though the pursued vessel "fired several shot," they were "to no effect"; the Chace "fired 8 guns at her; she struck." At this point, the *Chace* took command of the vessel, which "was a prize to the *Chatham*, a 50 gun," and the captain sent Lieutenant Silver and six men aboard the newly seized craft. The *Chatham* lost its prize vessel without knowing the capture had occurred. Such were the chances of sending a prize unaccompanied into a nearby port.[37]

When a port was close at hand, some privateer captains chose to escort their prizes to shore rather than risk losing them at sea. One "privateer from Philadelphia" who "brought in 2 prizes" to St. Pierre, "one a brigantine from Ireland, the other the *Longsplice*, a noted privateer schooner of 10 guns from Antigua," made this choice. When the *Hope* encountered a sloop and a brig in open waters, the crew made "every preparation for an engagement." But upon their approach, the two ships proved a fellow privateer from New London, Connecticut, and "her prize from England, taken at 8 o'clock this morning." Captain Fosdick of the privateer *Randolph* personally escorted his prize into port, for "her Cargo amounted to £20,000 Sterling," a sum much too high to risk losing. Solomon Drowne noted in his journal after capturing a snow, "How uneasy every one on board is, fearing to lose the prize." When they sighted land, the men erupted into "uncommon spirits."[38]

The journey of a prize vessel from capture to a safe port was perilous. When the *Pilgrim* took the ship *Hercules* "from Africa bound to Barbadoes . . . after a chace of 2 hours," two other vessels, the *Mohawk* and the *Swift*, arrived shortly thereafter and tried to claim "a porportion of the Prize."

Captain Robinson of the *Pilgrim* refused to allow men from the other privateer ships to board the *Hercules*, or to take any portion of its hold "loaded with Wood, Wax & Ivory, & a quantity of Gold dust." Instead, the captain sent the prize to "Martineco in charge of Mr Rand, p. Mast^r." Alas, upon the *Pilgrim*'s arrival in the harbor of St. Pierre, the captain received distressing news. Three prizes, the *Prince Wm Henry*, *Penobscott*, and *Friendship*, arrived safely in port. The *Hercules*, however, was "sunk at sea the day after . . . parting with her & Mr Rand & his crew were taken from her by the *Mohawk*." Such circumstances caused suspicion and "many severe reflections cast upon Mr Rand respecting the prize, and probably not without great Cause."[39]

At the end of its second voyage in October 1781, the *Pilgrim* returned home to the port of Beverly, Massachusetts, where the captain and crew learned "y^t 3 of [their] prizes had arived safe." While the arrival of these vessels was indeed good news, the crew was disappointed that there were "no more." In June 1782, on back-to-back days during its third cruise, the *Pilgrim* had exceptional good fortune and took two ships, the brig *Apledore* and the brig *Beaton*. The *Apledore* sailed "from Europe bound to Newfoundland laden with Prov^s," while the *Beaton* made way from London to Quebec "laden with Spirituous liquors, &c." Both ships were boarded by prize masters from the *Pilgrim* and sent to Beverly, Massachusetts. A month later, when the *Pilgrim* arrived back in port at Beverly, the crew learned "none of [their] prises as yet, except the Brigg *Neptune*" had arrived "to the no small satisfaction of a Ships company." The capture of a vessel did not always translate to the successful transport and sale of a prize.[40]

In addition to goods, ammunition, weapons, and supplies, prize vessels contained one other particular element: people, mainly in the form of prisoners and passengers. When the *Pilgrim* took the brigantine *Friendship* "from Newfoundland bound to Barbadoes" in January 1782, the vessel had "on b^d her . . . Dr Row & family." These individuals were passengers not prisoners, and they were sent into Havannah with the prize. Mr. Howland of the *Rambler* encountered "an old woman, and 2 small boys" aboard a captured shallop. The prize was stripped of its cargo of "salmon, butter, and eggs." When the vessel was readied for shore, the old woman "fell to lamenting and begging," arguing it "was too leaky to send home." Ultimately, the shallop was dismissed.[41]

On a "fair pleas^t" day, the *Oliver Cromwell* encountered "a fine Brig from Cork for Lisbon Laden with Butter & Beef." Upon inspecting the prize, the crew determined it was "formerly an American Privateer called the Montgomery mounting 18 Guns, taken & carried in to Gibralter." On board the former privateer, the sailors of the *Oliver Cromwell* discovered "several Laidys . . . boun[d] to Lisbon, whom [they] determined to take on Board . . . & together with all [their] other Prisoners land them [the ladies] (as they were effectionately desireous of it) on the British Shore."[42]

When Gustavus Conyngham took the *Prince of Orange* packet, he transferred all of the passengers, including the captain and crew, onto a Dutch fishing vessel and allowed them to maintain possession of their personal articles. While Conyngham treated his captured passengers with respect, other privateers felt differently. One letter writer reported the capture of a ship from England with "5 gentlemen, their wives, children, servants, and household furniture" on board; the passengers were "intending to settle on some pleasant part of the conquered lands." The author did not care to aid these travelers, noting, "I hope we shall be able to settle them all as these are settled (viz.) in a Goal."[43]

Prisoners were often taken in the middle of a vast ocean and far from land, which left American privateers with few choices in terms of their treatment. When the privateer *Hope* took a vessel sailing from Kingston, Jamaica, to New York, the captain sent "two prize Masters and ten men on board, [to] get the prisoners . . . and tak[e] the prize in tow." Prisoners could prove useful if they decided to change loyalties and serve as members of the privateer crew. The *Marlborough* already had "as many Prisoners as" it could accommodate when the privateer took the *Fancy*. Captain George Wait Babcock decided to give "the Major Part of the Prisoners Boats to go Whither they Pleas'd"—an uncommon grant of freedom without parole from an American privateer.[44]

For privateers lacking space, prisoners were transferred to other ships or given parole. After capturing the ship *Good Intent*, the *Pilgrim* needed to dispose of an influx of prisoners. A nearby Danish ship proved useful, as the *Pilgrim* "put all [its] prisoners on board her, to get to Europe, having taken their parolls and furnished them with provisions." Josiah Bartlett, log keeper aboard the *Pilgrim*, was impressed for the "behaviour of the Kings Officers on board . . . during their Stay, could not fail to give satisfaction, and the Generosity & Gratitude of Capt Smith & Mr Jackson at their departure extended to the most inferior Officer on b^d the Ship." In May 1781, after moving "everything valuable out of [the sloop *Stagg*] & put[ting] [it] on board the *Ann*," the crew of the *Pilgrim* "put all [its] prisoners to the amount of 55, on board the Sloop, taking their paroles, and gave them permission to go where they pleased, furnishing them with necessary provisions Liquors &c."

During the *Pilgrim*'s third cruise, on July 20, 1782, Bartlett noted, "At four p m put all our prisoners on board her, taking their parole."[45]

Transferring prisoners to nearby ships seemed to be a common practice for the *Pilgrim* and its crew, as it was for other privateers. The *Oliver Cromwell* of Beverly, Massachusetts, took "a Small sloop from Isle of Man bound to Port a Port in Ballast." The crew removed "some Sails, a Gun & Sundries" from the vessel, then "put . . . Prisoners on Board & sent her away." When the *Oliver Cromwell* encountered a French ship a few months later, the crew once again "put all . . . Prisoners on Board her," clearing space in the hold for the prisoners of the next prize. Sailing aboard the *Oliver Cromwell* of Connecticut, Timothy Boardman noted a similar experience with a French vessel. The captain of the privateer decided to "put 6 Prisoners on Board of Her" during the last month of the ship's second cruise. Zuriel Waterman recounted the dismissal of "Mr. D Ross and 5 men . . . also the mate and 3 men of the *Rachel*, giving them paroles and the brigt.'s long boat" during his service aboard the privateer *Chace*.[46]

Privateers moved prisoners to other vessels for various reasons. Space aboard ship was certainly a concern, as was the availability of provisions. Holds were stocked based on the number of crew members at the beginning of a voyage, not typically including the foodstuffs needed for potential prisoners. Prisoner uprising was another serious worry for privateers. A sufficient number of captives on board could create the opportunity for taking over a ship. On September 29, 1781, the captain of the *Pilgrim* "learned from One of the Prisoners, that at 4 Oclock, the prisoners had determined to attempt taking the ship." The decision was not hastily made; rather, the crew "found sundry matters [the prisoners] had secreted to facilitate their Design." Josiah Bartlett tried to make light of the situation in his log, noting, "Ever having been on our guard their attempt would have been in vain." However, Bartlett also admitted, "This inteligence doubled our vigilence, and we Ironed [the prisoners] hand & foot."[47]

Privateers serving on board the *Hope* had "their pistols hung up in the Cabin, to be in readiness for the prisoners, should they take it into their heads to rise upon the watch in the night." The privateer *Columbia* of New York placed a prize master and small crew aboard the newly taken sloop *St. Peter* and ordered the vessel to New York. During the cruise, prisoners still on board "secured the prize-master and people, and . . . [sailed] for Sinepuxent." After running aground, they arrived safely in port. Captives on board posed a certain risk, but the potential for danger was not enough to stop pri-

vateers from engaging and capturing prizes. The prospective profit and possible chance of hurting the enemy were enough to motivate these seafarers
in their prize-taking endeavors.[48]

Gustavus Conyngham and his crew experienced all of these aspects of
privateering during their cruises—chasing and engaging enemy vessels, risk-
ing life and limb, questioning what to do with prisoners, and achieving the
ultimate goal of bringing a prize safely into port. On July 16, 1778, the *Pennsylvania Packet* informed its readers, "The Peace and Harmony, Kennedy,
from Lisbon to London; the Betsey, Murphy, from the Streights to Newry;
the Fanny, St. Barbe, from ditto to London; the Hope letter of marque, from
ditto to Bristol; and the Enterprize, tender to the Enterprize frigate, are all
taken by the Revenge, Capt. Cunningham." Following his travails in the
North Sea and off the coasts of England and Ireland, Conyngham planned
to sail the *Revenge* to America. However, strong winds damaged his ship
and forced him to seek haven in a European port. Returning to France was
not an option, as Conyngham's actions at Dunkirk and subsequent time in
prison made him an unwelcome guest; certainly, the British ambassador,
Lord Stormont, could not and would not have tolerated the return of "the
Dunkirk Pirate." Instead, Conyngham and crew turned to Spain. Sailing
from El Ferrol and, later, Bilbao, Conyngham and the *Revenge* returned to
the seas seeking to terrorize and capture enemy vessels.[49]

During the late months of 1777 and early months of 1778, Conyngham
and the *Revenge* used these Spanish ports to mount their privateering operations. As long as the captain and his crew followed the unwritten rules concerning covert operations and refrained from overtly flaunting their prize
captures, Spain maintained a cordial and supportive relationship with the
American privateer. For a period of time, the *Revenge* ranged the seas and
acted in accordance with Spain's expectations, capturing four vessels during
the fall of 1777. Silas Deane noted in a letter composed January 15, 1778,
"Cunningham had, on the 20th. December, carried in two prizes to Carogne,
one of which sold for 6,000 & the other for 4,500, & was gone out on a second Cruize." The first sign of trouble with Spain emerged during that very
cruise when the *Revenge* pursued a French brig, the *Gracieux*. A French-
owned vessel should have been safe from seizure. However, the crew of the
Revenge was hankering for a prize. Conyngham justified the capture by noting that British vessels had taken French and Spanish ships with American
cargoes; the *Gracieux*, in Conyngham's mind, was carrying British cargo and
hence was liable to capture and sale.[50]

Spain did not react well to Conyngham's blatant violation of a neutral vessel—the French brig was seized and the privateer crew imprisoned. In addition, Conyngham received a strongly worded letter of reprimand from Silas Deane, who told him, "Every such adventure gives our Enemies advantage against us by representing us as persons who regard not the Law of Nations." Once again, one single decision the captain made and carried out caused an international incident and had the potential to swing the balance of power in the Atlantic World and the war. "Your Idea that you are at Liberty to seize English Property on board of French or other neutral Vessels is wrong," Deane continued, adding, "It is contrary to the established Laws among the maritime Powers in Europe." Deane admitted "that the English, in the last war, paid little or no regard to this Law." However, he reminded Conyngham, "[Britain's] situation and ours is very differnt in point of Force, tho not so in point of right." Conyngham must refrain from engaging with neutral vessels.[51]

Conyngham remained in port for the next few months while attempting to free his crew and reclaim his prize. Eventually, he was forced to drop his case. In March 1778, the *Revenge* and its captain returned to sea. The *Pennsylvania Packet*, printed in Conyngham's hometown of Philadelphia, kept readers apprised of the captain's feats, as evidenced by the list of captures printed on July 16, 1778.[52]

Though Spain was upset about the *Gracieux* affair, Conyngham was still well received in Spanish ports. One British seaman reported the treatment the American privateer received in Cadiz. As a British ship sat in the harbor for seven days awaiting recognition from the Spanish government, "the Revenge American privateer, commanded by Cunningham, who came swaggering in with his Thirteen stripes, saluted the Spanish Admiral, had it returned, and immediately got product; the Spaniards themselves [were] carrying on board wood, water, fruit, and fresh provisions." A letter from Cadiz published in the *Pennsylvania Packet* noted, "Cunningham in the Revenge Privateer, sailed from hence some days since on a cruize." Upon Conyngham's return to the Spanish port, the paper stated, "[The] Maria, Predoe, from London to Gibralter, is taken by the Revenge privateer, Capt. Cunningham, and carried into Corunna." Following the capture of the *Maria*, the crew of the *Revenge* demanded payment of their prize money. Conyngham, in need of sailors and forbidden to recruit in the Spanish port, conceded. The *Revenge* returned to the waters of the Atlantic, where it encountered the Swedish brig *Honoria Sophia*—the capture that spelled the end of Conyngham's privateering career along the coasts of Europe.[53]

The decision to pursue a vessel belonged to the captain of the privateer and his officers, as did the decision to leave off chasing a ship. The chain of command for privateers was self-contained on board a vessel; privateers waited for no one. On September 12, 1781, the *Pilgrim* spotted two ships nearby "which from their behaviour ... [it] judged to be Cruizers." Log keeper Josiah Bartlett recorded, "At noon one of them was within Musquet Shott of us, and fired a great number of Shott at us, some came very near, at One we made Sail, thinking not proper to Engage." The risks in this situation outweighed the potential for success. The following day, the *Pilgrim* "saw the Two Ship[s] again." Bartlett noted that the privateer once more "thought proper to avoid it, & ... therefore parted with them." While cruising near the island of Barbados in April 1782, the *Pilgrim* came upon a ship and "gave chace but finding her an Armed Ship (and judged to be a packet) Captain Robinson imagined she would endeavour to fight her way to the land & ... therefore hauld ... Wind: being not more than 5 or 6 Miles from the Shore."[54]

Captains of privateers examined each potential prize situation before determining whether to take or leave a vessel. The privateer *Providence* spoke with a vessel on the morning of September 18, 1779, that was "full of soldiers bound to New York." Initially, the *Providence* "fired about 24 shot at her," then left off a few minutes to assess the situation. The potential prize carried "4 guns," and the privateer decided not to take it, for "she would hurt ... [the *Providence*'s] cruise, because it would take so many men to man her and look after the prisoners." When the *Chace* encountered the *Robust* from England, the privateer initially engaged the enemy vessel. However, the captain and crew eventually reversed this decision: "She [the *Robust*] being so nigh Chebucto Head, we thought fit to quit her, there being many British ships in Halifax that could easily put out to retake her." Though the American privateer might succeed in taking the vessel, the chances of keeping it were quite low. Thus, the risk was too high and not worth the fight.[55]

While these decisions supposedly belonged to the captain, as Conyngham discovered, the crew often had more to say on the subject. Mutiny among crews was a real threat for privateers. Despite attempts to instill rules and regulations, the isolation of a ship left it vulnerable, and international crews could be harder to control. Aboard the *Fortune*, "the crew mutinied, intending to make the captain return and cruise off Halifax, threatening to go ashore." When Conyngham and the *Revenge* set sail from Cadiz, Spain, in May 1778, the vessel encountered the Swedish brig *Honoria Sophia*. Considering the late incident with the *Gracieux*, the *Revenge* should have left the brig alone. The crew, however, would not acquiesce and threatened to mutiny if the ship was not taken. Twenty-five sailors signed an attestation stating, "Whereas on this day we fell in with the Swedish Brigg Henerica Sophia Laden with British Goods from London to Tenerif & whereas Captn. Cunningham says that he has directions not to Insult any Neutral Flag yet, the Cargoe appearing so plain to be British property we have eng'd him to take her, & try her chance to America." The incident caused an uproar among European powers, and Conyngham was shunned when he tried to put in at Corunna to provision and refit the *Revenge*. The *Revenge's* time in European waters had come to an end.[56]

The reaction to Conyngham's seizure was not uncommon. British representatives in France and Spain complained at length about the actions of American privateers, but Conyngham was different. He offered a face to the issue; his success made him a household name. After the *Honoria Sophia* was taken, the Comte de Vergennes received a letter from the Comte de Creutz informing the minister of foreign affairs that "an American corsair named Cunningham, who seized [the *Honoria Sophia*] and sent the ship, with the Captain and three men of the crew, to America ... put [the rest of the crew] at the bottom of the hold as prisoners, and made [them] to experience all sorts of hardships." The Comte de Creutz asked for immediate action, "not only to obtain the restitution of that vessel and its cargo, with all suitable damages, but also to cause that corsair to be punished exemplarily."[57]

Benjamin Franklin assured his contacts, "We have no desire to justify [Conyngham] in any irregularities he may have committed." Franklin continued, "In the [congressional] commission given to privateers, ... it appears that sureties are taken of their owners that nothing shall be done by them 'inconsistent with the usage and custom of nations,' and those sureties are obliged to make good all damages." In a follow-up letter, he wrote, "It is a crime in our eyes to have displeased a power for which Congress is penetrated with respect, and although justified in seizing, by way of reprisals, the English prize which Conyngham had brought to Teneriffe to be sent to Martinique, we will none the less inform Congress of the grounds for complaint which this privateer has given to his Catholic majesty" of Spain.[58]

Arthur Lee wrote to the Committee of Foreign Affairs, "The court of Spain is so much offended at Captain Cunningham's conduct before this, that they write me orders have been sent to all their ports to prohibit his entrance." "From the beginning to the end of this business of Cunningham, it has been so bad," Lee postulated, "that Congress only can correct it by punishing those who are concerned." The American ambassadors to France were attempting to clean up the so-called mess Conyngham had made.[59]

The commander and his vessel, the *Revenge*, left Spain in September 1778 bound for the waters of the Caribbean Sea. Upon his arrival, Conyngham continued cruising against British enemy vessels. News from St. Pierre announced the appearance of "this intrepid Commander, so well known for his having an English Packet boat, and by that a Cutter of 18 guns, having spread terror through the coasts of England, Scotland, and Ireland." "In 18 month's cruize," the report noted, "he has taken 27 English vessels, and sent them into different ports, and has sunk or burnt 33." After a few months in the waters off Martinique, St. Lucia, Antigua, and St. Eustatius, Conyngham and the *Revenge* "returned from her cruize, bringing with her an English brig, the Loyalist, Capt. Morris, of 12 guns, and the sloop *Admiral Barrington*, Capt. Pelham, of 8 guns." A newspaper account added, "He has taken besides another vessel which he has sent to Guadaloop; and two small sloops which he ransomed."[60]

While Conyngham had recently lost the support of the Spanish, the Dutch seemed to welcome him. A letter addressed "to the Dutch Admiral commanding at St. Eustatius" asked, "Have you not summed up every mark of insolence and injurious behavior in your late reception of Cunningham, a known outlaw, who long infested the British seas, without so much as the flimsy pretence of a Congress commission, with which indeed he had no connection, and in whose quarrel he had no pretense to enter?" The missive continued, "Surely wherever such a fellow could have been seized, he should have been sacrificed to the violated rights of mankind." Apparently, the Dutch admiral did not concur.[61]

Captain Conyngham's final action in the Caribbean Sea consisted of sailing in convoy with the French fleet during the last weeks of December 1778. Contrary to the notion that they did not choose to sail in convoy, a myth perpetrated by the Penobscot Expedition, privateers often sailed and worked side by side in taking prizes. Seven vessels—the *Marquis*, schooners *Vengeance* and *Young Neptune*, and brigs *Trooper*, *Adventure*, *Randolph*, and *Betsey*—sought prizes in tandem. These privateers devised a system of signals used in pursuit of enemy ships. When the chase was on, a privateer should hang "a Pendant at Foretopgallantmasthead and hoist an English Ensign at Ensign staff." The sign for engaging an enemy vessel consisted of "haul[ing] down the English Ensign and hoist[ing] a Continental One." Privateer crews would "know Each Other after Boarding," for the "men [were] to have their shirts off." These signals proved especially useful at night, when it was difficult to see enemy and friendly vessels. Thus, sailors employed lanterns in privateer signs. To determine whether a ves-

sel was friendly, "the Enquirer . . . [gave] 6 flashes to be answered by One—
the Ship who hail[ed]. . . ask[ed] What Ship—the Hailed . . . Answer[ed]
Mountholly—then the other . . . repl[ied] Samboy." When the enemy was
"thought Superior" and separation deemed "necessary," "three flashes not to
be answer^d" were given.[62]

While Conyngham sailed with the French fleet under Jean Baptiste
Charles Henri Hector, Comte d'Estaing, the *Royal Gazette* reported an encounter with British ships. A reprinted letter from the ship *Martha* read as
follows: "The Count shewed a disposition to attack us a third time, but on
the appearance of a frigate standing for his fleet with several signals flying,
he plied to windward, and in the evening anchored off Gros Islet, about two
leagues from us. . . . He has been accompanied from his first appearance by
several American privateers, one of them commanded by the outlaw Cunningham." The letter concluded with a postscript noting the capture "of an
American privateer of 18 guns, called the Bunker Hill, which at day-break
was discovered within reach of . . . [the ship's] guns; and having struck, upon
finding she could not escape, the boats towed her within the line, before any
of the French fleet could get to her assistance. She saild from Salem the 2d
inst." Though sailing in convoy could prove profitable, privateers still risked
being captured.[63]

On June 3, 1781, the *Pilgrim* "saw a Sail to leward, & gave chace." After a
full day of pursuing the vessel, the *Pilgrim* "made private signals which she answered." The chased ship was the *Essex* out of Salem, Massachusetts, a fellow
privateer "out since 22^d Ap^r and no prize." The two craft "kept C^o" with one
another for the next week, adding the privateer *Defence* of Beverly, Massachusetts, to their fleet. The three vessels sailed together until Sunday, June 10, 1778,
when they "saw a large Ship to Windward running for the Midst of [their
convoy]." Noting in his log that the vessel showed "English Colours," Josiah
Bartlett further wrote, "Many were the conjectures respecting this Ship. . . . It
was generally supposed she was not a Kings Ship, unless she meant to deceive
us, which deception we sorrowfully experienced." The English vessel initially
chased the *Pilgrim*, but the privateer outran its enemy and "then altered her
Course for the *Essex*." When the *Pilgrim* attempted to aid the *Essex*, it did
so "without success." At this point, the *Pilgrim* and its crew prepared for action, expecting the *Essex* would make its way to them. Alas, "after a chace of
4 hours," the *Pilgrim* "had the mortification to see [the *Essex*] fall a prey." The
Defence, meanwhile, had made its escape "and was not in Sight."[64]

During the winter months of the following year, the *Pilgrim* spoke with
the *Scourge* from Salem, Massachusetts, under the command of Captain

Timothy Parker. The two sailed together for three weeks into the middle
of February, when the *Pilgrim* "at one p m saw a sail upon . . . [the] weather
bow & running" straight for the privateer. The ship proved "to be a line of
battle Ship under British colours." Though the *Pilgrim* attempted to communicate with the *Scourge*, the speed of the enemy vessel thwarted it. The
situation soon became clear to Josiah Bartlett aboard the *Pilgrim*: "that one
must unavoidably fall a prey." The *Scourge*, unluckily, bore that distinction.
The *Pilgrim* watched as "the *Scourge* was under command of [the British
vessel's] Shot." While Bartlett and the *Pilgrim* escaped, the crew "had the
great mortification to see . . . [their] Concert strike her Col^rs This disas-
ter put . . . [the privateers on their] guard," so they "carried a pressing sail
through the night." Sailing in consort with the *Pilgrim* seemed an ill-advised
endeavor, a fact both the *Essex* and the *Scourge* discovered.[65]

After the *Revenge* and Captain Gustavus Conyngham completed their
time in convoy with the French fleet, the privateer turned his vessel toward Philadelphia, Pennsylvania. He was finally heading home. Upon his arrival, Conyngham was greeted with the troubling news that his former crew
members had brought a complaint against him to the Continental Congress.
These sailors cited issues with his distribution of prize money. The Congress
attempted to address the issue, requesting financial accounts from the commercial houses of France and Spain, as well as an affidavit from Conyngham
himself. The case turned out to be far more complicated than anticipated,
and with a plethora of other questions, concerns, and cases before them, the
Congress decided to table the discussion and sell the *Revenge* at public auction. A group of Philadelphia merchants purchased the vessel, outfitted it as
a privateer, and employed none other than Gustavus Conyngham as their
commander. By April 1779, Conyngham was heading back into the open waters of the Atlantic. The reoutfitted *Revenge* did not meet with the same success on this voyage. Rather, Conyngham shortly found himself at the hands
of a British frigate, the HMS *Galatea*.[66]

Privateer ships sailed with the intention of pursuing and taking enemy
vessels, but even the best intentions went awry. Ships oftentimes found
themselves as the pursued rather than the pursuer. Zuriel Waterman recounted in his journal the day the *Chace* spotted "a brigt. northward of [the
craft]." The brigantine soon "bore down upon" the *Chace*, and the privateer
"put away before the wind." Initially, the *Chace* quickly separated from its
pursuer, so the captain shortened the sail to allow the vessel to approach. The
Chace then fired a gun in salute "under American colors." When the brig-

antine responded, its colors were difficult to see. Waterman noted, "She appeared to be a brigt. of force and endeavoring to get under our lee; we put away from her." The brigantine continued to pursue the *Chace*, but the privateer soon left the ship behind.[67]

When the *Oliver Cromwell* needed more speed to outrun a "British Man of War," the crew put "out Oars—[and] rowed several Glasses" to escape the enemy. In October 1777, the *Oliver Cromwell* "saw a Sail, [in] thick Weather." Soon the sail gave chase and "came up fast," revealing the hull of a frigate. The *Oliver Cromwell* received fire, but "many of the Shot went over us. Several struck our Hull & Sails." In an effort to gain speed and escape the frigate, the crew "hove . . . Guns overboard & stove some Water & by that means got a little from her." The following day, with the frigate still in pursuit, the *Oliver Cromwell* "rowed & kept at a Distance," losing sight of the vessel on the third day.[68]

Josiah Bartlett, serving aboard the *Pilgrim*, recorded an encounter with "a Fleet of 15 Sail of large Ships." Two of the vessels chased the *Pilgrim* "and for some time gained upon us," the sailor recalled. Sensing the peril of the situation, Bartlett wrote, the *Pilgrim* "at Evening made Sail, and left our prizes to Share their Fate." The survival of the *Pilgrim* at this moment outweighed the needs of the prize vessels.[69]

The *Pilgrim* experienced several more close calls during Josiah Bartlett's tenure aboard the ship. On December 31, 1781, the *Pilgrim* "at day light saw a Sail to Windward" near the island of Barbados. The privateer pursued the vessel until "a large Ship (judged to be a British frigate) [came] bearing down & gaining fast upon [the craft]." Wary of the ship's safety, the *Pilgrim* was "obliged to alter . . . [its] course." The frigate continued its pursuit until evening, when darkness halted its endeavors. The next month, the *Pilgrim* was "chaced all day by 2 Ships, judged to be British Men of War," but it escaped unscathed. In the midst of pursuing a vessel in early April 1782, the *Pilgrim* "saw 2 Sail to Windward in chace." Though the privateer was close to its prey, the two other vessels "gained fast" so the privateer "bore away & spread . . . [its] Canvas." One of the ships stopped to speak with the *Pilgrim*'s intended quarry. Bartlett said of the second vessel, "[It] kept pressing . . . & held way" until nightfall, when the privateer "fortunately & unexpectedly lost sight of her." The *Pilgrim* later learned "the Vessell . . . [it] chaced was loaded with Wines for Barbadoes. & that the Frigates were The *Fortune* of 40 & the *Pegasus* of 28 Guns belonging to his Brittainic Majesty." In these instances, the *Pilgrim* was lucky to escape intact and no worse for the wear.[70]

The *Revenge* under the command of Conyngham was not quite so lucky during its pursuit of British privateers on April 17, 1779. While following the enemy vessels, Conyngham was caught by the frigate HMS *Galatea*. Outgunned and unable to escape, Conyngham surrendered. The captain was taken to New York, clapped in chains, and placed aboard a prison ship—a fate many American privateers shared. Philip Freneau, captured aboard the *Aurora*, described the scene on the prison ship *Scorpion*: "At sundown we were ordered between the decks to the number of nearly three hundred of us. The best lodging I could procure this night was on a chest, [and I] almost suffocated with the heat and stench." "I expected to die before morning," Freneau continued, "but human nature can bear more than one would at first suppose. The want of bedding and the loss of all my clothes rendered me wretched indeed; besides the uncertainty of being exchanged, for who could assure me that I should not lie six or eight months in this horrid prison?" Some captured privateers lingered in anguish aboard prison ships for just such a time and longer. Treatment aboard prison ships was harsh. The *Scorpion*'s steward was "one of the most brutal of mankind, who abused [the prisoners] continually." Captives who escaped the prison ships reported, "The Americans are treated very ill and die fast, having the smallpox among them."[71]

Christopher Vail and his 109 fellow crew members from the privateer *Deane* were taken to the prison ship *Jersey* after their surrender. Many remained belowdecks wallowing in filth and oppressive heat or bitter cold, depending on the season. Vail described the intense suffering he experienced alongside 1,150 other prisoners who were kept in close quarters and "between decks at sun down." Movement was greatly restricted, Vail noted: "Only two people was allowed to go on deck at a time, and if a man should attempt to raise his head above the grate he would have a bayonet stuck into it." Vail also observed that sickness ran rampant, stating, "Many of the prisoners was troubled with the disentary." Vail recalled how those who were not allowed on deck to relieve themselves would be "obliged to ease themselves on the spot, and the next morning for 12 feet round the hatches was nothing but excrement." Death was a fact of life, and those who perished, he recounted, were "carried up on the forecastle and laid there until the next morning . . . when they were all lowered down the ships sides by a rope round them in the same manner as tho' they were beasts." The bodies were then taken onshore and buried in "a hole . . . 1 or 2 feet deep and all hove in together," an ignominious end for any man.[72]

Even after Cornwallis's surrender and the privateer's release from the ship, Vail continued to feel the effects of his imprisonment; he came down with "prison fever." "I staggered and realed like a drunken man," the former captive wrote; "I soaked my feet in warm water and I soon lost my senses for 27 days." Vail barely remembered a doctor taking his pulse and noting he "must have blisters drawn." Recovery from the fever took six weeks, but the memories of his time on the *Jersey* stayed with Christopher Vail for the rest of his life.[73]

Privateers captured at sea were held in various places throughout the Atlantic. Sailors experienced imprisonment on board man-of-war ships and prison ships, on islands of the West Indies, and in the jails of Great Britain, specifically Mill Prison and Forton Prison. Zuriel Waterman recorded his encounter with Lowry Aborn, who "was taken last December and carried into Jamaica; [he] got away from there in a Dutch vessel." Prior to his imprisonment on the *Jersey*, Christopher Vail was captured and held in a "stone prison" in St. John's, Antigua. Vail described the paucity of the captives' daily rations, which only included "1/4 lb. Salt beef and 3/4 lb. bread, and water that had been to Guinea and brought back again, and millions of worms in it." The beef was bony, and Vail recounted how he and his fellow prisoners "generally ate it raw, for if it was boiled . . . [there would be] no substance in it." Hunger plagued the captives, who hailed from various places; "Americans, Frenchmen, Spaniards, and Negroes, [were] all confined together." While many had the opportunity to walk the yard, Vail noted that "the poor Yankees was kept in close confinement." British jailers seemed to take particular pleasure in abusing their rebel prisoners.[74]

The acclaim privateers, especially captains, received in American and British newspapers proved a double-edged sword. While high-ranking officers of the Continental army were, in theory, supposed to be treated like gentlemen and held until an exchange was arranged, privateers were treated like pirates. Thomas Painter explained why he attempted an escape: "The Chance of our Exchange was Extremely bad, on account of our being Whale boat men (the worst kind of Privateers men)." Christopher Vail observed he was in a similar position, for he "found there was no exchange of Prisoners." Gustavus Conyngham, the man who had spread fear via his exploits in the Atlantic, was not worthy of exchange. The British intended to try him for acts of piracy.[75]

Word spread among privateers "that the men of war pressed all the sailors that came in." When Gideon Olmsted inquired of sailors on a brig out of New York "whether they pressed Americans," he received this response: "They told us that it made no odds what countrymen they was for they pressed all." Olmsted noted in his recollections the presence of "two English seamen and 3 Americans that was prisoners taken by Capt. Hill in the *Royal George* ... Artemas White, Aquila Ramsdell, [and] David Clark, who were put aboard by Capt. Hill as prisoners to work the vessel to New York." Christopher Vail spent "11 months and 9 days ... confined in a tight Gaol, and in a hot climate" before he was placed on board the *Aetna* bomb ship. While there, he "was stowed in a small Cable Tier ... [that afforded him] no light nor air." The conditions left Vail "very weak and hardly able to stand." The *Aetna* soon delivered the former privateer to the English fleet, where he was "put on board the Suffolk 74 gun ship." Subsequently, the British forced Vail to fight in engagements between the English and French fleets during the spring months of 1780. Vail recounted seeing "pleanty of blood on the Admiral's Ships sides" after one such battle. The situation was so dire that Vail petitioned the British admiral "to go to prison in Barbadoes or be sent [with] prisoners to England," but he did not receive a reply.[76]

American prisoners sometimes refused to fight on behalf of the British. Vail observed one instance when he and his fellow captives "were then called on the quarter deck and ordered to quarters but ... all as one refused to obey the orders." The *Suffolk*'s captain fumed at this act of insubordination, and threatened punishment. In reaction, Vail recalled, "We told him that we were American Prisoners of war and would not go to quarters." Vail claimed this decision earned the respect of the boatswain, who commented, "Damn them, I like them the better for their conduct."[77]

Vail soon found himself transferred aboard the frigate *Action*, where he had no proper lodging, was "exposed to all the rain that fell in squalls, and [had] nothing over ... [his] head ... but the ships boats and spare topmasts." Once again, the American prisoners refused to work, but this British captain would not take no for an answer. He called them "a damned sett of Rebels" and maintained he would "flog [them] until [they] would do duty." He made an example of one, Ebenezer Williams, whom he had flogged until "the poor man consented after being cut into a jelly." Though privateers were not pirates and were indeed legal combatants under the law of nations, the treatment they received upon capture proves their British foes regarded them as rebels, not American citizens. Some captive sailors were pressured to change loyalties and serve aboard British vessels of war, while others were transferred to places hundreds of miles from home.[78]

Captured privateers such as Conyngham were often transported across the Atlantic to prisons in Great Britain. Conyngham described his journey thus, saying that he was "sent to England in a packett in Irons Wt 55 lbs." The captain was initially imprisoned in Pendennis Castle, where he was kept shackled because he was facing charges of piracy. Eventually, the British moved him to Mill Prison. The conditions at the prison were deplorable, according to Americans held there. Conyngham wrote that his rations were "a rebel Allowance [of] 6 oz beef & 6 of bread for 24 hours, the least fault as they termed it, 42 days in the dungeon on half of the above allowance of beef & bread—of the worst quality." "[We] suffered a seveare & cruel treatment for [a] number [of] years," Conyngham opined in a narrative he wrote after the experience. He highlighted the "dogs, cats rats even the Grass eaten by the prisoners," remarking, "This [is] hard to be credited, but [it] is a fact."[79]

Timothy Connor, a prisoner taken from the privateer *Rising States* and held at Forton Prison, described the rations he and his inmates were provided: "[We] had three quarters of a pound of beef allowed us and some cabbage; one pound of bread, one quart of small beer for twenty-four hours. The cabbage is only every other day." William Widger of Marblehead, Massachusetts, was taken while serving aboard the privateer *Phoenix*. In his diary, Widger noted, "This day our Beef was brought and so poor that we refused, to Except it, the Agent would not Send it back." Widger also recorded, "The Number of americans, now in the prison are 186, between 20 & 30 are Sick in the Hospital, we are Greatly alarmd. at the Distemper, and are afraid, it will go through the prison." Connor recorded the loss of a fellow prisoner: "Last night one Philip Cory died in our hospital; he belonged to Rhode Island government."[80]

The day George Thompson was taken to the hospital at Forton Prison, he noted the arrival of new prisoners in his diary, writing, "60 American prisoners was commited privateers crew this prisoner was tacken in a priveter caled the Gennerall Glower commanded by Capᵗⁿ Barthlet." Such news of privateer ventures trickled into the prison via newspapers, including this account from New York: "[The] privateer Ship Genl. Mifflin, of 20 Guns & 150 Men, is taken off Charlestown, by his Majesties, Ship Rawligh, as also two prizyes."[81]

Some prisoners did not idly sit by and accept their fate. Thomas Painter, imprisoned aboard the *Good Hope*, determined to make his escape rather than face the possibility of contracting smallpox or worse. He and his former captain contrived to save their rations of rum "until . . . [they] had got a

Junk Bottle full with which" they planned to "make the Sentinels so happy that . . . [they] could be enabled thereby to Escape." In other words, one evening Painter and his coconspirator plied the guards with rum until the sentries were so drunk "as to wholly neglect their duties." By this time, other prisoners had made their way on deck, Painter recounted, so that there was a great deal of commotion and confusion.[82]

Painter had "lost his Companion," the captain, but he decided to make an escape attempt nevertheless. He found another man making his way down the cable, handed the man an oar, and quickly followed suit. As other guards rushed on deck to retake the prisoners, Painter was lucky; as he explained, "It [was] too dark for them to discover me in the water." Nearly drowned by the tide ripple, Painter clung to the oar as a life preserver. He and the other man "swam along together up the River and among the shipping, to try to get a Boat." Painter's fellow escapee found a boat first, but Painter was not sure if the vessel was friend or foe. Without hearing any "comforting words or reception" to allay his fears, Painter continued up the river, drifting to and fro twixt the Jersey side and the New York side. Finally, he "made up . . . [his] mind to swim for New York," where his feet finally found soil again.[83]

Painter continued his harrowing escape venture, eventually swimming back across the river to the New Jersey side. After taking "a last look at the little city of New York,—the shipping,—Especially of the Prison Ship, from which I had Escaped," Painter headed northwest hoping to quickly evade the British enemy. After further adventures, he finally arrived at his uncle's home to the great surprise of his friends, who, he noted, "supposed my Escape to be next to, utterly impossible." Thomas Painter was one of the lucky souls who escaped a prison ship alive and relatively well.[84]

Unfortunately for many prisoners, not all escapes proved successful. Christopher Vail described five separate occasions when he and his fellow captives attempted to break out of the stone prison in St. John's, Antigua. The first effort involved pulling "the stones loose under the back window so that we could take them out with ease and escape over the back wall," Vail said. Alas, the prisoners miscalculated when they bribed the sentinel, who quickly accepted the money, then threatened to "blow [any man's] brains out" that dared show his head at the window. The second attempt consisted of cutting a hole in the roof and lowering a man down via a rope; the first man to attempt this route was shot.[85]

The third plan, whereby a number of prisoners sawed through two iron grates, resulted in the escape of "about 12 or 14 . . . [men who] took a small row boat and committed themselves to the ocean in order to go to St. Eustatia." Alas, Vail recalled, they were captured by a British sloop of war. The fourth escape attempt included a great deal of digging—first, six feet beneath the wall partition, and then across an entire room to the outer wall of the jail. Vail noted with disappointment, "By some unaccountable means or other we were detected" before the plan was ever enacted.[86]

The fifth and final attempt, Vail remembered, entailed cutting through the top portion of a door above the locks so it would "swing in." The prisoners hoped to use the sound and fury of winter squalls to cover their escape. A group of six men successfully broke out by this method, lowered themselves down the rainspout, jumped to the street through "a large bunch of Prickey Pears," and ultimately made their way to the water. At this juncture, the men stole a canoe, commandeered a "small droger," and made their way to Guadeloupe, where they "sold the vessel for 50 half Joes." Though Christopher Vail had knowledge of these attempts, he never escaped from the prison himself.[87]

Vail was not alone as a prisoner in pursuit of his freedom. On the night of August 4, 1778, at Forton Prison, "twenty-five of the French prisoners made their escape out of their prison by making a hole through the wall; four of whom were taken the same night, the remainder not yet heard of at eight o'clock at night; among them were two Americans that were committed with them." Gustavus Conyngham also attempted to escape on several occasions, finding success on November 3, 1779, by digging a tunnel under the prison wall. Yet the captain's luck faltered once again. After sailing with John Paul Jones from Holland, Conyngham determined to make his way back home. However, the vessel that carried him was captured on March 17, 1780, and Conyngham was returned to Mill Prison. Even so, the mariner was undeterred. Widger recorded on March 17, 1781, "Captain Gustavus Conyngham went into the Office, and when he came down, Seeing the turnkey was not at the Gate, Went out and passed the Centinals." A local market woman named Sary "called John Good and informed him of it, [so] the Capt. Was brought back." The prisoners were allowed to purchase food, clothing, and other necessaries to supplement their needs, and they "determined not to purchase anything of [Sary] for the future."[88]

Prisoners received money from friends and relatives who learned of their plight, but they also received "relief as poor prisoners" from the "subscription books opened in many parts of England." Even in the Caribbean, citizens took up a subscription "for the relief of the American Prisoners in Antigua." Christopher Vail observed that "80 half Joes was collected," and earmarked for equal distribution in rations and clothes. Prisoners received "provision[s] . . . twice a week, which was one lb. pork, 1 quart Rice, and 1 quart of Rum for each man." In addition, every captive received "a shirt, trowse[r]s and blanket," all of which alleviated their discomfort and suffering.[89]

While parole or prisoner exchange seemed unlikely and escape appeared near impossible, some American prisoners chose to join the ranks of the British. Caleb Foot mentioned these individuals in a letter home: "Some others have entered on board of his majesty's ships, to get clothes to cover their nakedness, which is to the shame of America." Considering the actions of those who refused to serve, such as Vail and his fellow prisoner Ebenezer Williams—who was cut to ribbons for his refusal—American prisoners who turned coat were particularly odious to those who did not. Foot decided against trying to escape, as he feared the reprisal if recaptured. As he stated, "Sometimes they will keep him [a failed escapee] on board of their ships-of-war, and if we are brought back to prison again we must lie forty days in the black hole and upon half allowance which is only two pounds of beef and one pint of peas for one week to live upon; and likewise put upon the back of the list and will not be exchanged until the last, if there should ever be any exchanged." Despite these dangers, Gustavus Conyngham attempted escape one more time in June 1781, and this time, he succeeded in making the return journey home to Philadelphia.[90]

The lives of privateers during the American Revolution were fraught with danger and full of adventure and daring escapes. Seafaring men experienced a completely different war on the waves of the Atlantic than the one their counterparts waged on North American soil. This vastly dissimilar experience, examined in chapters 1, 2, and 3, led to an exceptional aftermath and postwar experience that many Americans could not—and did not—relate to in the years of the early republic. The battles of privateers did not feature fortifications, reinforcements, or retreats. The ships' crews were multinational and multilingual, fighting on foreign soil and in foreign waters for the Patriot cause and interacting with foreign governments in ways other combatants and civilians never experienced.

Isolated in the middle of the ocean, crews could influence their commanders through threats of mutiny or a refusal to work. There was no General Washington or Continental Congress to give or to clarify orders. Once a ship engaged in a full-on battle, sailors had few options. There were no field hospitals to treat the wounded. The dead were laid to rest at sea, where no scavengers could pick over the battlefield, for in this instance, there was no true field of battle. Rather, the Atlantic World at large was the stage of combat and war for privateers. One decision made by a privateer, particularly in the case of Gustavus Conyngham, could have Atlantic-wide ramifications. The contrast between experiences left privateers on the proverbial outs of the Revolutionary narrative. Chapters 4 and 5 delve into the postvoyage affairs of privateers and examine how legal proceedings, disagreements over prizes and prize money, and a legacy of less-than-savory methods ultimately hurt privateers in their efforts to be acknowledged as Patriots worthy of credit and recognition.

CHAPTER 4

Make Your Fortunes Now, My Lads

*A*n unidentified ship drew ever closer to the *Richmond*. Unsure of the enemy vessel's intent and operating under the belief that the craft was a British privateer, the captain of the *Richmond* threw all papers with proof of American ownership overboard. If the British took it, the *Richmond* would not be condemned as American property. Only as the privateer loomed before him did the captain realize his grave error.[1]

The privateer proved to be an American vessel sailing from Rhode Island. After capturing the captain and crew of the *Richmond*, the Americans took their prize into port and libeled the vessel in the state's Court of Admiralty. The *Richmond*'s captain tried to explain his predicament. His ship was indeed owned by loyal, patriotic Americans. In the summer of 1775, before hostilities broke out, the captain and his crew had sailed for London on a mission to settle personal affairs for the *Richmond*'s owners based in Nantucket Island. However, upon arrival in London, the captain learned that friendly relations between the two nations had ceased, and he could not clear out of the port of London under American papers. Hence, he put the *Richmond* and its cargo under papers from a London firm and claimed he was setting sail on a voyage to the West Indies and Halifax.

In actuality, the captain swore he was heading for Nantucket Island when the privateer overtook the *Richmond*. The captain and the owners of the *Richmond* convinced the Rhode Island Admiralty Court of their version of events, and the ship was acquitted. Its captors, however, appealed the decision to the Continental Congress, which decided the case on January 17,

1777. For the privateers, the appeal ended poorly; not only was the decision of the lower court affirmed, but the appellants had to pay all costs. The Court of Admiralty and the process of appeals to the Continental Congress could make or break a privateering venture. In this case, a privateer captain and his crew walked away with nothing to show for their efforts.

The voyage of a privateer vessel from port to port, including its day-to-day operations sailing various oceans, chasing and being chased by ships, facing climatological emergencies, participating in battles and engagements, dealing with injuries and deaths, and enduring the ordeals of prisoners of war, tells only part of the story of a privateer's overall experience. The other half of the story—that is, what happened once the prize was brought to port and before a Court of Admiralty—could be just as perilous, uncertain, and complicated as the endeavor to capture an enemy vessel, as the case of the *Richmond* demonstrates. Regardless of their ports of call, privateers often-times found themselves entangled in the court system. Whether as libelants or claimants, these seafaring men returned home not to shouts and cheers, but to struggles over property captured and prizes disputed, to fights over compensation for work already performed in the name of the American cause.

The colonies' Admiralty Court system during the Revolution was unstable and fragmented, particularly as regarded the numerous provisions concerning the establishment and regulations of said system. Individual colonies created their own courts and ran them according to their specific guidelines. Colonists tried to build on the Vice-Admiralty Courts of the colonial period; however, without a comprehensive knowledge of the British system, colonists struggled to create reliable continuity and commonality between courts. The Continental Congress found itself in a precarious position. Once the assembly authorized privateering, a process for claiming a prize—and potentially appealing a decision—needed to be established. The creation of the Court of Appeals in Cases of Capture was chaotic and piecemeal. While Congress approved the use of these sea raiders for the cause of independence, the question of how to handle their returns to dry land and claims to prizes habitually plagued the assembly. Privateer owners, outfitters, captains, and crews all found themselves fighting once again to take a prize. Simply put, victory at sea mattered not without affirmation in the courts.

Using the *Journals of the Continental Congress* and *The Revolutionary War Prize Cases: Records of the Court of Appeals in Cases of Capture, 1776–1787*, along with personal correspondence, newspaper articles, printed proclamations, and colonial and state court records, scholars can examine privateers' journeys as they took their cases to court in hopes of leaving with a capture deemed lawful prize. Records from state Admiralty Courts are difficult to locate, as many no longer exist—hence, the importance of the surviving documents from the Court of Appeals. Yet these sources are not perfect. There are 109 cases catalogued in the records, though four contain only the name of the case and have no pertinent papers on file. The danger of relying heavily on these sources lies in the fact that all concerned cases of appeal, meaning that for one reason or another a party involved was not pleased with the state court's initial verdict. In the process of transferring the case from a state court to the congressional court, papers might have been misplaced or lost. However, the records provide valuable insight into the workings of the Admiralty Court system in various colonies and states (excluding New York, which is the only one not represented by any case in the records). Coupled with the *Journals of the Continental Congress* and various other sources, these court papers reveal the process privateers encountered once they brought prizes safely to port and sought to bear the fruits of their labors.[2]

The court records—or, rather, the creation and evolution of the court system itself—also illustrate the complicated relationship between individual colonies and the Continental Congress. Colonies (and later states) struggled to maintain their powers and authority in the uncertain times of war. While some colonies built on traditional systems and laws from the pre-Revolutionary period, others sought to cement their authority and protect their individual powers in new ways. Meanwhile, the delegates in Philadelphia sought to wage an effective war while clarifying and strengthening their own powers. Resolutions outlined the right to appeal to the Continental Congress, yet not all colonies complied. Some placed restrictions on who could appeal and under what specific circumstances. Over the course of months and years, colonies changed their laws and updated their statutes, while Congress attempted to implement modifications across the board, particularly in terms of cases involving foreign powers. All of these developments resulted in complex court systems for privateers.

The happenings in court and the procedures by which sailors and owners claimed their prizes placed privateers on the fringes of the Revolutionary experience. In commonly claiming a prize, privateers opened themselves to the public judgment and scrutiny inherent in the process of fighting for their due. Newspapers ran stories of the next meeting of the Court of Admiralty and printed libels and announcements of sales. Filing a claim for a prize could be a long and arduous procedure lasting months or even years. The "battlefield" successes of a vessel and its crew depended greatly on politicians, lawyers, and jurors who could hardly relate to the privateer experience—if they could do so at all—and who ultimately cared more about the maritime military results privateers produced than about whether those same privateers were fairly compensated after the fact.

In the end, this experience, which differed vastly from that of other Revolutionary-era service members, inevitably helped create a public persona for privateers that was unique unto itself among the war's men-at-arms. This uniqueness, in turn, allowed the Founding Fathers to exclude privateers from the overall triumphant Revolutionary narrative. The system politicians and the courts set up for privateers required them to seek out their profits and rewards. Thus, by merely following the rules the new American government prescribed for them, privateers became unworthy, greedy, and unpatriotic in the eyes of their American peers and contemporaries. Continental troops and sailors fought for the cause, a cynical public's logic went, while privateers, however necessary from a strategic perspective, fought to line their pockets—a story perpetuated by their publicly displayed struggles in court.

✳✶☉◎☉✶✳

George Washington took pen in hand on November 11, 1775, to address a letter to the president of Congress, John Hancock. Washington, then serving with his troops in Cambridge, Massachusetts, inquired of Hancock, "Should not a Court be established by the Authority of Congress, to take cognizance of the Prizes made by the Continental Vessels? Whatever the mode is which they are pleased to adopt, there is an absolute necessity of its being speedily determined on." Washington referred Hancock to an act recently passed by the Massachusetts Provincial Congress. The enactment "respects such captures as may be made by vessels fitted out by the Province or by Individuals thereof," the general wrote, but it did not apply to "vessels fitted at the Continental expence." Washington also notified Hancock of a number of captures recently made by residents of Plymouth and Beverly, including "a Vessel from Ireland laden with Beef, Pork, Butter &ca." With the number of prizes taken on the rise, Washington's point about establishing a court was well worth noting, though Congress did not move with the speed he suggested.[3]

The Massachusetts act referenced by Washington in his letter, and discussed briefly in chapter 1, passed on November 1, 1775, and called for the outfitting of private vessels "to sail on the seas, attack, take and bring into any port in this colony, all vessel[l]s offending or employed by the enemy." Sections Four through Twelve addressed the formation of a "court of justice . . . to take cognizance of, and try the justice of, any capture or captures of any vessel[l] or vessel[l]s that may or shall be taken by any person or persons whomsoever." The act established courts at three locations in the province: Plymouth, Ipswich, and North Yarmouth. A jury of "so many good and lawful men" would decide each case. Any person or persons bringing the suit were charged with making "out a bill, in writing, therein giving a full and ample account of the time and manner of the caption of [such] [*said*] vessel[l]," including the status of the taken ship and its cargo. Massachusetts was the first colony to actively create a Court of Admiralty for the purpose of hearing and determining prize cases.[4]

The Continental Congress eventually appointed a committee to discuss the contents of George Washington's letters, as the general had written more than once requesting assistance in this matter. John Adams, Benjamin Franklin, George Wythe, William Livingston, James Wilson, Thomas Johnson, and Edward Rutledge presented a report to Congress on November 25, 1775, outlining eight resolutions concerning captures and courts. The fourth resolution "recommended to the several legislatures in the United Colonies, as soon as possible, to erect courts of Justice, or give jurisdiction to the courts now in being for the purpose of determining concerning the captures to be made aforesaid, and to provide that all trials in such case be had by a jury." The report also stated that prosecutions should occur in the colony where the capture was made. If a court was not available for that purpose, the resolution determined, "the prosecution shall be in the court of such colony as the captor may find most convenient." The sixth resolution provided for the right to appeal to the Congress, though the claim had to be made within five days and given to the secretary of Congress within forty days. A security from the party appealing was also required. With these plans, the Continental Congress laid the groundwork for the courts that would hear the cases of America's privateers.[5]

Following Congress's resolutions, colonies began establishing their own courts. Massachusetts, as mentioned above, created a court of justice before Congress even made its recommendations. In February 1776, however, Massachusetts repealed its previous act and passed another similar one with some differences, including a change of location for one of the courts from New Yarmouth to Falmouth. The February enactment also permitted private maritime citizens to bring captured ships into any port within the American colonies for trial, and it allowed appeals to Congress within a specified time frame. A month later, Massachusetts repealed the February act. On April 13, 1776, legislators passed "An Act for Amendment of an Act, Made and Passed by the Great and General Court, at their Session in November Last," which redefined legalized captures as follows: "all armed and other vessels, that have, at any time since the nineteenth day of April, seventeen hundred and seventy-five, been engaged in making unlawful invasions, attacks and depredations on the sea-coast of America, or used in supplying the fleet and army which have been employed against the United Colonies," or in carrying supplies. Unlike Congress, which had resolved that privateers could legally capture only those ships belonging to British subjects, Massachusetts deemed any vessel involved in aiding the enemy, regardless of ownership, as subject to seizure. In addition, the act limited the cases that could be appealed to Congress. Only vessels outfitted by the Continental Congress could appeal to its court; all others were required to take their cases to the Massachusetts Superior Court of Judicature.[6]

Massachusetts is a prime example of the ever-changing legal and court system in regard to captures. Privateers had to reckon with varying acts, resolutions, and laws, many of which depended on the port of call and the colonial authority governing the harbor. Even though the Continental Congress tried to prepare for the chance of appeal, regulations across the board were not uniform. The instability and, oftentimes, randomness of the court system created havoc, misunderstanding, and prejudice against privateers. Claimants in prize courts faced issues and judgments that other combatants and colonists never had to contend with or address. In creating a public venue in which privateers had to fight and argue for their lawful prizes, the colonies and the Congress might have unknowingly prejudiced the public's opinion. If they took prizes lawfully, then why should privateers have to argue their cases, and in some circumstances, why would privateers have to appeal? Rather than accepting their actions as inherently legal, the system itself made these mariners justify their deeds.

Many of the other colonies followed in the footsteps of Massachusetts, creating the suggested courts or revamping current systems to address the needs of prizes privateers, state vessels, and Continental ships brought in. Though not all of them restricted the right to appeal to Congress, each colony had its own particular regulations. Rhode Island created one court in March 1776 to try captures and amended this action in May 1776 to follow the resolves of Congress. In 1780, Rhode Island restricted the right of appeal, allowing no appeal to Congress if the appellant came from a state that prohibited appeals. Connecticut also passed an act in May 1776 establishing five county courts. New Hampshire borrowed heavily from the act passed by Massachusetts and likewise limited the right of appeal to vessels owned in part by the Continental Congress. In 1779, Congress forced New Hampshire to modify its act and allow for appeal in cases where a friendly foreign power or citizen was involved. Pennsylvania initially followed the resolves of Congress. However, in 1778, the state passed an act that shortened the time allowed for appeals to Congress, and in 1780, Pennsylvania removed the trial by jury requirement. New Jersey prevaricated on the subject for several years. Finally, when four cases were appealed to Congress in the fall of 1778, New Jersey established an act similar to that of Pennsylvania, though it did not restrict appeals to Congress or implement a time change.[7]

Virginia revised its regulations of the court system multiple times, in May 1776, December 1776, and finally in 1779. Ultimately, Virginia allowed appeals to Congress except in cases where both parties were residents of the state. South Carolina continued using courts already established for maritime matters, though the state constitution did not follow the resolves of Congress in regard to the proportion of a recaptured prize given to those who retook the vessel. The statutes of Maryland did not explicitly establish a Court of Admiralty, though four cases from the state were appealed to Congress. As was the case with South Carolina, Maryland most likely used the court system from its colonial roots.[8]

North Carolina closely followed the congressional resolves except for one noteworthy change. In cases of appeal, the appellant had to pay triple the amount if the decision of the North Carolina court was affirmed; for owners and privateers without the necessary funds, an appeal could prove quite difficult under these terms. Georgia allowed for appeals to Congress after a second jury trial. In the cases of New York and Delaware, there are no session laws regarding Admiralty Courts. New York did not appeal any cases to Congress, but Delaware did petition the court in five, which suggests that the courts of the colonial period continued in their regular duties during the war. The plethora of various regulations and rules in nearly all of the colonies highlights once again the chaos that oftentimes surrounded prize-case proceedings. Privateers found themselves embroiled in a system based on these ever-changing statutes, acts, and session laws, all of which contributed to a public conflict over lawful prizes and numerous judgments passed on the character and rights of said privateers.[9]

Once courts were established in the colonies, privateers began submitting prize cases. The *New England Chronicle* printed an advertisement of libels from the Middle District in Massachusetts that announced, "Notice is

hereby given. That the Maritime Court for the Middle District will be held
at Boston in the County of Suffolk, on Thursday the fifth Day of September,
1776, at the Hour of Ten in the Forenoon." Cases on the docket that day included "the Sloop named the *Isabella*, of about Seventy Tons Burthen, lately
commanded by one Nathaniel Kirk, and her Cargo and Appurtenances,"
taken by the privateer sloop *Revenge*. In Philadelphia, the *Pennsylvania Evening Post* publicized similar proceedings: "A Court of Admiralty being to be
held to-morrow morning at ten o'clock, when the Martial and Crier must
attend, the Sale of the cargo of the prize ship *Friendship* is postponed until to-morrow afternoon, at three o'clock when a quantity of Sugars, Coffee,
Rum and Cocoa, will be sold." The *Connecticut Gazette* announced a change
of date for one prize case, declaring, "The Court of Admiralty for the Trial
of the Cargo of the Ship *Nathaniel & Elizabeth*, will be held at the Court
House in New-London, on the 20th Instant, instead of the 22d, as mentioned in the Advertisement in the last Page of this Paper." Judge J. Brack-
ett of Portsmouth, New Hampshire, announced the libels of the *Glasgow*
and *Neptune*. This statement followed the announcement: "Notice is given,
agreeable to the laws of said state, that the maritime court erected to try and
condemn all vessels found infesting the sea coasts of America, and brought
into the county of Rockingham, will be held at the court house in Portsmouth, the 29th day of October instant, at 10 o'clock before noon, to try the
justice of said captures, that all persons concerned may appear, and shew
cause (if any they have) [that] the said vessels, their cargoes and appurtenances should not be condemned."[10]

Once a court deemed a prize lawful and its goods subject to auction, papers printed notices of sale. One such advertisement in the *Pennsylvania
Gazette* informed readers, "On Friday next, the 20th instant, will be sold at
public vendue, on or near Plumstead's wharff, Rum, Sugar, Coffee, Cotton,
and Cocoa, the cargoe of the prize Schooner *Peter*, condemned in the Court
of Admiralty." Some announcements gave detailed descriptions of the vessel and its cargo in an attempt to entice potential buyers to the auction. The
Maryland Gazette described "the Ship *Caroline*, of London, lately made a
prize by the *Harlequin* privateer, capt. Woolsey, of Baltimore, with her sails,
rigging, and materials, being about 200 tons of burthen, plantation built,
[and] about six years old." "Having been stranded on the coast of England,"
the paper reported, "[the *Caroline*] has been since rebuilt, and her keel, stern
and stern-post, many of her futtocks and floor timbers of English oak, she
is supposed to be equal, if not superior, to a new American built vessel."
The cargo of the *Caroline* consisted of "choice Muscavado sugars and rum,

shipped on board said ship from Jamaica . . . [and] 400 hogsheads of sugar, and 117 puncheons of rum." The announcement also noted the ease of access to the location of the sale: "Pitt's landing on Pocomoke river, in Chesapeake bay . . . lies convenient for transportation to any part of Virginia, Maryland, or Philadelphia markets." A privateer outfitter and owner might have won his case in court, but the venture was only successful if the goods sold for a decent price at auction.[11]

Successful cases could result in the sale of a prize vessel, but for those who were unsatisfied with the court's decision, the process of appealing to the Continental Congress began soon thereafter. This procedure changed during the course of the war as members of Congress attempted to create and firmly establish a coherent, fair system. Initially, appeals to Congress were referred to an ad hoc committee. Such was the case with the first recorded request to Congress from the Court of Admiralty for the port of Philadelphia. "A committee of five" was appointed to hear "the appeal against the verdict and sentence of condemnation passed against the schooner *Thistle* and her cargo." The committee consisted of Richard Stockton, Samuel Huntington, Robert Treat Paine, James Wilson, and Thomas Stone. The following month, a petition from Jacob Sheafe was "referred to the commissioners appointed to hear and determine upon the appeal in the case of the *Elizabeth*."[12]

Continuing appeals to Congress from claimants in New Hampshire and Massachusetts Bay to Pennsylvania and Virginia quickly revealed the need for a more permanent committee. On Thursday, January 30, 1777, the Continental Congress "*resolved*, That a standing committee, to consist of five members, be appointed to hear and determine upon appeals brought against sentences passed on libels in the courts of Admiralty in the respective states, agreeable to the resolutions of Congress." This resolution also noted that appeals should be "lodged with the secretary," who would deliver each one to the standing committee "for their final determination." The standing committee appointed by Congress included James Wilson, Jonathan Dickinson Sergeant, William Ellery, Samuel Chase, and Roger Sherman.[13]

Congress amended the system a few months later, calling the current "standing committee, for hearing and determining appeals . . . too numerous." The group was discharged, and a rule of three was put in place stating "that a new committee of five be appointed, they or any three of them to hear and determine upon appeals brought to Congress." The panel appointed on May 8, 1777, included James Wilson, James Duane, John Adams, Jonathan Dickinson Sergeant, and Thomas Burke. The next Monday, Congress "*resolved*, That the committee on appeals be authorized to appoint a

register to attend the said committee." Slowly, Congress made progress toward establishing a structured legal institution, but the process would last
several more years before the formation of a formal Court of Appeals.[14]

The Continental Congress first addressed the possibility of instituting
an appellate court on Tuesday, August 5, 1777. Delegates passed a resolution "that Thursday next be assigned to take into consideration the propriety
of establishing a court of appeals." The following Thursday "there was only
one State present represented" when the Congress was supposed to meet at
ten o'clock in the morning. A half hour later, representatives arrived from
New Hampshire, Massachusetts Bay, Rhode Island, Connecticut, New Jersey, Pennsylvania, Maryland, and South Carolina. One hour after the official
beginning of the congressional meeting for the day, delegates from Virginia
and New York presented themselves. At a quarter past eleven o'clock, Delaware's representatives arrived, followed by those from Georgia at half past.
The postponement of the debate concerning a Court of Appeals is of little
wonder when one considers the nature of the Continental Congress. Delegates barely arrived on time, if at all, which sometimes meant no one was
present to discuss the matters at hand. In fairness, the Continental Congress
had a great many issues to argue, analyze, and ultimately decide. However,
in terms of the Court of Appeals, the Continental Congress tabled the issue
for two and a half years. Circumstances with the Congress as they were, privateers grappled not only with undefined state courts, but also with an appeal system that did not adequately serve their needs.[15]

The lack of an established Court of Appeals was not the only issue facing
privateers involved in appellate cases. The ad hoc committee and the Standing Committee on Appeals appointed to hear such cases faced a chronic
problem of membership turnover. Representatives to the Continental Congress did not always serve extended tenures in their positions. For example,
John Adams served from 1774 to 1777 prior to his appointment as joint commissioner to France, a post he assumed in early 1778. Adams, as noted above,
was chosen for the standing committee of May 1777, having also served on
the revised committee of March 12, 1777. Following his appointment as joint
commissioner, Congress once again revised the membership of the standing
committee. On November 17, 1777, John Harvie of Virginia, Francis Dana
of Massachusetts, and William Ellery of Rhode Island were selected to re-
place Henry Laurens of South Carolina, John Adams of Massachusetts, and
Henry Marchant of Rhode Island. During the course of the Committee
of Appeals, thirty-seven different members of Congress were appointed to
serve in forty-two cases. The composition of the special committees and the

standing committee changed on at least twenty occasions. Such a high rate of turnover offers some explanation for the inconsistent nature of the appeals process. Nevertheless, the changeable composition of the committee added to the difficulties privateers faced in appellate cases.[16]

While Congress dragged its feet on the formation of a formal court, privateers and questions concerning privateering continued to swirl. On Wednesday, July 24, 1776, delegates issued an amendment concerning the resolutions of March 23, discussed in chapter 1. The Congress noted, "Whereas these United States have by a long series of oppressions, been driven into a war with Great Britain . . . and it is impossible to distinguish among the subjects of the same sovereign, between those who are friends and such as are enemies to the rights of America and mankind, it is become necessary to consider as enemies all the subjects of the King of Great Britain." For privateers, this meant that all ships and vessels, including "their tackle, apparel and furniture, and all goods, wares and merchandises," were subject to seizure if they belonged "to any subject or subjects of the King of Great Britain, except the inhabitants of the Bermudas, and Providence or Bahama islands."[17]

On February 3, 1778, the Committee of Commerce was charged with "recommend[ing] to Congress proper persons in the respective states to act as attornies in each State . . . for claiming the continental share of all prizes libelled in the court of admiralty of the State where they may respectively reside." The first order of business on the twenty-sixth of that same month charged "captains or commanders of privateers, to annoy the enemy by all the means in their power, by land or water, taking care not to infringe or violate the laws of nations, or the laws of neutrality." A month later, Congress asked the Marine Committee to revise the instructions issued to privateer commanders and report their findings to the body at large.[18]

On May 8, 1778, Congress issued a proclamation concerning foreign powers' objections lodged against privateers. Neutral nations claimed American privateers attacked and captured their ships without cause and in violation of the laws of war and neutrality. The exploits of Captain Gustavus Conyngham, particularly his encounter with the *Honoria Sophia* discussed in chapter 3, certainly played a role in the complaints Congress received. The proclamation cited American vessels' "unjustifiable and piratical acts, which reflect[ed] dishonour upon the national character of these states." Commanders of any American vessel were to conduct themselves in a dignified manner as laid out in their commissions and instructions. Vessels of neutral powers were not liable to seizure unless, the proclamation stated, "they are employed in carrying contraband goods or soldiers to our enemies." Enemy craft seeking sanctuary and protected by neutral coasts and nations were also off limits. In closing, the decree threatened consequences for people who participated in such illegal activities: "If taken by foreign powers in consequence thereof, [they] will not be considered as having a right to claim protections from these states, but shall suffer such punishment as by the usage and custom of nations may be inflicted upon such offenders." The proclamation responded to the protests from foreign powers and gave the air of authority and control to the Continental Congress. However, issuing a pronouncement was much easier than enforcing its contents.[19]

Congress continued to hear complaints from overseas nations and their citizens. A letter from the minister of France received attention in April 1779. Its contents referred to "two Spanish vessels captured by an American privateer and carried into the State of Massachusetts bay." The case was set for a trial in the said state, which, as discussed above, only allowed appeals to the Continental Congress when a vessel in service to the United States was involved. Despite the fact that the case included a foreign citizen's property, the Continental Congress could not intervene.[20]

The matter was then referred to the Committee on Appeals, which reported to the body at large, "It is of the highest importance to the welfare and interests of these United States, that there be an uniform and equal administration of maritime law within the said states." Committee members noted that Congress was supposedly "invested with the Supreme Sovereign Power of War and Peace," which included determining the legality of captures on the high seas based on the law of nations. However, with the Articles of Confederation not yet ratified by Maryland, the vested powers of Congress were not in full effect. The committee proposed that the states enact a law providing that "the United States in Congress assembled . . . have the sole and exclusive right and power of establishing rules for deciding in all cases what captures on land or water shall be legal . . . appointing Courts for the Trials of Piracies and Felonies committed on the high seas and establishing Courts for receiving and determining finally appeals in all cases of captures."[21]

On May 22, 1779, Congress passed a resolution to transmit instructions to the states in regard to "the legality of captures on the high seas." Delegates focused in particular on the state of Massachusetts Bay, which should "take effectual measures to expedite and facilitate an appeal from the decision of their courts on the cases of vessels or cargoes, claimed as Spanish neutral property, if . . . demanded by either party." In this instance, Congress tried to impose rules and regulations concerning capture on the states, but the lack of authority and true power within Congress meant very little came of the representatives' request.[22]

A resolution on Thursday, August 26, 1779, called for the appointment of "a committee of three . . . to report a plan for establishing one or more supreme courts of appeal in all maritime causes within these United States." The group's members included Samuel Huntington, William Paca, and John Dickinson. Two months later, the committee made their report, which included a plan for the formation of four districts: the Eastern, Northern, Middle, and Southern. This proposal included provisions for two sets of judges, each consisting of "three persons learned in the law, . . . commissioned by Congress during good behaviour, and sworn to execute the office of Judge faithfully and impartially." Judges would sit in either the Eastern and Northern Districts or the Middle and Southern Districts, with the proviso that only two need be present to hear a case. The judges and courts would have the power to appoint registers, levy fines and terms of imprisonment, and determine the time and place of the court meetings. All appeals the district courts received would "be heard and determined according to the Civil Law, the law of nations and the usage and practice of the Courts of Admiralty in Europe." Congress took the committee's report under consideration.[23]

In similar fashion to its protracted process of outfitting and commissioning privateers in 1775 and 1776, Congress took its time creating a Supreme Court of Appeals. On December 4, 1779, Congress agreed on the report titled "Ordinance for establishing a Court of Appeals for finally determining captures." The ordinance contained an important change from the initial document: there would be one court "established for the trials of all appeals from the Courts of Admiralty in these United States in cases of captures," not four different district courts. However, the judges were charged with holding sessions at Philadelphia, Pennsylvania, Williamsburg, Virginia, and Hartford, Connecticut. The usage of nations determined the outcome of a trial, not a jury, and "all exhibits, evidence and proceedings" were to be "in writing and at full length." Representatives' agreement on this ordinance signaled progress, but they put off the debate once again.[24]

When Congress took up deliberation of the Court of Appeals on January 5, 1780, the first order of business concerned adding a member to the committee, as William Paca was absent. Congress chose Oliver Ellsworth, after which Robert Livingston made a motion: "The judges of the said court [shall] hold their sessions at such time and place, as shall appear to them most advantageous to the public . . . provided that the court shall at no time be held to the southward of Williamsburg in Virginia, or to the eastward of Hartford in the State of Connecticut." The proposal was put to a vote. Perhaps not surprisingly, Virginia's, North Carolina's, and South Carolina's representatives voted in the negative, as did Maryland's and Rhode Island's delegates. With the states equally divided, the motion did not pass.[25]

Congress then moved on to consideration of the phrase "that the trial of all captures in the courts of admiralty be according to the usage of nations and not by jury." The debate did not last long, as the question "was put off by the State of Pennsylvania," and the session adjourned thereafter. Three days later, deliberations continued. James McLene made a motion to add a stipulation stating, "Nothing in the foregoing resolutions shall be construed to admit an appeal in any case where all parties concerned are citizens of one and the same State, unless allowed by the legislature of the said State." A vote was taken, with the states once more equally divided. Delegates read the resolutions in their entirety before another vote; again, the states were split "and the question lost."[26]

William Churchill Houston presented a motion that a new committee of four be appointed to address the question of forming a Court of Appeals, "and that the papers before the House on that subject be referred to them." This new committee consisted of Oliver Ellsworth, Thomas McKean, William Churchill Houston, and Robert R. Livingston. The creation of a Court of Appeals was subsequently postponed yet another time. While privateers continued capturing prizes and sending them to port, the system by which they could claim their fair share faltered in the hands of Congress.[27]

Congress continued to debate, tweak, and change the resolutions presented regarding a Court of Appeals. On January 15, 1780, representatives voted to strike phrases, reword sentences, and confirm paragraphs. After further debate, "the remainder of the report" was "postponed." However, Congress did take an affirming step in assigning "Saturday next ... for electing the judges of the court of appeals," and in determining "that in the meanwhile, nominations [would] be made." For once remaining on schedule, on Saturday, January 22, Congress appointed George Wythe, William Paca, and Titus Hosmer as the judges of the Court of Appeals. The following Thursday, a committee was appointed to prepare commissions for the judges. On February 2, 1780, Congress approved the commissions, telling the new designees, "Reposing special trust and confidence in your ~~patriotism~~ learning, prudence, integrity, and abilities, we have assigned, deputed, and appointed you one of our judges of our Court of Appeals, to hear, try, and determine all appeals from the court of admiralty, in the states respectively, in cases of capture." The commission also provided that the judges were "authorized and empowered by Congress to do and perform, [that] which shall be necessary . . . for the execution of the said office, according to the law and usage of nations and the acts of Congress; to have, hold, exercise, and enjoy, all and singular, the powers, authorities, and jurisdictions . . . also the privileges, benefits, emoluments, and advantages to the said office belonging, or in any wise appertaining." The Court of Appeals was nearly complete.[28]

The official establishment of the Court of Appeals might be dated January 15, 1780, when the resolutions were revised, or January 22, when the judges were appointed, or even February 2, when the commissions for the judges were drafted. The penultimate date in the creation of the court may very well be Wednesday, May 24, 1780, when Congress "*resolved*, That the stile of the Court of Appeals appointed by Congress, be, 'The Court of Appeals in Cases of Capture.'" On this same day, representatives passed oaths for the judges and the register, as well as strict guidelines for the timeline of appeal. Congress declared, "Appeals from the courts of admiralty in the respective states, [will] be, as heretofore, demanded within five days after definitive sentence; and in future such appeals [will] be lodged with the register of the Court of Appeals in cases of capture within forty days thereafter, provided the party appealing shall give security to prosecute such appeal to effect." Delegates also noted that all future appeals were the sole concern of the "newly erected Court of Appeals." The case of the *Sandwich* packet, brought forth in a memorial from James Wilson, was the first "transmitted to the said Court of Appeals." Six years into the war—not weeks or even months, but *years*—privateers finally had a supreme authority in cases of capture.[29]

Questions concerning privateers and the newly formed Court of Appeals continued to occupy the meetings of Congress. George Wythe declined his appointment as a judge, whereupon Congress elected Cyrus Griffin of Virginia to the post. On May 2, 1780, Congress agreed to revised commission and bond forms presented by the Board of Admiralty, as well as "instructions to the captains and commanders of private armed vessels . . . [who had] commissions or letters of marque and reprizal." These directives reminded captains of their right to "attack, subdue and take all ships and other vessels belonging to the crown of Great Britain or any of the subjects thereof," except those belonging to Bermuda.[30]

The second point of the instructions stressed the importance of respecting the rights of neutral powers, an issue that still plagued Congress. Captured vessels should be brought to a convenient port with the master or pilot and one other person as witnesses. Instructional points six, seven, eight, and nine addressed treatment of prisoners, written accounts, and the percentage of landmen. In closing, the directives noted, "[Commanders] shall observe all such further instructions as Congress shall hereafter give in the premises." Captains were also warned that any actions "contrary to these instructions" would result in the forfeiture of the commission and liability "to an action for breach of . . . bond." These sailors would then "be responsible to the party grieved, for damages sustained by such malversation." Congress charged the Board of Admiralty with printing copies, and the president with transmitting them to the governors and presidents of the states. During the summer of 1780, Congress also created a committee "to report the salaries of the judges of the court of appeals . . . and of the commissioners, clerks and others." Delegates passed a resolution discharging two prize agents in Pennsylvania. Upon the death of Titus Hosmer, Congress "*resolved*, That Friday, the 1st Sept. next, be assigned for electing a member of the Court of Appeals," Hosmer's replacement.[31]

The following year, Congress addressed further issues from France, amended instructions for privateers, and answered questions concerning capture. Members of the Board of Admiralty drafted a reply to the French minister stating that all prizes taken by French vessels and brought into American ports would receive the same treatment as prizes seized and brought in by American vessels. This was a gesture of reciprocity and respect, as the French allowed American captured prizes the same courtesy in their courts. The question of Hosmer's replacement received attention on February 27, 1781, inasmuch as Congress announced, "To Morrow be assigned for electing a third judge of the Court of Appeals." The next day passed without any such election.[32]

Congress revised the instructions for privateers on April 7, allowing for the capture of all British ships with no exceptions for Bermuda or for vessels carrying settlers. James Madison proposed changes to the Court of Appeals in hopes of establishing a stronger, more defined system. He suggested specific locations and dates for sessions, as well as rules for court costs and provisions for the judges, such as black robes. Though the recommendations were referred to a committee, the majority of Madison's applications never passed. In the final months of the war and in the six years thereafter, Congress modified, adapted, and addressed ordinances relating to capture, as well as instructions to armed vessels and privateers. Finally, on December 5, 1782, Congress elected a replacement for Titus Hosmer, as well as one for William Paca; John Lowell and George Read took up the positions.[33]

The question of compensation for judges also arose in 1784 and 1785. As the court had not conducted any business for over a year, Congress ultimately declared, "The Salaries of the judges of the Court of Appeals shall henceforth cease." Cyrus Griffin, who was sitting on the bench at the time, was offended by the lack of tact and appreciation Congress showed the court. Hence, on February 9, 1786, representatives issued a resolution: "[Members of] Congress are fully impressed with a sense of the ability, fidelity and attention of the judges of the court of Appeals, in discharge of the duties of their Office; but . . . as the war was at an end, and the business of that court in a great measure done away, an attention to the interests of their constituents made it necessary that the salaries of the said judges should cease."[34]

The Court of Appeals met for the final time in May 1787. A system that took years to build ceased to exist as some of the representatives from Congress looked toward building a new form of government at the Constitutional Convention. With the end of the war, privateers no longer fulfilled an economic or military need. Rather, their exploits took on the veneer of piratical ventures, and they themselves took on the guise of individualistic entrepreneurs seeking fortune and fame at the expense of others.

❋⊱◈◉◎◉◈⊰❋

The various Special Committees of Appeals, the Standing Committee of Appeals, and the Court of Appeals heard over one hundred cases during their terms. In cases for which the outcome is known, the Court of Appeals reversed the lower court's determination on forty-four occasions and affirmed the decision in thirty-eight instances. The case at hand was dismissed in eleven appeals, while three cases were settled by the parties, two were denied on appeal, one was struck from the docket, one was granted a rehearing with the ultimate decision unknown, and one was affirmed in part and reversed in part. Men and women from throughout the colonies lodged their petitions and grievances with the Continental Congress in hopes of securing a different outcome than that judged by the colonial and state Admiralty Courts. The success of a privateer venture depended on the court's determination in the sailors', owners', and outfitters' favor. Four such cases— *John Barry vs. The Sloop Betsey, Thomas Rutenbourgh vs. The Schooner Frank, Peter Norris vs. The Schooner Polly and Nancy,* and *Babcock vs. The Brigantine Brunette*—are chronicled below as case studies of the different obstacles, tactics, and international complications that privateers faced in the legal system, and the ways in which they approached this final phase of their voyage.[35]

Congress received the case of *John Barry vs. The Sloop Betsey* on November 7, 1776. The matter was "referred to a committee of five ... impowered to hear and determine upon the said appeal." Andrew Robeson, the registrar of the Court of Admiralty in the state of Pennsylvania, created "a true and exact Copy of the Record, or Minutes of the Proceedings of the said Court," which Congress received upon the lodging of the appeal. The facts presented in the Court of Admiralty at the port of Philadelphia in Pennsylvania were as follows: John Barry, commander of the armed brigantine of war *Lexington*, and James Robertson, commander of the privateer sloop of war *Chance*, sought the condemnation of the sloop *Betsey* as lawful prize. The *Lexington* was "fitted out and armed at the Continental Charge," while the *Chance* was "equipped victualled fitted out and armed at the Expence of sundry Persons Inhabitants of these United States." While sailing on the high seas in August 1776, Barry and his crew "did discover pursue apprehend and as lawful Prize take the Sloop or Vessel called the Betsey commanded by Samuel Kerr." William Lewis, proctor of the court for the libelants Barry and Robertson, claimed the *Betsey* was property of a subject or subjects of the king of Great Britain. During its cruise, Lewis maintained, the *Betsey* "was employed in transporting provisions and Necessaries to the British Army and Navy within the United States of America." In addition, the cargo hold of the *Betsey* contained several African slaves. Lewis petitioned for the condemnation of the *Betsey* and its apparel, tackle, furniture, and cargo, including the six enslaved persons.[36]

Judge George Ross asked his court marshal to "summon twelve honest and lawful Men of the County of Philadelphia" to serve as jurors in the case; they were told to appear in court on September 29, 1776. The judge also ordered the registrar to give public notice of the case according to the resolves of Pennsylvania. An announcement appeared in the *Pennsylvania Packet* on September 10, 1776, stating, "Notice is hereby given, That a Court of Admiralty will be held at the State-House in the city of Philadelphia, on Thursday, the twenty-sixth day of September inst. at ten o'clock in the forenoon" for the purpose of hearing the case of *John Barry vs. The Sloop Betsey*. The notice requested "that the owner or owners of the said sloop, cargo and slaves, or any person concerned therein ... appear and shew cause, if any they have, why the same should not be condemned according to the prayer of the said bill."[37]

Meanwhile, William Lewis planned to make his case on behalf of his clients, Barry and Robertson. The court prepared questions for possible interrogations, and Lewis readied various exhibits. The first exhibit was a signed statement from John Hancock confirming John Barry's appointment as commander of the *Lexington*, "fitted out at the Continental charge." Next, Lewis presented the privateering commission of James Robertson, dated July 2, 1776, in Philadelphia. The final exhibit contained the moniker of John Murray, Earl of Dunmore, of the state of Virginia. Dated July 31, 1776, the license stated, "We do hereby take into his Majesties Service the Sloop Betsey Samuel Kerr Master." Kerr was ordered to proceed to St. Augustine, Florida, with his family, other passengers, and a cargo meant "for the Use of his Majestie or for the Use of the Inhabitants of any Town or Place governed and possessed by his Majesties Troops and no others." The license was in effect for a period of three months. With this last document, Lewis sought to prove the *Betsey* was an enemy vessel.[38]

The first and only witness called was Samuel Kerr, commander of the *Betsey*. Kerr explained during his examination that the brigantine *Lexington* had captured the *Betsey* while the privateer *Chance* was in sight, which explains why Barry and Robertson jointly sought condemnation of the prize vessel. Kerr explained "that the said sloop [*Betsey*] was not fitted for War" at the time of capture. According to Kerr, the cargo on board belonged to inhabitants of Virginia and North Carolina including himself, his brother George Kerr, Robert Sheddon, and Henry and Thomas Brown, among others. The commander confirmed that the *Betsey* had sailed from the Portsmouth River in Virginia and was bound for St. Augustine when the *Lexington* captured it. Kerr further asserted that the slaves on board were set for delivery to various owners in Florida. For example, "Phillis the property of Mrs Bruff of Hampton in Virginia who had ran away from her Mistress . . . had been taken on board for the purpose of redelivering her to her said Mistress." Lastly, Kerr testified that "no papers or Writings [were] thrown overboard or destroyed on board the said Sloop to [his] knowledge except some in the presence and by the permissions of Captain Barry aforesaid and not at all relating to the said Vessel or her Cargo." Thus concluded the commander's testimony, given in court on September 26, 1776.[39]

The case then rested in the hands of the jury and Judge Ross. After examining all of the exhibits and taking time for deliberation, the jury returned a verdict that "all the Facts alledged and set forth in the Bill aforesaid [were] true." Whereupon, Judge George Ross gave his "definitive Sentence or Decree," which ruled "that the Sloop or Vessel called the Betsey with her Tackle Apparel and Furniture and the Goods Wares and Merchandizes found on board the said Sloop at the Time of her Capture and the Negro Slaves in the said Bill named and mentioned be condemned as lawful Prize." In addition, Judge Ross ordered the marshal "to sell the same at publick Vendue." The monies deriving from the sale of the *Betsey* were to be divided into 135 shares. Forty-one shares went to James Robertson and his officers, mariners, and seamen. The other ninety-four shares belonged to John Barry and his crew; however, according to his Continental commission, two-thirds of those portions were "for the use of the thirteen United States of North America."[40]

Two days later, on September 28, 1776, Samuel Kerr filed an appeal with the court via a proctor. On behalf of himself and several others who owned cargo aboard the *Betsey*, Kerr "appeal[ed] from the Verdict and Sentence given in this Cause to the honorable Continental Congress." Kerr offered a security "in the sum of six thousand pounds lawful money," after which Andrew Robeson created his "true and exact Copy" of the case record. A congressional Committee of Appeals, consisting of George Wythe, Robert Treat Paine, James Wilson, and William Hooper, reviewed the case. Written on the final page of the case records, below Robeson's attestation, the committee gave their ruling on November 23, 1776. The verdict reads, "The committee of congress who were appointed to hear and determine this appeal have heard the parties by their counsels and the record and proceedings being seen and diligently inspected, and by the committee fully understood, it seems to the committee that there is no error in the verdict and sentence aforesaid: therefore it is considered by the committee that the same be affirmed." Kerr lost his appeal; Barry and Robertson successfully claimed their prize.[41]

The case of *John Barry vs. The Sloop Betsey* highlights the significant role the courts played in the success of a privateer venture. Captain James Robertson and his crew seemed to be in the right place at the right time as the *Lexington* captured the *Betsey*. However small, their role entitled the officers and sailors to a share of the prize. The confirmation by the Committee of Appeals of the Pennsylvania Court of Admiralty's decision ensured a successful cruise—and decent payday—for the privateer vessel. Yet not all privateering efforts were as lucky, as the following case illustrates.

On October 29, 1776, the sloop *Montgomery*, commanded by Captain Thomas Rutenbourgh, captured the schooner *Frank*, commanded by Sylvanus Waterman, during the latter vessel's return journey to Jamaica. Rutenbourgh and his crew carried their prize into the port of Providence, Rhode Island, where they brought suit in "the Court of Justice for the Trial of Prize Causes in and throughout the State of Rhode Island and Providence Plantations in America." Rutenbourgh claimed that the *Frank* had been "employed in carrying supplies to the Enemies of the said united States contrary to the Resolves of Congress the Laws of this State and the Law of

Nations." He asked Judge John Foster to grant the *Frank* as lawful prize to the *Montgomery*.[42]

Matters were quickly complicated when Mary Alsop entered the picture. Mary Alsop was the widow of Richard Alsop, formerly of Middletown, Connecticut, and owner of the *Frank*. As her husband's administrator, Alsop claimed that the *Frank* had "never [been] the Property of any of the Subjects of the King of Great Britain neither was the aforesaid Schooner in the Employ or Service of the Enemies of the United States, neither was the Cargo of said Schooner Destined to Supply the Fleet or Armies of the King of Great Britain or any of the Enemies of the United States." Rather, her husband, Waterman, and his crew were "good subjects of the United States of America." The case at hand was significant, for the cargo of the *Frank* included "91 Casks of dry Fish about 40 Quintals of Fish loose Stowed in the Aft Hold about 12 Casks and 3 Barrels of Oile and 5 Barrels of Herrings," in addition to the vessel with all its apparel, tackle, furniture, and appurtenances. Mary Alsop sought the restoration of her ship and property.[43]

At first glance, the facts of the case appear simple enough. A commissioned private vessel, the *Montgomery*, took the *Frank* on the high seas under the rule that ships aiding the enemy were considered fair game. Mary Alsop claimed the *Frank* was property of a loyal subject of the United States and therefore not a legal prize. Yet the story of the *Frank* was anything but simple. When the vessel first left the port of New London, Connecticut, it was sailing under the name *Dolphin* and with papers to that effect. Waterman was charged with commanding the ship on a voyage to Jamaica, where he would discharge his cargo. He was subsequently to gain "a Cargo of The Produce of s^d Island and then return with s^d Schooner directly to New London and Middletown." However, while anchored at port in Jamaica, Waterman claimed he had heard news of the Battles of Lexington and Bunker Hill. According to his deposition, the commander feared for the safety of his vessel and believed the *Dolphin* would fall prey to a British ship. Therefore, Waterman made a decision "without Orders from his said Owner & with intent only to save said Schooner & Cargo from Condemnation as American property"; he sold the *Dolphin* to a local merchant in order to gain new papers. The craft was renamed the *Frank*.[44]

Waterman maintained he had departed Montego Bay in Jamaica with the aim of sailing directly for New London, Connecticut. However, just as the *Frank* came within sight of Long Island, the crew "discovered an armed Ship lying at anchor which he judged to be a British Sloop of war." The *Frank* changed course to avoid the enemy. According to Waterman, an unfriendly wind caused him to change course again, this time for Newfoundland, where he and the crew arrived on October 4, 1776. The captain asserted that he had tried to make it to New London once more but had been thwarted by "two British frigates." Instead, the *Frank* had made several trips between Newfoundland and Jamaica before the *Montgomery* ultimately captured it. Waterman's deposition ended with his insistence that he had "constantly endeavoured in every method he thought safe . . . to comply with his Original orders & return with said Schooner to New London & Middletown." The original ship's papers, which proved Alsop's ownership of the *Dolphin*, were "destroyed when [the vessel] was chased by s^d Sloop of war." Thus concluded the deposition of Captain Sylvanus Waterman.[45]

The records also contain depositions from several additional individuals presented for the court's consideration. Jeremiah Wadsworth of Hartford offered that he had known Richard Alsop well before his death and that the deceased had often spoken of his ship, the *Dolphin*. Wadsworth also contended that "Waterman always bore the Character of a Friend to the united States of America and son of Liberty, and also that of a man of inflexible Integrity and Truth." Nathaniel Shaler of Middletown concurred with Wadsworth's testimony. Both depositions were "taken at the request of Mrs Mary Alsop," who attempted to prove her captain's loyalty and her husband's ownership of the vessel. In addition, a sailor who joined the voyage in Montego Bay, Jamaica, gave a statement confirming Waterman's story of sailing for New London and encountering the British enemy. The seaman claimed he had initially served aboard a different vessel owned by Richard Alsop, then transferred to the *Frank* in hopes of returning home sooner; at that time, the sailor had the "understanding that she [the *Frank*] belonged to the same owner," Alsop.[46]

In his deposition, Ashbel Burnham noted his and other mariners' reactions when word of Lexington and Bunker Hill had arrived in Jamaica: "[The news] allarmed us very much and [we] was informd that all american Property was Seized and taken by the man of War cruising on our Coast." Burnham affirmed that he had encouraged Waterman to change his papers "by altering the Register," and to take out new ones in the name of someone who was friendly to America but not an American citizen. Furthermore, Burnham contended that he had brought home a copy of the receipt "to Mr Alsop [him]self." After these facts were presented, Mary Alsop asked for a dismissal of the libel and exoneration of the ship.[47]

The judge declared against her and a jury was impaneled. In the case of Thomas Rutenbourgh vs. the *Frank*, the jury declared, "The aforesaid Vessel has been employed in carrying and Supplying the Enemies of the United States of America contrary to the Resolves of the Congress the Laws of this State and the Law of Nations." Upon hearing the jury's findings, the judge proclaimed the ship "condemned" for the use of Rutenbourgh and his crew and called for auction "at [a] Public Vendue to the highest Bidder or Bidders as soon as may be ... first giving Publick Notice of the Time and Place of Sale." Mary Alsop appealed the decision to the Continental Congress.[48]

Theodore Foster, clerk of the Rhode Island Court of Justice, compiled a packet of nineteen pages that "make and contain a True Copy of the whole Cause as the same was heard and Tried ... on the Libel of Thomas Rutenbourgh against the Schooner Frank." This record was submitted to the Continental Congress. Alsop's appeal was lodged with Congress on March 6, 1777, and referred to the Standing Committee on Appeals on Thursday, April 24, 1777. James Wilson, John Adams, and Thomas Burke heard the case and handed down their judgment on May 20, 1777. "Having heard and fully considered as well all and singular the Matters and Things contained and set forth in the Records or Minutes of the Proceedings of the Court of Admiralty" of Rhode Island, the committee pronounced that the decree of the Rhode Island court "be in all its parts revoked reversed and annulled." The *Frank*, all its appurtenances, and the cargo on board at the time of capture were to "be restored and redelivered unto Mary Alsop and Sylvanus Waterman the Claimants in the said Cause." In addition, the judges charged Thomas Rutenbourgh with paying Alsop and Waterman ninety-five dollars "for their Costs and Charges by them expended in sustaining and supporting their said appeal."[49]

Thomas Rutenbourgh and the crew, owners, and outfitters of the privateer *Montgomery* lost their hard-earned prize in this case of appeal. Rutenbourgh had no further recourse—the decision of the standing committee was final. Thus, a venture that had seemed fruitful a year earlier turned out for naught. In fact, the cruise operated at a ninety-five-dollar loss. Privateers ran such risks with every voyage they undertook. The crew did not receive any prize money, and the owners did not receive any return on their investment. In the world of privateers, there were no guarantees. As this case illustrates, even if a privateer voyage resulted in a prize in port, that did not automatically convert into prize money.[50]

Threats to a voyage came not only from the owners of a prize vessel, like Mary Alsop and her deceased husband, but also from members of the privateer crew itself. In October 1777, Captain John Porter and the privateer *Rutledge* set sail from Charleston, South Carolina. Two weeks into the voyage, the *Rutledge* made prize of the sloop *Pallas*, "which was Armed and fitted out as a Tender to the said Sloop Rutledge for the more Successfully Cruizing against the Enemy." Over the next few weeks, the *Rutledge* and the *Pallas* fell in and out of contact with one another as each pursued potential prizes. The *Pallas* took prize of "a small schooner on board of which prize, Captain Porter the Commander of the said Sloop Rutledge put" Peter Norris "as Prize Master." After parting ways again due to heavy winds, the *Pallas* and its prize regained contact, upon which "they descried a Sail, to which the Tender gave Chace, and in about an hour afterwards took her." The new prize "proved to be a Schooner Called the Polly and Nancy Commanded by Captain John Davis from Mobille bound for Jamaica." Matthew Smith, captain of the *Pallas*, ordered Peter Norris to transfer to the *Polly and Nancy* as prize master. All three—the *Pallas*, the first prize, and the *Polly and Nancy*—set course for Charleston on Smith's orders.[51]

Of all three ships in the company, the *Pallas* was the only armed and outfitted vessel. It also carried the majority of prisoners from the *Polly and Nancy*, including its captain, John Davis. Davis led the other mariners aboard the *Pallas* in an attack against Smith and his crew. "With his Mutineers in full possession of the Tender," Davis bore down on the other prize schooner and recaptured it. He then turned his attention to the *Polly and Nancy*, which he eventually overpowered. John Davis controlled all three vessels at this time. He placed Peter Norris aboard the *Polly and Nancy* as prize master and ordered the vessel to Jamaica. After a day or so on this heading, Davis decided to change course and sail for Mobile. Norris followed in the *Polly and Nancy* as he was ordered. Five days later, Norris and four other seamen rose up and retook control of the vessel; they immediately changed course and sailed for the port of Charleston, South Carolina.[52]

Upon arrival in Charleston, Peter Norris brought his case to the Court of Admiralty. He sought the condemnation of the *Polly and Nancy* as lawful prize to himself and the other sailors: William Thomas, Patrick McLean, James McDaniel, and Daniel Russell. According to his version of events, Norris "was threatened with the loss of his head if he should open his Mouth to speak" when Davis overtook the *Polly and Nancy*. Davis then appointed Norris master of the ship. During their short voyage together, Norris told the court, Davis had "spoke[n] with [him] and with imprecations and menaces [had] threatened to blow out his brains in Case he should attempt to run away and again fall into his [Davis's] hands." Despite these threats, Norris claimed he had vowed to retake the ship. He subsequently accomplished this feat and then sailed into Georgetown. William Thomas, a mate on the *Polly and Nancy*, affirmed Norris's account, as did Daniel Russell.[53]

Judge Hugh Rutledge ordered Edward Weyman, the marshal of the court, to announce the case to the public. Such notice gave anyone with just cause the opportunity to present themselves and "to shew . . . why the said Schooner her Tackle, furniture, Apparel and Cargo should not be Condemned as lawful prize according to the prayer of the said Libell." Jacob Read, the man appointed proctor for Norris and his fellow sailors, then presented several papers taken on board the *Polly and Nancy*. These included a certificate from the port of Mobile that stated the vessel would not unload in any European port north of Cape Finisterre unless it be in Great Britain or Ireland. The papers also included a clearance from His Majesty's Customs House in Mobile. Read presented both documents as proof that the vessel belonged to subjects of the king of Great Britain and thus was an enemy of the United States and subject to capture. On Friday, February 20, 1778, Edward Rutledge, on behalf of John Porter, captain of the sloop of war *Rutledge*, lodged a claim in the case. Porter was not challenging the condemnation of the *Polly and Nancy*; rather, he was challenging who had right to the prize vessel.[54]

Porter argued that he and "the Owners, Officers, Seamen & Mariners of and belonging to the said Sloop Rutledge" had the definitive claim over the *Polly and Nancy*. The men sailing aboard the *Rutledge*, including Norris and his comrades Thomas, McDaniel, Russell, and McLean, had signed articles of agreement prior to setting sail on their voyage, the captain maintained. These articles of agreement, presented to the court by Porter's representative Edward Rutledge, "agreed that all prizes taken on the said Cruise, should be divided between them [the owners, captain, and crew of the *Rutledge*] in such proportions as were Settled by the said Articles." On behalf of Porter, Rutledge asked the court that the prize and its appurtenances "be divided by and between them in such Shares and proportions as if the same had been taken by the said Sloop Rutledge and Justice may be done." On Monday, February 23, the judge ordered a drawing of the jury. Norris responded to Porter's claims via his proctor Jacob Read, who stated, "The said Petition and Claim of the said John Porter to the said Libel are very untrue imperfect and insufficient to be replied unto." Norris was prepared to defend his claim to the *Polly and Nancy*.[55]

Edward Weyman summoned all of the jurors, save two who could not be found, and made public announcement of the case. Two witnesses, William Williamson and James Cavannah, were called on behalf of Norris in an attempt to bolster his claim. Williamson, who was part owner of the *Polly and Nancy* prior to its capture, was taken prisoner when the vessel was seized, and he corroborated most of Norris's initial claim. However, Williamson could not "say who were or could be said to be owners thereof" of the *Polly and Nancy* after Norris and his fellow sailors captured it the final time. Cavannah had joined the crew of the *Polly and Nancy* at Kingston, Jamaica, and had been aboard during the voyage to Mobile when taken by the tender *Pallas*. He confirmed that Norris had been placed on board the *Polly and Nancy* as prize master, and that Captain Davis had retaken the vessel and appointed Norris "as Master and Navigator." Perhaps most importantly for Norris and his case, Cavannah testified "that the said Norris and others after they so took her [the *Polly and Nancy*] became owners thereof." Rutledge and Read both presented further evidence and "cited Cases" in support of their claims and causes before the case was handed over to the jury for deliberation. The jury returned shortly thereafter with a verdict: "We find for the Claimants, and that the Actors be intituled to their shares agreeable to the Articles . . . John Scott foreman."[56]

The judge ordered the *Polly and Nancy* into the hands of Porter's agent, who was charged with selling the vessel, giving notice of payments "in one of the Publick Gazettes of this State," distributing the correct payments and shares to those involved in the case, and returning "an account of the Sales of said Schooner and Cargo" to the register of the court within twenty days. Judge Rutledge also ordered Norris and his fellow actors to pay the court costs for the claimants; any remaining court costs were to be paid from the money gained from the sale of the *Polly and Nancy*.[57]

Peter Norris was not satisfied with the judgment handed down by the Court of Admiralty in the state of South Carolina. Less than a week later, Jacob Read lodged a petition on behalf of Peter Norris for the right to appeal the verdict. The proctor argued that ownership of the *Polly and Nancy* changed hands over the course of its capture and recapture. When John Davis had mutinied against the *Pallas* and taken the *Polly and Nancy* as prize, Read contended, the vessel had returned to the hands of British owners, enemies of the United States. Read cited the resolves of the Continental Congress, which stated, "Any vessel or Cargo the Property of any British Subject not an Inhabitant of Bermuda, or any of the Bahama Islands brought into any of the Ports or Harbours of any of these United States, by the Master of Mariners shall be adjudged Lawful Prize & divided among the Captors." Furthermore, Read reasoned, the evidence presented during the case and the examination of witnesses illustrated "that the Schooner Polly and Nancy

was British property, bound on a Voyage to Mobille on the day of her be-
ing taken and seized by my Party Actors in this Cause." According to Read,
John Porter and his crew lost any right to the *Polly and Nancy* when Captain
John Davis, a British owner, retook it and kept it for days.[58]

Norris's proctor also took issue with an opinion Judge Rutledge issued to
the jury that said the resolution should not "operate in this Cause," for the
articles of agreement signed by the crew, owners, and officers specifically addressed the division of prize shares. Read summarized his argument made
during the case that the arms and ammunitions of the sloop of war *Rutledge*
were not used to capture the *Polly and Nancy* the second time, nor were the
Rutledge's crew or the "implements of War" under its commission used in the
seizure. Peter Norris and the other actors of the case captured the *Polly and
Nancy* after they had been taken as prisoners of war, Read continued. Norris
seized the vessel under his own initiative after a British owner and captain,
John Davis, had placed him on board. The sloop of war *Rutledge* was not involved in the second capture of the prize, according to Read's petition.[59]

Read took his party's claim a step further during the case, quoting an act
of assembly passed by the state of South Carolina in regard to recapture and
salvage rights. If a ship owned by subjects of the United States was taken on
the high seas by the enemy, then retaken and brought into any port in the
state, those who retook the ship were owed a salvage fee based on the number of hours the vessel spent in British custody. This circumstance would remain true so long as the court found in favor of the original owners or claimants. In the case of Peter Norris, Read postulated, the *Rutledge* gained legal
rights over the *Polly and Nancy* when it initially captured the vessel. However, the ship had then spent "upwards of Ninety six hours in the hands of
the British owner" before Peter Norris and his mates recaptured it. Hence,
Read proclaimed, Norris and his fellow actors were "intitled to one half of
the said schooner in lieu of Salvage for the same." Yet Judge Hugh Rutledge
once again ruled against Norris and his proctor and stated that the act of assembly did not apply in this case. Read then concluded, "Whereby the Jury
were as aforesaid Induced to find against the Actors, nor did they allow the
Actors any manner of Salvage for the said Schooner contrary to Right and
Justice and the said Resolutions of Congress and Laws of this State." On
these grounds, Jacob Read lodged his appeal. Edward Rutledge, proctor for
John Porter, protested "against the admission of said Appeal," which was entered in the court records. Nevertheless, the case was brought to Congress
and received on April 20, 1778.[60]

No papers survive regarding the committee's consideration or the reasons for their decision. The only note contained in the papers concerning the case states, "Decree of ye Court below Confirmed Augt 14, 1778." The case of *Peter Norris vs. The Schooner Polly and Nancy* highlights the perils of a privateer venture beyond the ebb and flow of the high seas. Members of the privateer crew could pose potential hazards, not just as mutineers, but as appellants in a court case. A prize taken could easily turn into a prize lost, whether lost in the Atlantic or in the courtroom. Luckily for John Porter and the owners and crew of the *Rutledge*, their prize was restored to them. However, for Peter Norris and his fellow sailors on board the *Polly and Nancy*, their additional efforts in retaking the prize amounted to nothing more than their initial share of the vessel and its cargo.[61]

Even if a prize was successfully sailed into port, matters in Courts of Admiralty were rarely simple. Further complications often arose when the proceedings turned on the question of a neutral nation. Such was the situation for George Wait Babcock, commander of the private armed ship *General Mifflin*, and Mungo Mackay, a merchant of Boston, who submitted their case to the Massachusetts Bay Middle District Maritime Court on February 23, 1780. According to the captain's initial account of events, "on the 19th day of August" 1779, he and his crew "attacked, seized and took" the brigantine *Brunette* while sailing "on the high seas." Babcock and Mackay argued that the vessel of 150 tons was "the property of and belonging to subjects of the King of Great Britain," and that it carried cargo "freighted, insured, and risqued" by British subjects. Furthermore, the captain and the merchant claimed that the commander of the *Brunette*, Thomas Griffien Moses Welch, had known the cargo to be British property, had known a war existed between Britain and the United States, and had still decided to sail from Oporto, Portugal, to Ireland.[62]

If these circumstances were not enough to condemn the vessel, the libelants also argued that Welch had refused Babcock's request to search the vessel and had "attempted to cover and secure the said vessel and her cargo from capture, by false papers and false pretences." Though Welch claimed his vessel and its cargo belonged to and was employed by subjects of the United Provinces of the Netherlands, Babcock contended otherwise. He noted that Welch had thrown important papers that might have proved ownership into the sea. These documents, Babcock lamented, were "irrecoverably lost." He also alleged the *Brunette* had been "carrying supplies to the Enemies of said United States." All of these reasons, declared Babcock and Mackay, illustrated why the ship and its cargo were a lawful prize.[63]

Seven weeks later, on April 12, 1780, Jonathan Williams arrived in the

Middle District Maritime Court. A merchant of Boston, Williams appeared "on behalf of the owners and others concerned in the brigantine *Brunette*." He argued that the libel presented by Babcock and Mackay's attorney, William Tudor, was "altogether false." Williams further contended the vessel and its cargo did indeed belong to subjects of the United Provinces of the Netherlands—a neutral nation at the time of capture, a nation not at war with the United States. Therefore, neither the ship nor its cargo was subject to seizure. Williams requested the return of the vessel and cargo to its owners, in addition to repayment of the expenses the owners had incurred from his services and from the damages they had suffered from "the unreasonable and groundless arrest, seizure, and supposed capture" of the *Brunette*.[64]

The case was held over until Friday, July 29, 1780, when both parties returned to court. A jury of twelve men was impaneled with Judge Nathan Cushing presiding over the trial. Each side presented "proofs and exhibits" in an effort to convince the jury of its version of events and claimed truths. Babcock and Mackay offered the captain's instructions from Congress for commanders of private armed ships dated April 3, 1776, which stated, "You may by force of arms, attack, subdue, & take all vessels belonging to the subjects of the King of Great Britain." The instructions also noted that the captain should let a vessel "pass unmolested" if the commander of said ship allowed "a peaceable search" and gave "satisfactory" answers regarding the cargo and destination of the cruise. In Babcock's account, the *Brunette* was a vessel of British subjects whose captain had refused a search and provided false answers regarding his ship's cargo and destination—hence, Babcock's claim that his prize was lawful and legal.

The libelants continued their case with testimony from officers aboard the *General Mifflin*. First Lieutenant James Eldred recounted how he had boarded the *Brunette* "to examine her and her papers" immediately following its capture. Eldred testified the captain of the taken vessel, who "appeared to be a Dutch man but talked English," had produced only one paper when asked for the ship's records. The document appeared to be a bill of lading, Eldred noted, which was the only record ever found as far as Eldred knew. Captain Babcock corroborated the first lieutenant's story in his interrogation. The supposed commander of the *Brunette*, the Dutchman, boarded the *General Mifflin* and delivered the single paper. As Babcock described it, the document was "a memorandum something like but not exactly resembling a bill of lading ... which was in Dutch." The captain maintained he had found no other papers and had given the only one he did receive to Edward Kirby,

In CONGRESS,

WEDNESDAY, April 3, 1776.

INSTRUCTIONS *to the* COMMANDERS *of Private Ships or Vessels of War, which shall have Commissions or Letters of Marque and Reprisal, authorising them to make Captures of British Vessels and Cargoes.*

I.

YOU may, by Force of Arms, attack, subdue, and take all Ships and other Vessels belonging to the Inhabitants of Great Britain, on the High Seas, or between high-water and low-water Marks, except Ships and Vessels bringing Persons who intend to settle and reside in the United Colonies, or bringing Arms, Ammunition or Warlike Stores to the said Colonies, for the Use of such Inhabitants thereof as are Friends to the American Cause, which you shall suffer to pass unmolested, the Commanders thereof permitting a peaceable Search, and giving satisfactory Information of the Contents of the Ladings, and Destinations of the Voyages.

II.

You may, by Force of Arms, attack, subdue, and take all Ships and other Vessels whatsoever carrying Soldiers, Arms, Gun powder, Ammunition, Provisions, or any other contraband Goods, to any of the British Armies or Ships of War employed against these Colonies.

III.

You shall bring such Ships and Vessels as you shall take, with their Guns, Rigging, Tackle, Apparel, Furniture and Ladings, to some convenient Port or Ports of the United Colonies, that Proceedings may thereupon be had in due Form before the Courts which are or shall be there appointed to hear and determine Causes civil and maritime.

IV.

You or one of your Chief Officers shall bring or send the Master and Pilot and one or more principal Person or Persons of the Company of every Ship or Vessel by you taken, as soon after the Capture as may be, to the Judge or Judges of such Court as aforesaid, to be examined upon Oath, and make Answer to the Interrogatories which may be propounded touching the Interest or Property of the Ship or Vessel and her Lading; and at the same Time you shall deliver or cause to be delivered to the Judge or Judges, all Passes, Sea Briefs, Charter Parties, Bills of Lading, Cockets Letters, and other Documents and Writings found on Board, proving the said Papers by the Affidavit of yourself, or of some other Person present at the Capture, to be produced as they were received, without Fraud, Addition, Subduction, or Embezzlement.

V.

You shall keep and preserve every Ship or Vessel and Cargo by you taken, until they shall by Sentence of a Court properly authorised be adjudged lawful Prize, not selling, spoiling, wasting, or diminishing the same or breaking the Bulk thereof, nor suffering any such Thing to be done.

VI.

If you, or any of your Officers or Crew shall, in cold Blood, kill or maim, or by Torture or otherwise, cruelly, inhumanly, and contrary to common Usage and the Practice of civilized Nations in War, treat any Person or Persons surprized in the Ship or Vessel you shall take, the Offender shall be severely punished.

VII.

You shall, by all convenient Opportunities, send to Congress written Accounts of the Captures you shall make, with the Number and Names of the Captives, Copies of your Journal from Time to Time, and Intelligence of what may occur or be discovered concerning the Designs of the Enemy, and the Destinations, Motions, and Operations of their Fleets and Armies.

VIII.

One Third, at the least, of your whole Company shall be Land Men.

IX.

You shall not ransome any Prisoners or Captives, but shall dispose of them in such Manner as the Congress, or if that be not sitting in the Colony whither they shall be brought, as the General Assembly, Convention, or Council or Committee of Safety of such Colony shall direct.

X.

You shall observe all such further Instructions as Congress shall hereafter give in the Premises, when you shall have Notice thereof.

XI.

If you shall do any Thing contrary to these Instructions, or to others hereafter to be given, or willingly suffer such Thing to be done, you shall not only forfeit your Commission, and be liable to an Action for Breach of the Condition of your Bond, but be responsible to the Party grieved for Damages sustained by such Mal-versation.

By Order of CONGRESS.

JOHN HANCOCK, *President.*

Instructions issued by the Continental Congress to commanders of privateer vessels.
Courtesy of the Library of Congress, Rare Book and Special Collections Division,
Continental Congress & Constitutional Convention Broadsides Collection.

prize master of the brigantine *Brunette*, who was charged with bringing the vessel into port at Boston.[65]

Kirby was the third witness questioned on behalf of Babcock and Mackay. The prize master confirmed he had received one paper from Babcock in addition to a copy of his captain's commission. After parting company with the *General Mifflin*, Kirby explained, the *Brunette* had sailed on, but it soon found itself in bad shape. The ship received relief from two privateers. Captain McLacy of the privateer *Lady Spencer* took those two documents—the bill of lading and the copy of the commission—from Kirby, and the prize master avowed he had not seen them since. Thus, the supposed papers that might have proved Babcock's and Mackay's story were not presented as evidence.[66]

While Eldred, Babcock, and Kirby testified regarding the *Brunette*'s papers, the next witness, Captain James Tew, recounted the sequence of events aboard the *General Mifflin* following the capture—events that supposedly confirmed Babcock's account and refuted Williams's claims. Tew was a passenger aboard the *General Mifflin* when it sailed from Nantes in August 1779. He witnessed the capture of the *Brunette* and saw Eldred board the brigantine. Three men from the captured vessel gave different stories concerning the circumstances of the *Brunette*, Tew explained. The first, a Dutchman, declared he was the captain but had no papers to give. The second, "one Welch," stated the ship's destination was Holland. The third, an Irishman named Moloy, said he had taken passage on the *Brunette* because he was headed for Dublin, Ireland—the ship's true destination—and he had made arrangements with Captain Welch. The story continued, as Tew described how Lieutenant Eldred had brought on board a young lad who "confess'd the whole matter to him"—that is to say, the true destination of Dublin, Ireland, and the captaincy of Welch. Tew further declared that the aforementioned Dutchman had corroborated the story upon hearing the lad's tale. When Welch was confronted with these facts, Tew elaborated, the supposed captain had "sat still for some short space" before confessing the destination was indeed Dublin and the vessel belonged to John English of that port. Welch bemoaned his confession "would ruin him" and his trade.[67]

The testimony of James Tew delivered important components of Babcock's and Mackay's account of the capture, but it was not over yet. The following day, Tew's account continued, the *General Mifflin* had come across a Portuguese vessel, one the Irishman Moloy had initially booked passage on. Captain Babcock "told Moloy he should go on board said ship," but

the Dutchman and Welch would continue on to America. The two condemned men pleaded for mercy, Tew explained. Moloy even spoke on behalf
of Welch, who apparently had "a large family at home." The doomed men
feared "they should die on board a prison ship in America." Though Babcock
had known he might face issues redeeming his prize, Tew noted, the captain had ultimately decided to let all three men—Moloy, the Dutchman, and
Welch—board the Portuguese ship bound for London. Tew further testified
that he had often spoken with the sailors taken from the *Brunette*. They not
only confirmed the ship's destination and ownership, but also explained how
on several occasions they entered the port of Dublin with secret signals and
new papers delivered upon their arrival. At least, these were the facts according to James Tew.[68]

The next witness, Joseph Lunt, another passenger aboard the *General
Mifflin*, mostly reiterated Tew's story. Lunt added that Captain Babcock had
promised the young lad no harm would come to him for telling the truth
about the ship's destination and captaincy, then had "sent [the boy] on board
of the prize brig." Three pieces of evidence bolstered these two passengers'
testimony: certificates supposedly signed by Thomas Griffien (the Dutchman), Moses Welch (the captain), and John Chiddell (the lad). All of these
items attested to various aspects of the story, including the destination, ownership, papers, and cargo of the *Brunette*. All three were "objected to as illegal evidence" by the claimants. With this, the libelants rested their case.[69]

The stage was now set for the claimants to deliver their side of the story.
According to documents presented, the true owner of the *Brunette* was
James Turing, a respected and "very well known" Burgher and merchant of
Veere, in the province of Zeeland in the Netherlands. Turing bought the
vessel for 5,900 guilders from a broker, Habertus Hallewaand, who represented Brother and Antichan, merchants of Bordeaux. These claims were
submitted as evidence and supported by notarized reports from John Siver-
uius Halffman, notary of Veere, and the Bürgermeisters and the Council of
Vere. In addition, a letter from Lambert Kingston to Turing & Son dated
July 20, 1779, noted the safe arrival of the *Brunette* in Oporto, Portugal. The
missive also discussed the cargo of wine, fruit, and cork loaded aboard the
vessel "by order and for account and risk of Messrs. James Turing & Son."
The ship would set "sail [at] the first fair wind." By all these accounts, the
Brunette did indeed belong to a subject of the United Provinces of the Netherlands. Not surprisingly, the libelants objected to all three pieces, citing
them as illegal evidence.[70]

Captain Thomas Griffien, via a notarized description, shared a different account of events from those presented by Captain Babcock and his crew members and passengers. Griffien declared he was indeed the captain of the *Brunette*, which had set sail from Oporto, Portugal, on August 1, 1779, "the wind being SE . . . bound for Drontheim in Norway." The *Brunette* sailed in company with a Portuguese vessel, the *May de Deos Santa Anna*, for nearly two weeks when both were hailed by a Bristol privateer "having American colors" and commanded by Captain Peter Wade. Griffien claimed "three officers and about eight or nine men armed with naked swords" had boarded his ship and questioned him about his destination, provenance, and papers. The privateer officer seemed satisfied with Griffien's replies and "assured them he had no objection against them." Nevertheless, Griffien complained, the privateer had detained his ship for five hours and had ultimately taken wine, a dozen fowl, lemon juice, lemons, and oranges from the *Brunette* before allowing it to continue on its voyage.[71]

While sailing solo off the coast of France near Brest in the wee hours of the morning on August 18, 1779, the *Brunette* was attacked and seized by the Boston privateer the *General Mifflin*. Despite his explanation, papers, and pleas, Griffien contended, Captain Babcock had refused to believe the *Brunette* was "neutral property" and instead "did insist to make prize of her." Babcock sent the vessel and one cabin boy to port and kept Griffien and the remainder of the crew on board the privateer. The following day, Griffien noted, the *General Mifflin* had come upon the aforementioned Portuguese ship. Babcock decided to place Griffien and two other passengers on board the London-bound craft and provided them "a small allowance of provisions." Griffien swore that as soon as the ship landed at Dover, he had made every effort to return home to the Netherlands, where he gave his testimony in front of a notary. He also maintained that there had been no misconduct or neglect on his part. Rather, the *Brunette* was taken by the "obstinate will" of Babcock, who "would not be convinced" that the ship and its cargo were neutral property.[72]

While these two versions of the same event shared commonalities—the seizure of the *Brunette* by the privateer *General Mifflin*, the decision to send the former in as a prize, the presence of a third vessel that ultimately transported three men—other facts remained in dispute. These details included the central question regarding the nationality of the owners of the *Brunette* and its cargo. As per the commission granted to Captain George Wait Babcock, he was allowed to capture vessels belonging to subjects of the king of

Great Britain, but he must let those belonging to neutral nations pass by un-molested. Did Babcock err when he seized the *Brunette*? Or was he justified in his actions? The jury had to decide who actually owned the vessel and its freight based on the testimony and evidence both sides presented.

On Monday, July 31, 1780, the jury returned with its judgment. The *Brunette*, the jurors found, "was the property of some of the subjects of . . . the United Netherlands" and therefore must be returned to its owners. The cargo, however, belonged to British subjects and thus was "lawful prize to the captors." Two days into the new year of 1781, Judge Nathan Cushing con-firmed the jury's findings and "decreed that the said brigantine *Brunette* with her appurtenances be restored for the use of the owners." The cargo was "for-feit" and should be sold; "the monies thence arising," after deducting neces-sary charges, should be granted to Babcock and those involved in the cap-ture. Three days later, Jonathan Williams filed an appeal on behalf of the owners of the *Brunette*. Isaac Mansfield, the clerk of the Massachusetts Bay Middle District Maritime Court, prepared a complete record of the case's documents, including the original notarized files from the claimants, and sent it to the Court of Appeals.[73]

After waiting nearly seven months, Williams and the *Brunette*'s owners finally learned the fate of their petition when on August 4, 1781, the Court of Appeals rendered a decision. Williams's appeal was dismissed, and the decree of Judge Nathan Cushing was "in all its parts confirmed and estab-lished." To add insult to injury for Jonathan Williams (and the owners of the *Brunette*), the court ordered that he pay Babcock "the sum of fifty spe-cie dollars for his costs and charges" that amassed due to the appeal. On the one hand, Babcock and his privateer crew, along with Mungo Mackay and the other owners and investors in the *General Mifflin*, were victorious in their pursuit of a prize. The cargo was theirs, and they would benefit from its sale. On the other hand, they lost out on an even larger payday, as they were forced to watch the vessel they had worked so hard to secure sail out of the harbor. The case of *Babcock v. The Brigantine Brunette* once again highlights the risk-reward potentials and hazards of a privateer venture.[74]

The convoluted, and at times controversial, story also serves as a reminder of the importance of the instructions distributed by the Continental Con-gress to privateers, and the complications that often arose when neutral ves-sels carrying supposed neutral cargo were seized as prizes. In theory, priva-teers should have easily learned the provenance and ownership of a vessel, but a ship's papers could be altered, lost, or intentionally tossed overboard.

The ownership of the cargo might also prove difficult to determine. The onus lay on the privateer captain to prove his prize was indeed legal; in the case of Captain George Wait Babcock, he only partially succeeded.[75]

⁂

After a prolonged process of creation, the Admiralty Court system in place during the American Revolution was functional at best. As a result, privateers habitually grappled with the ever-changing resolves of the Continental Congress and the resolutions of various state governments. Massachusetts led the initial charge in the call for privateers, as well as the creation of courts to handle questions regarding captured vessels and lawful prizes. Though Congress soon followed suit with its own set of resolutions, the regulations laid out were never truly set in stone. Other colonies established courts as well, with varying degrees of success. The Continental Congress set forth its own ability to appeal cases, but the delegates could not promise that the states would allow proceedings in every circumstance. To be sure, not all states permitted these appeals. As described above, some states initially granted that right, then changed their tune and disallowed it, and vice versa. No government—colonial or otherwise—wanted to truly cede power; hence, the colonial resolutions and acts contained a plethora of restrictions and caveats.

This tepid cooperation between colonies and the Continental Congress might seem to suggest a growth of American nationalism, or perhaps even to serve as a harbinger for future cession of state powers to the federal government. However, this would imply the actions outlined above were taken with those specific ideas in mind. In the moment, colonists, delegates, and governments were simply trying to deal with the matter of privateers and prize cases in the best way they knew how. They followed the British model where applicable, but they also made their own distinct choices and decisions based on the demands and desires of the colony in question.

While members of Congress grasped the need for an official Court of Appeals, they probably did not understand what was at stake on an individual level for those involved in privateering ventures. Privateers fought simply for the opportunity to receive payment, albeit a potentially greater one if fortune and the courts favored their cause. Thus, the outcome of a case could often mean the gain or loss of thousands of dollars for privateer captains, owners, outfitters, and crews; one well-endowed cargo hold and well-equipped and well-outfitted prize could mean the difference between success and devastation for merchants and sailors.

The struggles over sovereignty and power among the thirteen colonies and the Continental Congress spilled over into the court system and the cases of privateers and their prizes. Though some of these seafarers successfully libeled their suits, others walked away empty-handed. The cases delineated above offer insight into those that did receive appeals at the highest level, but they also only represent a small percentage. Indeed, the 109 cases filed with the Court of Appeals are a mere fragment of those that were heard throughout the colonies during the course of the war. Nevertheless, they offer insight into the complex motivations, experiences, and efforts of privateers.

The court system presented a situation ripe for public opinion to fall against the positions and legacies of privateers. The Continental Congress and state governments commissioned, ordered, and encouraged privateers to capture enemy vessels on the promise of receiving a financial incentive for the taken prize. Yet when these sailors returned their captured vessel to port, a convoluted system of claims awaited them. In other words, privateers were forced to publicly and legally justify their actions—actions Congress bolstered and supported in the first place.

Some of these cases lasted long after the final shots were fired at Yorktown, leaving privateers in what was often deemed an unpatriotic position. Despite the risks they took on behalf of the American cause, privateers came to be viewed as profiteers more often than not—and as men who had not sacrificed in the manner of their land-based counterparts in the army, or even resembling the sailors of the regular Continental navy. The damage done to the legacy of privateers had consequences in the Revolutionary period; the apparently unseemly actions of these marauding vessels and crews left privateers on the outskirts of the triumphant Revolutionary narrative.

CHAPTER 5

To Glory Let Us Run

M ansel Alcock, owner and outfitter, struggled with his conscience over his interest in privateers. Early in the war, Alcock was a "warm advocate for privateering." He witnessed the positive effects of the enterprise: the prizes, goods, and money brought into the maritime ports and towns of New England. The sea was a way of life in the coastal areas of Massachusetts, and Mansel Alcock was a part of that legacy.[1]

Yet recent events and reports in the spring of 1778 from Salem privateer and shipowner John Baptiste Millet prompted Alcock to doubt his involvement. He became "almost a Convert to the Interests of the Army" and declared, "I should always have been so." The army needed men—men that privateers eagerly took without a second thought to the consequences of their actions. Privateers could be unpredictable and act in unlawful ways. Alcock explained that he did not realize the threat these sailors posed: "I had such a high Opinion of Our Virtue & Our strength, that I only look't on Privateering as the exuberance of both." However, he had seen the error of his ways. "I find myself mistaken," Alcock admitted, "[and] stand rectified in my Opinion & shall act accordingly, tho' I cant entirely give up Privateering, as its confin'd but to few States." Even though Alcock recognized his faults, he also realized the profits he would forfeit if he quit the privateering business altogether.[2]

Such was the dilemma that many Americans faced during the Revolution. To support privateering was to support what many viewed as a legalized form of piracy. To give up the venture was to relinquish any potential prizes and prisoners that might come from the numerous cruises—not to mention the possibility of losing what little martial presence the Americans, devoid of a well-developed navy, had on the high seas. Privateers occupied this grey area during the war. Despite their efforts on behalf of the colonies, they were later whitewashed by men like Alcock who ultimately decided that privateering was not a pastime of gentlemen.

Privateers faced numerous obstacles in their ventures, including enemy ships, poor weather, capricious European governments, and a complicated court system that occasionally left the adventurers empty-handed. Yet the final obstacle such mariners encountered was the court of public opinion. Despite their patriotic, and sometimes heroic, undertakings during the war, privateers eventually accrued an enduring legacy of faithless and fickle actions and intentions. In the early years of the Revolution, investors, owners, captains, and crews brought the war directly to the coast of England, inflicting damage to British merchant ships and causing insurance rates to rise. Some Americans in the colonies cheered the efforts of privateers; they understood that the fledgling Continental navy could not compete with the British juggernaut that was His Majesty's fleet. Yet over time, colonists like Mansel Alcock changed their view of those commerce raiders. Privateers became a problem, rather than part of the solution.

Privateers were an ever-present threat, annoying and harassing the British at every turn. However, these marauders were also unpredictable, unruly, and self-interested. Privateers did not always follow their instructions. Some crews sought profit whatever the cost, whether from an enemy vessel or, as Gustavus Conyngham's experiences highlighted, from a neutral vessel. Such actions were contrary to the law of nations, which left the Continental Congress in a difficult situation. Public perceptions of privateers were both positive and negative throughout the entirety of the war; a prize brought into port might be hailed by one colonist and denigrated by another. At the war's inception, individual reports of successful voyages filled colonial newspapers and bolstered opinions toward privateers. Yet at the end of the war, due to the unsavory actions of some seafarers, the contemptuous perceptions of leading men—like George Washington, John Paul Jones, and those elites who did not want to include seemingly piratical actions in the overall narrative of the nation's founding—strengthened negative feelings about privateers so that these combatants were eventually—and intentionally—overlooked.

Americans and Europeans held complicated feelings and points of view in regard to privateers, their choices, their actions, and their ultimate place within the Revolution's legacy. These various perceptions were ultimately overwhelmingly negative, and they led to a postwar narrative of the conflict relegating privateers to the outskirts. The mariners were considered unworthy of inclusion alongside the likes of George Washington, John Paul Jones, Thomas Jefferson, Benjamin Franklin, and John Adams, not to mention the so-called patriotic Continental troops, navy sailors, and state militias that fought and died on behalf of the American nation.

Privateers served an important purpose during the Revolution. While the Continental navy struggled to get off the docks and stay afloat for the entirety of the war, these privately armed vessels continually plied their skills and kept the British Admiralty, navy, and citizenry on high alert. The effects of privateering are not in question. Rather, the issue in the postwar period was what to do with these privateers, or, better still, how to remember them, if at all. Many had committed illegal actions during the war, and contemporary correspondence illustrates European nations' ire, disgust, and indignation in regard to these sailors. Following the conflict, the newly minted American nation sought recognition from and reconciliation with its former mother country. America needed Britain's approval and, perhaps more importantly, its trade. The threat of privateers and the memories of their illicit actions—at least from the English perspective—created a problem for the Americans. Privateers could not be part of the triumphant narrative of patriotism and independence. They represented piratical actions in the eyes of the British. American representatives could not openly celebrate privateers while courting the favor of the British Crown. Nor did the elite gentlemen who had worked tirelessly to create this new nation want their own reputations and legacies tainted by these seamen. A rebellion such as the one fomented in the colonies only becomes a successful revolution if all the pieces fall into place. The privateer piece of the puzzle simply did not fit the commemorative picture the Founders had in mind.[3]

✴✿◎◎◎✿✴

Elbridge Gerry, a strong proponent of privateering, penned a letter to Samuel Adams on October 9, 1775. Months before the Continental Congress officially declared independence, Gerry wrote, "My attention is directed to the fitting out of privateers, which I hope will make them swarm here." Gerry inquired of Sam Adams, "Is it not time to encourage individuals to exert themselves in this way?" Gerry noted that General Thomas Gage of the British army had already attacked supplies collected for the Continental army. Privateers were the quickest and surest way to fight back. Indeed,

Gerry asked, "Can we hesitate at this time about the propriety of confiscating vessels employed by him [Gage] to infest the coasts, or supply his troops, or can we doubt the propriety of encouraging individuals by giving them the advantage resulting from their reprisals, when it is certain that other plans will not meet with such success as will probably attend this?" Gerry was not concerned with the moral correctness of fitting out privateers. Rather, he saw the potential victories that could result from swiftly taking action in the private sphere. In the eyes of Elbridge Gerry, privateering was a worthy endeavor as long as the British suffered in the end.[4]

Early in the war, a number of Gerry's fellow leading colonists shared his outlook on privateering. Jack Thompson, residing in St. Eustatius, wrote in disbelief on April 13, 1776, "The merchants at New-York, Philadelphia, and other places on the Continent do not fit out privateers as last war, with commissions from Congress to take all vessels coming from or going to Europe, from any part of the world whatever, as English bottoms." Thompson noted the British admiral was handing out commissions at Antigua and Dominica. "I must say," he opined, "I do wish the Americans would return the compliment." He further speculated that "if two or more privateers did once appear in the West Indies, all kinds of produce, particularly sugar and rum, would fall 25 per cent." Thompson understood how the mere threat and presence of privateers could affect the British economy.[5]

In a May 1776 letter, William Hunt informed Elbridge Gerry of privateering operations that had captured "fifteen hundred whole barrells of Gun Powder, containing about—seventy five Tons, one Thousand stands of Arms a large quantity of intrenching Utensils—a Number of travelling Carriages, a quantity of English Goods &c." Hunt continued, "The Privateers are gone after more," and he further remarked that intelligence indicated that General Howe and the British had evacuated Boston and were headed for Halifax. Hunt added, the "Privateers intend doging of them & find[ing] out who they are [and] where they are bound." Samuel Phipps Savage received a letter from D. Ingraham Jr. also relating the event: "Yesterday Morning one of our Small Privateers Gave Chase to a Ship and follow'd her almost up to the Light House and Boarded her and to our Surprize she made no resistance." Ingraham vented, "While we are humbling ourselves for our Sins, and beseeching the Pardon of them [the English]; and intreating the Assistance of Heaven, we receiv'd an answer, and to me a very Striking one." The success of the privateers convinced Ingraham that the cause of independence, rather than the path of seeking forgiveness, was the correct course of action.[6]

News of a large cache of goods taken by privateers traveled quickly through personal correspondence. On June 5, 1776, Robert Morris informed Silas Deane of the success of two Pennsylvania privateers in seizing "three large ships bound from Jam[aic]a to London with 1082 hhds Sugar 260 Puncheons Rum 300 Casks Piemento, 22000 hard dollars, 70 pipes Mad[eir]a Wine & a Number of other Valuable Articles." Morris posited, "Many more West India Men will be taken this Summer & probably Great Britain may have Cause to Repent of the prohibitory acts, especially as they have much more property to loose than we have." That same day, William Whipple composed a letter to John Langdon in which he also reported on the good fortune of the privateers. Whipple noted that the vessels' contents amounted to "24000 dollars in specie" and remarked, "The money is arrived at Egg Harbour but the ships are sent to the Eastward." A few weeks later, the *Virginia Gazette* printed a letter from Philadelphia, dated June 5, that also highlighted the incident. The anonymous author provided the names of the three captured ships, "the *Lady Juliana, Juno,* and *Reynold[s]*, having on board as underneath ... 22,420 dollars, 187 lb. of plate, 1052 hogsheads of sugar, 246 bags of pimenta, 396 bags of ginger, 568 hides, 25 tons of Cocoa, 41 ditto of fustic, and 1 cask of turtle shell." Although the particulars of the cargo did not match up exactly in the accounts, news of the capture was important enough for inclusion in multiple letters; the actions of privateers occupied the thoughts and correspondence of land-bound colonists.[7]

Positive reports on privateers circulated throughout the colonies. While Washington gathered his troops in the early days of the war and struggled to earn victories against British regulars, privateers offered morale-boosting stories of success and bravery to those at home. Captain Lambert Wickes wrote to Samuel Wickes, "A large Ship from Jamaca [was] taken by the Sloop *Congress* a Privattear belonging to Philad, the Prizes Cargo was very valueable as it concisted of Sugar & Rum." Josiah Bartlett penned a letter to John Langdon from Philadelphia a month later with further news on the *Congress*. Bartlett informed Langdon, "A small privateer from this City called the *Congress* has taken a vessel bound from the West Indies to Halifax and sent her safe into port." The captured vessel, Bartlett continued, contained "1078 Joes—672 guineas and some other gold coin." The Committee of Secret Correspondence wrote Silas Deane with updates on outfitting operations. "Our small privateers," the group's members told Deane, "have Already had great success as the papers will shew you." The committee also offered this supposition about its privateering activities: "By abstaining from Trade ourselves while we distress that of our enemy's, we expect to Make their Men of war weary of their unprofitable and hopeless Cruises, and their Merchants Sick of a Contest in which so much is Risk'd and Nothing gained." David Cobb, writing from Boston, told Robert Treat Paine, "The Spirit for Privateering is got to the highest pitch of enthusiasm, almost every Vessel from 20 tons to 400 is fitting out here." The owners of one privateer offered Cobb "20 £ p Month & 4 shares, to take the Surgeon's birth on board" the ship. Benjamin Franklin heard from Samuel Cooper in Boston, "We have Nothing new here except Captures from the British Trade, which are likely to increase." "Our own Navigation," Cooper explained, "is almost Wholly turn'd into Privateering, so that their Cruizers can take little or Nothing from us but empty Hulls, while their Ships come fast to us richly laden'd."[8]

William Bingham, an American agent in the West Indies, wrote a letter to Silas Deane touting private maritime citizens' achievements: "Our Privateers have met with uncommon Success. they have made great Havock among the West India men; so that upon casting up Accounts, the Ballance will be immensely in our Favor." In a letter of his own from Paris, Deane reminded John Jay, "Do not forget, or omit, sending me blank Commissions for Privateers, under these, infinite damage may be done, to the British Commerce, & as the prizes must be sent to you, for Condemnation, the eventual profit, will remain with you." Even George Washington was kept apprised of the situation. John Langdon wrote the general, "Our Privateers doe great execution, and had we guns for our Continental Ships, they would give great Assistance to your Excellency's Opperations, by Cuting off, the Supplies, of the British Army." News of dashing privateers filled colonists' letters in the early years of the conflict, when success—in any form—was of utmost importance for the ongoing war effort.[9]

One colonist in particular sought details of privateer actions—John Adams of Braintree, Massachusetts. Adams, as chapter 1 notes, was a tireless advocate for the building of a strong Continental navy. However, he understood that in the absence of such a force, the efforts of privateers were an important component of the broader American fighting contingent. Adams informed Benjamin Rush, "If I could have my Will, there should not be the least obstruction to Navigation, Commerce, or Privateering." "I firmly believe," Adams argued, "that one Sailor will do Us more good than two Soldiers." Writing to Major Joseph Ward in July 1776, Adams noted, "Our Privateers, have the most Skill or the most Bravery, or the best Fortune, of any in America." Adams supported the determination of privateers to take more enemy vessels. He told Ward, "Our People, may as well fight for themselves as the Continent." Ward informed Adams of "the agreeable news of . . . Privateers having brought into Nantasket a Ship and Brig from Glasgow with two hundred and ten Highlander troops on board." Ward also relayed the results of the capture, writing, "We had four men wounded, the Enemy had three privates killed and a Major, and eight or ten wounded." He then concluded his letter with more news: "The Providence Privateers have taken two Store Ships from the Enemy."[10]

James Warren, a close friend of Adams's, wrote, "A large Sugar Ship from Jamaica with 300 hhds. sugar 80 Puncheons rum some Madeira wine &c. &c. is taken and got into the Vineyard. . . . It is said that 4 or 5 others are taken by two Privateers who took this." In another epistle composed in Boston, Warren shared, "We have nothing going forward here but fixing out privateers, and condemnation and sale of prizes sent in by them, so many that I am quite lost in my estimate of them, and West India Goods are falling at a great rate." Warren informed Adams that a prize had recently arrived containing "several hundred bags of cotton (a capital article)."[11]

Alas for Adams's naval dreams, Warren regretted, "While all this is going forward, and whole fleets have been here, and might have been taken by your ships at sea, I can't sufficiently lament the languor, and seeming inattention to so important a matter" as the Continental navy. According to Warren, ships were laid up at Portsmouth and Newburyport simply waiting for guns and men. "This delay," he argued, "disgusts the officers, and occasions them to repent entering the service." While the navy remained at the docks, privateers were sending in prizes on a daily basis. Adams responded to Warren's missive a few weeks later. "The success of your Privateers is incouraging," Adams wrote. "I lament with you," he continued, "the Languor and Inattention to the Fleet. I wish I could explain to you my Sentiments upon this Subject, but I will not. I am determined you shall come here, and see, and hear, and feel for yourself."[12]

Adams corresponded with numerous associates regarding privateers. In a letter to his cousin Samuel Adams, he implored, "Above all let me beg of You to encourage Privateering." Benjamin Hichborn composed a letter to John Adams sharing this news: "Our privateers have made so many Captures that it is impossible for me to be particular, most of those from Europe I am informed have considerable quantities of Coal in them." In response to a question regarding America's gains and losses in the capturing of ships, Adams wrote Henrik Calkoen, "America has gained." Adams went on to observe, "Privateering is a great Nursery of Seamen, and if the Americans had not imprudently Sacrificed Such a Number of their Frigates and Privateers in the Attack and defence of Places, these alone, would by this Time, well nigh have ruined the British Commerce, Navy and Army." Adams also received updates from Isaac Smith, who wrote, "There is here and the Towns round About a doz privateers Out, a small One took a brigantine from Ireland bound to Halifax with beef butter &c." Adams informed Smith in a letter from Amsterdam, "I think our Commerce as well as Privateering is on the rising hand, and I hope that next year, it will increase considerably, and that We shall hear oftener from home." "Nobody need be afraid of Privateering, from Apprehensions of Peace," he declared, adding, "There is not Peace to be had."[13]

Adams often discussed the subject of privateers in letters to his wife, Abigail. In an August 1776 note, he posited, "Thousands of schemes for Privateering are afloat in American Imaginations." "Some are for taking the Hull ships, with Woolens for Amsterdam and Rotterdam," Adams remarked, while "some are for the Tin ships—some for the Irish Linnen ships—some for the outward Bound and others for Inward Bound India Men—some for the Hudson Bay ships—and many for West India sugar ships." He predicted, "Out of these Speculations many fruitless and some profitable Projects will grow." Abigail responded with an update on the privateer *Independence* from Plymouth, which had "taken a jamaca man laiden with Sugars and sent her into Marblehead last Saturday." In other news, Abigail wrote, "I hear the Defence has taken an other." "I think we make a find hand at prizes," she told her husband. The following spring, he informed Abigail, "The Privateers act with great Spirit, and are blessed with remarkable Success." Clearly, privateers were on John Adams's mind.[14]

The inclusion of such positive reviews of privateer ventures in correspondence illustrates that the Revolutionary leadership believed privateering would be an important factor during the war. Elite colonists, like John Adams, who were staunch supporters of the war effort wanted to learn of victories, whether on land or at sea. In the early years of the conflict, privateers offered some of the only positive reports from the front. Many praised the efforts of privateers, particularly when their Continental counterparts in Washington's army failed to win on the battlefields of New York. Yet personal correspondence was only one of the ways colonists learned of success at sea.

News of the arrival of a prize in port elicited ovations in letters and high praise from American newspapers reporting the actions of privateers. The *Constitutional Gazette* printed an extract from a letter that noted, "The privateer *Congress*, fitted out of this port, had taken and sent into Sinepuxent a schooner from Pensacola for Grenada, loaded with flour and lumber, and a bout 200 Half Joes." Two months later, the *Connecticut Gazette* apprised its readers of the event where "two . . . privateers took a ship and a sloop from England, and carried them into the South-Bay." The exploits of Captain White and his privateer schooner made the *American Gazette*, which reported he had "taken and sent into Beverly a large Sloop with One Hundred and Fifty Puncheons of Rum said to be bound from Antigua to Ireland, which he took in his Passage for the West-Indies." "This is the second Prize he has taken and sent home," the paper said of White. On September 7, 1776, Rhode Island's *Providence Gazette* included news of "Capt. Jabez Whipple, in the privateer Independence, of this Place," who had "taken three valuable prizes, viz. a Ship, Brig and Sloop, and convoyed them into a safe Port." Accounts such as these found their way into newspapers throughout the colonies. Many simply reported the names of the privateer vessel and the captured vessel, if available, and the cargo contained aboard the prize.[15]

The *Freeman's Journal* of Portsmouth, New Hampshire, informed its readers, "Wednesday last was bro't into Falmouth, by Capt. Crabtree, a sloop from Anapolis bound to Halifax, taken off the Grand Passage, loaden with Lumber, Hand-Spikes, Butter, Cheese, Potatoes, &c." A few months later, the same paper included a list of prizes taken by the privateer *M'Clary*, including "the Prize Snow Three Friends . . . laden with 210 hogsheads of sugar . . . [and] the ship Live Oak . . . laden with Mahogany & logwood." On January 2, 1777, the *Independent Chronicle* of Boston, Massachusetts, reported, "Two Prizes are taken by a Privateer from this State, and carried into Cape-Ann.—One of them has on board upwards [of] 1400 Firkins of Butter, &c. and was from England bound to Gibraltar, for the Supply of the Garrison there." The same day, the *Continental Journal* published news of "a Prize Ship taken by the *American Revenue* Privateer, Captain Samuel Champlin." The vessel was "a light Guineaman . . . homeward bound from the West-Indies, [that] mounted 6 Carriage Guns and made some Resistance." According to the piece, Captain Champlin was already back in action in pursuit of "16 Sail of Ships from the West-Indies bound to England," which the prize had parted with one day prior.[16]

However, some reports, such as one in the *Boston-Gazette and Country Journal*, included stories of danger and loss. According to an article dated January 19, 1778, a privateer under Captain Connolly of Manchester engaged with "a Ship of 20 Guns, with 40 Men, during which the Ship blew up." On a voyage from London to Antigua, the surviving crew estimated the worth of the prize "at upwards of 80,000 l." The survivors also informed the privateer captain that "there was a Lady of an immense Fortune on board, who likewise perished." The paper admitted, however, "We have not learnt her Name." Articles such as this one told a story of battles on the seas and richly laden vessels. Other reports were sparse, perhaps including rumors rather than known facts. Despite these variations in quality, newspapers continuously included the actions and effects of privateers in their printings. Readers seemingly wanted to know about the war in the Atlantic, and these positive reports could potentially sway public opinion in favor of privateers.[17]

Articles often described the cargo brought in by prizes; this cargo could help replenish dwindling supplies and aid hard-hit cities. The *Pennsylvania Evening Post* notified readers, "A brigantine laden with provisions, one of the Cork fleet, is safe arrived in Beverly, sent in by a small privateer belonging to that port." News of the sloop *Comet* and its prize, "a brig from Jamaica, bound to New-York, laden with rum, sugar, coffee, and cotton," made the first page of the *Connecticut Journal* in September 1778. The *Providence Gazette* of Rhode Island, on January 30, 1779, printed a list of prizes taken and sent into Boston. The list included the capture of a prize taken by the *Monmouth*, commanded by Captain Nichols, that was "laden with rum and sugar." Two other prizes "laden with coffee and melasses" were sent into port. The ship *Nancy* was sailing "from Glasgow for Jamaica" when "first taken by the Marlborough privateer, retaken by the Experiment man of war, and last by the Providence." The hold of the prize ship was "richly laden, to the amount of 30,000 sterling." The article mentioned four other prizes with holds ranging from "rum, sugar, &c." to "fish" to "black oats."[18]

In an effort to stay apprised of recent privateering ventures and to keep various owners informed, newspapers in one region frequently reproduced letters and articles from papers of other regions. The *Gazette of the State of South-Carolina* reprinted an account from New York relating the engagement of a privateer schooner belonging to the port of Charles Town with a British frigate and the subsequent sinking of said schooner, the *Volunteer*. The *Gazette* published the New York report in full, but it also added this opinion: "There does not appear [to be] much humanity in firing a whole broadside, of a frigate's cannon, upon a small scooner, that appears to have been within musket-shot." In this instance, the paper could not resist taking its own shot at the conduct of the British vessel.[19]

In another instance of reprinting reports from various cities, the *Pennsylvania Evening Post* included news from Kingston in its August 6, 1778, issue. A schooner belonging to an inhabitant of St. Thomas "was taken off Saltpond Bay, by an American privateer of twenty swivel guns and forty men." The captured vessel included "a load of hard timber . . . [and] five valuable sailor Negroes . . . belonging to Mr. Christie," the owner of the prize. According to the article, the privateer "carried off" these sailors "together with the vessel." A report from Philadelphia, Pennsylvania, reprinted in the *Connecticut Journal* announced the arrival of "a prize sloop, the Northamton, Moses Ventris, late commander, from Charlestown bound to New-York, laden with tar, rice, &C. She was taken by the Fair American privateer, Captain Jackways" in the spring of 1781. Even London papers took news from colonial outlets. The *Public Advertiser* received a copy of the *Virginia Gazette* from a Bermudan's recent arrival in England. The *Gazette* included a story declaring, "The Goods of the West-India Ships, lately taken being sold, the Owners of the Privateers shared 5000 1. each, and each Sailor had for his Share 500 1." The article also noted, "This great Success has infused into most a Spirit for Privateering; and they are fitting out a great Number, in Hopes of picking up many of the next West-India fleet," a fact the British *Public Advertiser* chose to include for its readership.[20]

The frequency of articles on privateer incidents shows how important such actions were to the news-reading public. Clearly, readers of papers throughout the colonies from New England to South Carolina wanted to see stories about these mariners, and newspaper editors knew such accounts sold. Otherwise, editors would not have continued to include similar accounts during the entirety of the war. Stories of prizes brought into port ran in two veins: either they were boilerplate or, in some instances, tales of engagements and battles that made for a good story. Many of the articles related events simply, including a list of information rather than a detailed narrative. However, there were some exceptions to this rule. Overall, articles describing privateers were straightforward without any flourish of masculinity or courage. Instead, these papers, many of them published in seafaring towns and major port cities, sought to inform their readers of local men in local ships making a difference in the war effort. Whether or not readers supported privateers, their exploits and, perhaps more importantly, their captures proved exciting reading and highlighted patriotic success even when Washington and his troops faced defeat. At least in temporary intervals, these sailors gave the people something to cheer for and to take pride in.

Personal correspondence and newspapers might have included positive portrayals of privateers, as noted above, but they also focused on the negative aspects of these ventures. Privateers during the Revolution were a polarizing lot. Depending on one's point of view, they were heroes or villains, patriots or self-interested entrepreneurs, privateers or pirates. For many Americans, privateers were a drain on the war effort; they were men engaged in private ventures focused on personal gain rather than American glory and unification. For many Europeans, American privateers were a diplomatic nightmare, a problem that needed to be dealt with swiftly and assuredly. These negative perceptions tainted the seafarers' actions during the war and led to a postwar metanarrative of the nation's founding that intentionally excluded them.

British newspapers such as the *Public Advertiser* and *Lloyd's Evening Post* reported deleterious aspects of American privateering from the outset of the war, a point of fact that is not surprising. The reading public in England wanted updates on the war effort, particularly since the majority of fighting was taking place an ocean away. American and British privateers' exploits filled the papers of London. One article in the summer of 1776 noted, "All the Ships at Barbadoes, homeward bound, wait there for the Arrival of men of war from England to convoy them home, they not daring to stir on account of the Multiplicity of American privateers." Another reported, "They write from Boston, that the Privateers yet at Sea are mostly small; but there are a great many on the Stocks, which will be soon launched, to carry from 16 to 24 Guns." An account from Bristol reprinted in the *Public Advertiser* relayed information that the British vessel *St. James* "was taken by a Provincial Privateer." A British man-of-war pursued both vessels, upon which the Americans "ran her [the *St. James*] on shore." To prevent the Americans from gaining the vessel again, the British "set fire" to it.[21]

London papers frequently reprinted letters with information on privateers. The *Public Advertiser* included one from Plymouth that informed readers of "an American Privateer, mounting twelve Carriage Guns, spread[ing] a great deal of Canvas, full of Men, and . . . painted Black." An extract from a letter penned by Captain Underwood noted that "off the Rock of Lisbon" the British vessel faced "an American sloop privateer, mounting eight guns, having a stern of her a brig . . . judged to be a prize." The engagement was cut short by the appearance of a Portuguese frigate "sent out to cruise against three privateers that infest[ed] the coast." An epistle from Dominica included this detail: "The American Privateers have ventured amongst the Islands." When one vessel took another carrying a flag of truce, the general "ordered the Privateer not only to give up every Vessel and Cargo, but to pay back the Ransom Money, and at his Peril to presume interrupting any English vessel in the Neighbourhood of that Island for the future."[22]

Articles concerning privateers also included information about the actions and intentions of these private armed vessels, albeit with a clear inherent bias. The *London Chronicle* explained how the *Ann*, a British vessel sailing from Dominica to London, "was decoyed in the following manner." The

American privateer lowered a boat carrying men who claimed to be from the *Isis* man-of-war. These sailors then asked to see the *Ann*'s papers. Once on board, the men from the American ship took the British vessel as their prize—an action of deceit not befitting private gentlemen. Another report noted, "One of the Owners of the American Privateers that took our West Indiamen so richly laden, on receiving his Share of Prize Money, immediately deposited 3000 l. towards building larger and more complete Vessels for intercepting and annoying our Trade."[23]

The British newspaper perspective on American privateers was not a particularly positive one. The *Public Advertiser* asserted, "[The merchants of Lisbon] are fitting out armed Ships to cruize against the Americans, and those they take they are determined to treat as Pirates." Reports claimed, "The Success of the first Outset of Privateers from the Provincials, had raised such a Spirit among them, that Hands were soon found to man the Vessels; but now the King's Ships have taken a few of them, they begin to relax greatly of their piratical Scheme, and seem contented with what they have already got." Yet just a few months later, a periodical declared, "Letters by the West India mail bring Advice, that the American Privateers are cruizing in every Part of the West Indies." Even the *New-York Gazette*, a Loyalist paper printed in the colonies, informed readers about the actions of privateers. One article told of "His Majesty's Sloop of War the *Falcon*," which "had a smart engagement in the West-Indies . . . with a Rebel Privateer Ship of 28 Guns, and a Sloop of 12." The sloop escaped, according to the account, but the ship was "struck." The British captain with "his Boat shot to pieces, and several of his Crew killed and wounded . . . left the Rebel a Wreck to the Mercy of the Sea." There was no love lost among Loyalists, British subjects, and American privateers.[24]

Even at home, among other so-called Patriots, privateers found an unwelcoming atmosphere at times. The June 27, 1776, entry of the memorandum book for the Pennsylvania Committee of Safety noted "taking measures to bring back the Boat men from the Privateers fitting out at Egg Harbour." One main issue facing privateers, vessels of the Continental navy, and troops of the Continental army was the question of manning these various forces. Privateers offered one important advantage the other two did not: the possibility of a very high payday. However, this prospect also came with the chance of great loss; no captured prize could mean no money. Yet for many seamen, the potential payoff was worth the risk. Unfortunately for these newly minted privateers, their choices greatly upset those who sought to build the navy and win the war using methods deemed more patriotic.[25]

Isaac Smith succinctly summarized this dilemma in a letter to John Adams, noting, "As to the Massachusets raising more Men—[I] would say the sea ports are draind very much by those going a privateering &c." Smith explained that men flocked to privateers for one reason: "the late success of One belonging here (Cap. White) who with Another has taken four ships &c." Brigadier General Benedict Arnold sought "at least One Hundred good Seamen . . . as soon as possible." He described his current status as follows: "[I] have a wretched motley crew . . . the Marines, the Refuse of every Regiment, and the Seamen, few of them, ever wet with salt Water." Unbeknownst to Arnold, however, was the fact no better seamen were available. John Langdon complained of the dearth of men attainable for the Continental fleet, admitting, "I am verry fearful we shall not have a hand left on board unless the Guns are forwarded soon & a prospect of the Ship's going to Sea, there-being the Greatest Demand for Officers & Seamen to Man the Privateers." Langdon bemoaned the present situation, stating, "Hardly [a] week passes but more or less leave the Ship, tho' we keep the best look out possible to prevent them & some severely punished."[26]

Not even the threat of bodily harm could keep men from signing up for privateering ventures. "I do not expect to have one Man left in few days," Langdon wrote William Whipple. "In short them want to be excused, as they have great offers every Day in the Privateering way." While Continental vessels waited for guns, ammunition, and supplies, privateers set out daily. Langdon complained, "There is scarce now one single man out of employ fit for Midshipman [as] Privateers [are] every Day calling for Men." Not only were privateers exhausting the sea towns and ports of available recruits, but they were also causing the cost of a voyage to increase. As Langdon declared, "Such has been the Demand for Seamen within these few days that there Wages have risen to abt Twenty Dollars P month—the Privateers give one hundred Dollars P man Advance." Continental vessels simply could not compete.[27]

Esek Hopkins, commodore of the Continental navy during its infancy, encountered this problem of manning ships with sailors, seamen, and landmen. He consistently wrote to the Continental Marine Committee on this account. "The whole attention of Merchants and Seamen at present seems to be on Privateering," Hopkins observed, adding that such focus had taken root "through the whole New England Colonies." He further stated that the only way to encourage sailors onto Continental vessels was "to give the same Prize Money which [was] one half as they do"; this would make it "a great deal easier to Mann the Continental Vessels." Two ships were ready to sail in September 1776, but Hopkins could not get them out to sea. He explained

Commodore Esek Hopkins, commander-in-chief of the Continental navy during
the early years of the American Revolution. Courtesy of the Library of Congress.

why he found himself in this situation: "It will be very difficult to mann any
of them [the ships] without ... the Chance of Prize Money as good as they
get in the Privateers, which is one half and large Sums advanc'd to the People before they go to Sea."[28]

Letter after letter highlighted Hopkins's crew problem. He explained
why ships sat at port, opining, "There are so many Privateers a fitting out
which give more encouragement as to Shares; it makes it difficult to mann

the Continental Vessels." Hopkins soon began sounding like a broken record. Two vessels, the *Columbus* and the *Providence*, were nearly ready to sail, and he hoped to "get them out as soon as possible." At the same time, he admitted, "[I] expect to meet with great difficulty in getting Men—The Privateers being so plenty, and having great Success that the Men look on their Shears better than what they have in the Navy." Without men to sail in his fleet's vessels, Hopkins could not adequately do his job, and he blamed this failure on the presence and practices of privateers.[29]

Weeks later, Hopkins was still "at a loss how . . . [to] get the Ships Mann'd, as . . . near one third of the Men which have been Shipp'd and receiv'd their Month's pay, have been one way or another carried away in the Privateers." Hopkins suggested drastic measures be taken; he wanted an embargo on privateering until the Continental fleet was fully manned, and he wanted orders from the committee "giving . . . leave, whenever [he] found any man onboard the Privateers, not only to take him [the paid sailor] out, but all the rest of the Men—That might make them more Cautious of taking the Men out of the Service of the States." Captain John Paul Jones undertook such actions without the approval of the committee. Hopkins learned that Jones had taken hands from a "privateer a coming in from a Cruise." After sending men on board the vessel, Jones "found two Men belonging to the Fleet, and two More belonging to the Rhode Island brigade, all four of whom he took out." Hopkins defended Jones's actions and explained to the committee "that Captn Jones knew that the Privateers made a constant practice of carrying away the Men belonging to the Fleet, thought it would put some Stop to that practice, and not be any damage to the Owners as she was coming in from a Cruise." "I can't but believe," Hopkins declared, "that Captn Jones did as he thought best for the good of the Publick—and I must Confess I shall be glad if it meets your approbation."[30]

The idea of an embargo on privateering gained traction in personal correspondence among the governing elite in the fall of 1776. Major General Charles Lee wrote to the president of the New Hampshire State Council, "The Officers (and indeed it must necessarily be so,) are of [the] opinion, that nothing impedes the recruiting of the Army so much as the present rage for privateering." "Unless this is in some measure check'd," Lee continued, "it is vain to expect any Success." He therefore suggested that the council consider "a temporary Embargo on Privateers until the Regiments of each State [were] compleated." "Our situation is so delicate and alarming and the absolute necessity of the Army's being raised without delay so obvious," Lee contended that an embargo was the only course of action he could think of to address this issue of losing men to privateers.[31]

Shortly thereafter, Major General Lee was captured, which prompted Benjamin Rush to pen a letter to Richard Henry Lee. Rush confided, "Since the captivity of General Lee, a distrust has crept in among the troops, of the abilities of some of our general officers high in command." According to his sources, Rush wrote, "The four Eastern states [of New England] will find great difficulty in raising their quota of men, owing to that excessive rage for privateering, which now prevails among them." Rush did not blame enlistment issues on the skills of the high command. Rather, he claimed, "Many of the continental troops now in our service, pant for the expiration of their enlistments, in order that they may partake of the spoils of the West Indies." Rush estimated the number of New Englanders aboard privateers as "not less than ten thousand men." "New England, and the continent, cannot spare them," he argued, noting, "They have a right at this juncture, to their services, and to their blood." Rush was determined that the continent "have an army; [and that] the fate of America must be decided by an Army." In Rush's eyes, privateers were nothing more than a siphon of men.[32]

An embargo was discussed at a meeting of commissioners in Providence, Rhode Island, following the fall of New York City. Officials "recommended an Embargo upon all privateers and merchant Vessells, except those sent after Necessaries by permit, untill the Army was raised." The prohibition did not hold water, however, as some colonists did not believe in stifling the efforts of privateers, and some states did not follow through. Esek Hopkins noted, "[Several of my officers] had been Induced to Sign some paper or Petition greatly to my Disadvantage; which they were perswaded to by some of the Gentn of this Town, I supposed the Owners of the Privateers, to who I am sorry to Say are greatly prejudiced against me since I endeavoured to get an Embargo laid upon Privateering in order that the Continental Ships might be Mann'd." Captain Thomas Thompson wrote to the New Hampshire Committee of Safety, "An Embargo is laid & strictly adhered to in the other States, of all private property. All Privateers are stopp'd for the purpose of manning the Continental Ships of War & filling up the army." According to Thompson, while other states enforced an embargo, New Hampshire allowed privateer vessels to outfit and set sail from various ports. "How different here!" he exclaimed, adding, "A Privateer launch'd, Rigg'd & Mann'd since the Embargo was laid (if it may be so called)." "While the other States stop all Privat—strictly relying on their sister States to preserve the same Virtuous conduct," Thompson observed, New Hampshire was neglecting its duty. He feared that outfitting privateers would "bring a Reflection on this State . . . and manifestly tend to the disadvantage of the public service."[33]

Thompson would not be able to man his vessels without a stronger enforcement of the embargo. John Adams, on the other hand, expressed his displeasure with the embargo idea in a letter to James Warren, writing, "I hope your Embargo is off, before now, that the Privateers may have fair Play." "Indeed," Adams stated, "I am sorry it was ever laid. I am against all shackles upon Trade." He urged Warren, "Let the Spirit of the People have its own Way, and it will do something." Adams did not believe the ban even worked: "I doubt much whether you have got an hundred Soldiers the more for your Embargo, and perhaps you have missed Opportunities of taking many Prizes and several Hundreds of seamen."[34]

Other efforts were made to keep men away from privateers. The Massachusetts Council appointed a "water Bailiff" whose job was "to make due Search through out" an appointed ship. "If he find any persons on board who are enlisted or engagd in the Land or Sea Service of this or the United States," the order designating the bailiff declared, "he is to apprehend & secure them untill the further Order of the Council." The Massachusetts General Court passed an act and resolve stating that private vessels of war could only be outfitted by towns that had "raised their full proportion of the Continental Army." Owners and commanders were charged with giving a six-hundred-pound bond to this effect: "They will not Ship or receive any Men on board said Vessels, that are the Inhabitants of any Town within this State, that have not raised their proportion of the Continental Army." If a person signed on to a private vessel "after having inlisted themselves into the Continental Army," the general court's act stated, "he or they shall forfeit to the use of this State all their Share of any Prize or Prizes that may be taken by such Armed Vessels during their Cruize."[35]

The New Hampshire Committee of Safety resolved, "No Soldier nor Seaman [may] be permitted to Enter on board any Vessel of war belonging to any other State untill our own Quota of men in the Continental armey is compleated, and the *Raleigh* and other Vessels of war belonging to this State is fully mann'd." In an exchange between the Portsmouth Committee of Safety and the New Hampshire Committee of Safety, the city chapter complained that ships were "to this day unman'd occasion'd by Private Arm'd Vessells being man'd in this Port & Persons from other States coming here to carry away our Men." Members of the Portsmouth Committee maintained, "These things have been and are unhappy circumstances attending this Matter"; they simply sought an answer to this ever-present problem.[36]

The South Carolina Legislature passed an ordinance on January 26, 1778, in an attempt to address the issue "that many seamen and mariners ha[d] been prevented from entering on board Continental vessels of war and armed vessels in the service of this State, by reason of their having previously engaged to serve private persons." The ordinance declared that no seaman who signed on to a Continental vessel could be sued for breaking his contract with a private vessel: "All such articles and agreements shall, as to such seamen and mariners, be absolutely null and void." Sailors aboard Continental and state ships were also due wages and shares from the private ships they served. The seafarers did not forfeit any of their earnings by leaving the craft. In this way, the state of South Carolina tried to encourage mariners to leave private vessels for public ones. The New Hampshire Council also tried to find a solution. Its members voted "for a Committee to consider of some method to prevent so many good Landmen fit for the army from Entering on board Privateers." The Massachusetts Council ordered any person who took out a commission for an armed vessel to pay a bond "in the sum of two thousand pounds" with this condition: "They shall not carry out with them any person in pay of this State or any Officer or Soldier belonging to the Continental Army." The council tried to put a stop to the recruitment of already-enlisted men by hitting owners where it hurt most—in their wallets.[37]

Despite all of these efforts, correspondents still complained of privateers acquiring and luring away able-bodied soldiers and sailors. Captain Thomas Thompson observed, "What engages Seamen's attention is Privateers, not seeing the Wages & other Encouragement given by the Continent far exceeds any other Service whatever." Even when Continental and state vessels were manned, William Whipple complained about their circumstances, remarking, "[They are not] so well manned as I could wish, owing to the Spirit of Privatiering which still prevails & has carried off most of the Seamen." Captain Nicholas Biddle took matters into his own hands when he chased down a privateer that had "been detected in carrying off [his] People." He knew that an incoming privateer contained four of his men on board, so he went after the vessel and "was Determined to Sink him if he did not [bring to] and fired at him." Biddle eventually retrieved two of his four men from the ship, but he could not receive further fulfillment, for he was not at liberty to "stay for a tedious Law Suit." The question of manning vessels was so heated that Biddle was willing to engage an American vessel to gain satisfaction. In this instance, he did not believe the privateer fought for the same patriotic cause; rather, the other captain was a purloiner of able sailors.[38]

William Whipple repeatedly complained of manpower issues in his correspondence with Josiah Bartlett. "I could wish we had a sufficient body of soldiers there [in Rhode Island] to prevent the ravages," Whipple opined, "which I doubt not would be the case, were it not for the infamous spirit of privateering that so generally pervades at this time." He also lamented the drain on land forces. Clearly, Whipple thought privateers were more of a problem than a solution. "I wish some method could be adopted to abate the rage for that business," Whipple entreated, "which appears to me the most baneful to society of any that ever a civilized people were engaged in." Whipple maintained the officers aboard privateers were "the most profligate fellows," and he said of a mariner who might have had moral standards before setting sail, "[He] very soon degenerates and falls into all the vices of his associates." Though an embargo had faltered, Whipple argued, "Unless some measure can be adopted to check the voracity of these people, they will exceedingly disgrace the American flag." He claimed the only way to solve the privateer problem was to stop the business altogether. Otherwise, the navy would continue to lose men.[39]

Josiah Bartlett sympathized with William Whipple's point of view. He knew that there were "some very essential alterations . . . necessary" in terms of marine affairs, and he agreed that better management might improve the position and power of the navy. However, he did not take Whipple's side in respect to putting a full stop to privateering. "I think experience has shewn that privateers have done more towards distressing the trade of our enemies and furnishing these States with necessaries," Bartlett contended, "than continental Ships of the same force." "At this early period," he continued, "*we* cannot expect to have a Navy sufficient to cope with the British."[40]

Whipple did not agree with Bartlett's assessment. He argued that American public ships would have done just as well if privateers had not sailed the seas. Nevertheless, Whipple continued to plead for a way to stop privateering ventures at that moment. He noted that the adverse effects of the practice harmed not only the navy, but also those fully engaged in privateering. "No kind of Business can so effectually introduce Luxury, Extravagance, & every kind of Dissipation," Whipple posited, "that tend to the destruction of the Morals of people." According to Whipple, privateering siphoned men from public ships and caused prices in labor and agriculture to increase. There will be no gentlemen left to serve as officers, Whipple proclaimed, for "every Officer in the public service (I mean in the navy) is treated with general contempt . . . [and] therefore to avoid those indignities quits the service & is immediately Courted to go a Privateering." Eventually, the navy would either employ "tinkers, Shoemakers, & Horse-Jockeys," Whipple pre-

dicted, or it would cease to exist. He believed it would be better to "set fire
to the ships now in port then pretend to fit them for sea" under such dire
circumstances.[41]

Captain Hector McNeill also complained of privateers. He addressed the
Continental Marine Committee and explained why finding crew members
for his vessel was his "main difficulty," declaring, "We are daily robb'd of our
men by both privatiers, & merchant men & the Extravigant wages given by
the Latter, & the great Encouragements given by the former." The committee also received word from John Bradford that manning ships continued
to be an issue. "Men are not to be had at any tirms unless her [a Continental ship's] appearance may be an inducement to the Tarrs to Quit the Privateers to go on board her," Bradford said. But that inducement would mean
an increase in wages and money the committee simply did not have. Continental vessels sat in port ready to sail but lacking crews, and many believed
vessels "wo^d be compleatly manned in a very few days were it not for the Privateers." Word spread of "60 seamen [who] marched . . . for Newbury this
day to go on Board Privateers."[42]

Issues with manpower continued throughout the war. When France officially joined the conflict as an American ally, French naval officers noted,
"Continental frigates at Boston . . . awaited only to be able to complete their
crew before going out." "They are in shortage of sailors," noted one lieutenant commandant, "because of the enormous number of privateers that
they have at sea." "The hope of plunder," he concluded, "is found more easily among seamen than among soldiers." For outfitters and captains trying
to set sail in Continental and state vessels, privateers proved ruinous. Sailors
did not simply sign on for patriotic reasons, as these letters illustrate. Wages
and prize shares were additional motivating factors in a privateer's mind.
These factors did not sit well with the American people at large who, at least
publicly, offered patriotism and independence as motivations for fighting
the British.[43]

The fact that privateer vessels took sailors, seamen, and mariners from
ports—and from Continental and state vessels—cannot be denied. Perhaps
the public could have forgiven these actions if privateers had always acted
purely out of patriotism. However, numerous letter writers of the Revolutionary era took these sailors to task for their other actions and decisions,
which for many were unbecoming of Americans fighting for independence.
Robert Morris initially refused to participate in privateering ventures. He
contended, "Those who have engaged in Privateering are making Large Fortunes in a most Rapid manner, I have not meddled in this bussiness which

I confess does not square with my Principles for I have long had extensive Connections & dealings with many Worthy men in England & Could not consent to take any part of their property because the Government had Seized mine, which is the case in several instances." However, as discussed in chapter 1, Morris did change his mind later in the war, when he began losing his vessels, and his money, and his profits to British ships.[44]

William Rotch wrote to Nicholas Brown, an outfitter of numerous privateers, complaining about the conduct of one of Brown's captains. According to Rotch, the captain of a small sloop known by the inhabitants of Nantucket as the "*Willful Murther* . . . with his Company in a Ruffain like manner took possession of [a] Vessell & Cargo" belonging to the town's citizens. The commander and his men carried out their attack "with Swords & guns." Rotch claimed the privateer captain refused to return the vessel and its cargo to the rightful owners. Deeming this conduct "unjust," Rotch asked Brown, if he was indeed still one of the privateer's holders, to aid in giving "impartial justice" to the ship and its owners. Rotch could not believe that Brown would "be partaker of the Spoils of such wicked plunderers." He also reprimanded the outfitter for his involvement in the business of privateering. "I beg you to consider the consequences of it," Rotch implored, "& how often honest Men are depriv'd of their Rights; it is not sufficient in my opinion to say that the innocent must suffer with the guilty." He asked Brown to consider all of these things, as well as the recent news of the sufferings in Nova Scotia, stating, "The Calamitous situation of some of our real friends & Country men that are settld there, brot on them by the Destruction from privateers, must be a very moving scene to a mind susseptible of but a small degree of Humanity." Not only did Rotch blame the privateers for their actions, but he also held Brown accountable as an owner. He played upon the morality and humanity he hoped Brown still possessed. In a postscript, Rotch explained that the Nantucket owners decided to unload the vessel and would allow the courts to determine the fate of the cargo. When privateers assaulted and attacked those who were not the enemy, their actions convinced many that they were indeed no better than pirates.[45]

The activities of privateers had logistical and military consequences beyond the sea. Esek Hopkins observed in Providence, Rhode Island, that the coast and the city were "almost with out people to Defend them." He explained, "The milishe Refuses to Come in on acct of the high Prices of Goods and the Low Wages the State gives them and the princable men that have maid fortens by Priviteren have bought Estates back in the Cuntrey & have and are now Moving a way which Must Leave the town in a Defencless

Condition." William Whipple, too, expressed concern: "Marine affairs seem to be in a bad situation & I am fearfull ever will be, while those who have the conducting them are concern'd in privateering." Whipple held that private interests, particularly those in the privateering way, would trump public interest. While he believed "the servants of the public sho^d be well paid," he also maintained "their whole attention should be given to the service of their imployers." Members of the Continental Congress were also worried, for they declared, "It is exceedingly distressing to Congress to hear of Misconduct in any of the Commanders of Armed Vessels under the American flag." The Committee for Foreign Affairs asked the American commissioners in France for "every authentic information " they could provide, and "every means" would be taken "to punish the Offenders and make reparation to the Sufferers."[46]

Even men who boarded, and served aboard, privateers looked unfavorably on them as they experienced the costs and perils of private ventures. The Reverend Henry Alline spent one day on a privateer and at the end of his experience warned, "Let them that wish well to their souls flee from privateers as they would from the jaws of hell, for methinks a privateer may be called a floating hell." Solomon Drowne, whose experiences were discussed in chapters 2 and 3, served as surgeon on board the sloop *Hope*. He signed on for service because his family was in need of money; it was the first—and only—privateer venture Drowne underwent. In his journal, Drowne noted, "If Virtue is the doing good to others, privateering cannot be justified upon the principles of Virtue." "I know it is not repugnant to THE LAWS OF NATIONS," he admitted, "but rather deemed policy amongst warring powers thus to distress each other, regardless of the suffering individual." "But however agreeable to, and supportable by the rights of war," Drowne surmised, "yet, when individuals come thus to despoil individuals of their property, 'tis hard:—the cruelty then appears, however, political." Drowne had made up his mind about the nature of privateering.[47]

Thomas Painter took stock of his life and his chosen profession after his narrow escape from a prison ship (discussed in chapter 3). He recalled, "[I witnessed] boats go from the Privateer to which I belonged, on board Neutral Vessels, and plunder them, under false colors, and other outrageous acts." In other words, Painter knew of and served aboard privateers who knowingly took neutral vessels and cargo, claimed their bounty as legal prize, and used the state of war as cover for their devious ways. Painter decided "that Privateering, was nothing better than Highway Robbery, under the Protection of Law." Furthermore, he proclaimed, "Forcibly taking the property of peaceable, unoffending Citizens, and squandering it away, (as is usually done, by Privateers men), is worse than lost to the whole Community." He then concluded, "[Privateering] cannot be justified, in a moral point of View." Therefore, Thomas Painter, a man who had been "considerably Engaged" in privateering operations, declared he would "follow it no more." Instead, he would "follow the sea, in the Merchant service, and only to act on the defensive, if use was to be made of Weapons, at all." Privateering was often deemed an unworthy or ungentlemanly exploit, even by those who sailed on voyages.[48]

George Washington and John Paul Jones, leaders of the Continental army and navy respectively, took issue with privateers during the war. Out of necessity, Washington was one of the first to encourage privateers in defense of the colonies, but even he noted, "Our Rascally privateers-men go on at the old rate, Mutinying if they can not do as they please." Privateers were inconsistent and disloyal, according to the general; their ultimate goal was to look out for themselves rather than fight for the American cause. John Paul Jones, sailing upon the same Atlantic waters as American privateers, had even greater issues with the commanders and sailors on board private vessels. "It is to the last degree distressing," he wrote, "to Contemplate the State and Establishment of our Navy." "The common Class of mankind are Actuated by no nobler principle than that of Self Intrest," Jones believed, further stating, "This and Only this determins all Adventurers in Privateers; the Owners as well as those whom they Employ." He was desperately trying to build up the might and manpower of the Continental navy, but to no avail. As Jones pointed out, "Unless the Private Emolument of individuals in our Navy is made Superiour to that in Privateers it never can become respectable—it never will become formadable.—And without a Respectable Navy—Alas America!" He even went so far as to suggest that enlisted seamen should have all of the prizes and prize money they captured if that would prove incentive enough to outfit the entire navy.[49]

Jones was concerned that men involved in outfitting frigates for the Continental navy were also involved in privateering; this was an obvious conflict of interest from Jones's point of view. These men, he observed, "not only Wink at, but encourage, and Employ deserters from the Navy." "What punishment is equal to such Baseness?" Jones asked, exclaiming, "And Yet these men pretend to love their Country!" Privateer owners, outfitters, and sailors exasperated him and stymied his efforts to properly outfit and man the Continental navy. "The care and increase of our Seamen is a consideration of the first Magnitude, and claims the full attention of Congress," Jones told Rob-

John Paul Jones, captain in the Continental navy.
Courtesy of the Library of Congress.

ert Morris. "That our Seamen have decreased is a sad reality," Jones continued, "[and] that they will continue to decrease is as certain, unless effectual
measures are taken to prevent it." He placed the blame for this loss of men
squarely on the shoulders of privateers: "I have seen with Indignation, the
sordid Adventurers in Privateers sporting away the Sinews of our Marine."[50]

Jones also complained of the lack of enemy prisoners private vessels brought in. "Publick Virtue is not the Characteristick of the concerned in Privateers," he observed, exclaiming, "No wonder then that they let their Prisoners go, in such a manner, that they immediately augment the Strength of the Enemies Fleet." "Their selfishness furnishes them with Reasons for this conduct," Jones explained. He added, "Were they to keep their Prisoners, their Provision would be the sooner consumed; which might perhaps oblige them to return home before they had sufficiently glutted their Avarice." Finally, Jones believed that privateers feared uprisings from prisoners, asserting, "These and the like are with them all-prevailing motives and bear down every Public consideration." Privateers cared not about the cause or victory in the war, as Jones saw it. Rather, they only cared about themselves and the safety of the prizes they could procure.[51]

While their fellow Americans took privateers to task for their motivations and actions, European nations including Great Britain, France, and Spain found these crews infuriating and frustrating throughout the war. British vice admiral Samuel Graves, serving in the colonies during the early years of the Revolution, noted, "Many Rebel armed Vessels infest the Coast of America particularly about Providence, Rhode Island, Long Island, Long Island Sound, Mechias, and the Bay of Fundy, who have already taken two of his Majestys Schooners and several Trading Vessels." Graves therefore ordered his captains, "Use every means in your powers to take, burn, sink and destroy all and every Pirate or Rebel you meet in Arms whether on Shore or at Sea; And you are to do your utmost to lay waste and destroy every Town or Place from whence Pirates are fitted out, or shall presume to harbour or shelter them." In Graves's mind, American privateers were no better than rebels and pirates; hence, they deserved to be treated as such, even though privateering was an accepted practice of war at the time.[52]

British major general William Howe was aware of the privateering situation too. He wrote to Lord Dartmouth, "I am also concerned to observe that the Uncertainty of defenceless Vessels getting into this [Boston] Harbour is rendered more precarious by the Rebel Privateers infesting the Bay, who can take the Advantage of many Inlets on the Coast, where His Majesty's Ships cannot pursue them, and from whence they can safely avail themselves of any favorable Opportunities that offer." Howe admitted that British ships could not block all of the ports "which afford Protection to these Pirates without the Assistance of a Land force that [could not] at present be spared." American privateers were not worthy opponents; they were unworthy foes—in a word, pirates.[53]

British intelligence reports contained news of privateers as well. In New Haven, Connecticut, "two Brigs [were] fitting out as Privateers . . . 12 or 14 Guns each." Further information was reported by deserters from Philadelphia who noted, "Then there was Six Privateers laying there." A letter from Baltimore described "two Ships of Twenty Guns each, then fitting out as Privateers at that place." Information from a captured Rhode Island captain included word "that there were forty Privateers carrying from 12 to 32 Guns" fitting out at Providence. The captain, asserted, "The Rebels [are] arming all the Captures they can make serviceable for the purpose."[54]

One intelligence summary included an "abstract of Advices lately received respecting Privatiers which have gitted out or refitted, in the Ports of France; or which have arrived at, or sailed from, some of those ports." Gustavus Conyngham, sailing from Dunkirk, was included in this intelligence. The author of a report from Martinique stated, "I had heard before I went there much of the protection given by the French at that Island to the American Privateers; and was astonished to find that there had been no exaggeration in the Reports." This writer also noted, "The Number of Privateers fitted and fitting out is scarcely credible. Every prize vessel proper to be converted into a Privateer is fitted out as one, for which Trade the Americans find every thing at St Pierres." Governor Valentine Morris of St. Vincent informed Lord George Germain, "The American Privateers have taken a fresh start in these seas, six of them, of these two Large ones, having put to sea from Martinica ten days ago; and fourteen more were preparing to go out to be in readiness to intercept the soon expected West India fleet."[55]

Other reports stated that American privateers were cruising off the coast of England. One British ship "being to the Southward of Scilly eight or ten Leagues" spied "a Rebel Privateer Brig, and chac'd her" until the enemy vessel was ultimately taken. Captain John Macartney at Halifax conveyed this following information: "A small privateer from Salem about the 20th of February says there are 25 or 27 Vessels of the same kind . . . ready to sail to line all the Coasts of Nova Scotia and destroy the Trade wherever they can." "These Vessels are principally manned with Marblehead and Salem Fishermen," Macartney warned, "who are well acquainted with every small Harbour and Creek on the Coast . . . where they can run in one way and out another, in case of being pursued."[56]

News such as this put Vice Admiral Graves and the English government in a precarious position. Graves was charged with protecting the American coastline, but his captains reported they "[could not] put A stop to the Insolence of the Privateers without more force." Vice Admiral James

Young asked for more men and vessels: "Send out some Ships to reinforce the Squadron under my Command, as with the few now here, it is impossible for me to carry on the Kings Service in the manner I could wish." Major Francis Hutcheson reported from Staten Island, "The Rebells have several privateers at Sea, that have taken some West India Men homeward bound that are great prizes for them." Captain George Collier complained of the "piratical Robberies of Crabtree," captain of the schooner *Harlequin,* "and other little privateers." Despite their efforts, the British could not contain or stop American privateers.[57]

Great Britain could not—and did not—tolerate illegal actions taken by privateers, as evidenced by their experiences with Captain Gustavus Conyngham discussed in chapter 3. However, Conyngham was not the only privateer captain the British government encountered and addressed. Lord Grantham wrote to Lord Weymouth of "a North American armed vessel" that met with a French vessel off the coast of Lisbon, Portugal. According to Grantham, the vessel was "a pirate . . . a sloop called the *Union,* belonging to Cape Ann," that forced the French ship to take eleven sailors on board. "Incidents like these," Grantham posited, "ought surely to convince every commercial nation of the necessity of preventing such interruptions to their trade." British intelligence accused Benjamin Franklin of encouraging "seamen of every Nation" to enter into American service, declaring, "Pyracy is the Game, not Action, & where there is a Prospect of great Gain & little Hazard." General William Howe received intelligence to this effect: "The Pyrates which have done all the mischief on the Coast of this Province, appear as fishing boats, and have concealed arms."[58]

Elsewhere, Governor John Dalling of Jamaica complained to the secretary of state for the American colonies, Lord George Germain, of "a Rebel privateer" who took the mail from the *Grenville* packet. Dalling also explained, "The North side of this Island had hitherto been much exposed to the depredations of privateers fitted out by the Rebels themselves, or by persons in the French Islands using Commissions of the North-american Congress." Lord Stormont informed Lord Weymouth of "many Marks of Evident collusion" between the French and the Americans. "The American Pirates made Signs when they came near the Coast of France," Stormont reported, "and People went out in Boats to meet them." France gave aid to these American pirates in the form of safe harbors, repairs, and supplies, which infuriated Stormont, for it was clear the French "wilfully shut their Eyes" to the illegal actions those vessels took. American privateers seemed to be everywhere, thwarting British efforts at each turn, while the British complained of the piratical actions of these rebel vessels. In the eyes of Great Britain, privateers were the worst of the rebels.[59]

Privateers affected martial strategies and diplomatic approaches not only in Great Britain, but in France and Spain as well. These European nations grappled with the same question: What should be done, if anything, about American privateers? France wanted to aid the American effort against Great Britain, but in covert ways initially. In June 1776, M. Garnier informed French foreign minister Vergennes that Congress had authorized the capture of any British vessel. "This bait should cause the Privateers to multiply and should be detrimental to the trade of Great Britain in the West Indies," Garnier remarked. Vergennes responded, "The desire to make captures more easily may attract Privateers in the European seas where the English are less on their guard and it will be rather embarassing to decide what to do if they want to send their prizes to our ports for security."[60]

At first, the French government allowed privateers into their ports under the guise that Americans were technically still British subjects although they were in open rebellion. William Bingham, American agent in the West Indies, noted from St. Pierre, "Several privateers have been fitted out here, and except the Captain and first Lieutenant have been manned altogether with French men." The English governor complained about this international crew "as a direct Violation of the Peace subsisting between the two Crowns." Bingham described the French commander's response in these terms: "[He said] he is not answerable for the Conduct of the American Privateers—that they might have seduced Some of the subjects of France into their service, but that they fought under their own standard and in their own Quarrells."[61]

Eventually, however, even the French allies of the American cause found the actions of privateers inexcusable and unacceptable. French merchants sought retribution and recompense for a vessel taken by the privateer *Civil Usage*. They wrote to Benjamin Franklin, asking, "Reclaim our said goods, and ... use your best influence with the Congress in order that the captor indemnify us." If privateers did not follow the rules set forth by France, then the French government could not support them, secretly or not. Instructions to Jean Holker, a French merchant sailing to North America, included the following: "It must not be omitted to make known to them [the Continental Congress] how much France and Spain have reason to be offended at the various outrages committed by privateers against their flag." The directives continued, "French vessels have been captured in Europe, and taken to America, on the pretext that their cargo was English, a distinction to which the two powers cannot subscribe: others have been searched, ill-treated, despoiled in various regions: it is expected that most prompt reparation will be made."[62]

Holker himself relayed similar sentiments to Henry Laurens, president of the Continental Congress. Considering "the Insults committed by American Privateers against the French and Spanish Flags, who have searched and plundered several merchant Vessells belonging to those two Nations," Holker informed Laurens, "the Courts of France and Spain expect that Congress will take the quickest and most efficacious methods—to put a stop to such insults and give them the most compleat satisfaction on this head." Vergennes composed a letter to the American commissioners in France "regarding the behavior of an American privateer called John Warren toward a French snow or brigantine, Captain Rochel, which he seized quite near land and in view of the town of Madeira." "Such reprehensible proceedings," Vergennes wrote, "cannot remain unpunished, and I do not doubt, Gentlemen, that you will take most efficacious steps through Congress in order that not only may Captain John Warren receive the punishment that his conduct deserves, but also that the Captain of the French vessel may be given the satisfaction and compensation that are due to him." When American privateers crossed the line, ally or not, France had to respond.[63]

While France contended with the Americans and their privateers, Spain dealt with similar entanglements. Lord Weymouth of England wrote to Lord Grantham "of the supposed intention of the American Privateers to carry their Prizes into the Ports of Spain." Weymouth asked Grantham to remind the Spanish of "the Injury that will be done to the Commerce of this Country, if such proceedings were suffered." He added, "His Majesty cannot doubt from the Justice of His Catholick Majesty that proper steps will be taken effectually to prevent this measure, that is in a great degree designed to interrupt the good Harmony that so happily subsists between the two Countries."[64]

Spain was well aware of its precarious position. José Moñino, the Count of Floridablanca and chief minister of Spain, wrote to Pedro Pablo Abarca de Bolea, the Count of Aranda and ambassador to France, about "the most singular behavior that the American privateers observe[d] in [Spain's] European seas." "Their excesses," Floridablanca noted, "are notorious . . . and their disorder has reduced itself to the principles of imprudently abusing the protection which they found" in France and in Spain. He complained of the actions of privateers, particularly those accused of seizing the vessels of French merchants under the pretense that they carried British goods. The French, already "gravely offended by similar excesses," Floridablanca wrote,

"will take measures with the same American privateersmen on their returning to the port of that Kingdom . . . to obtain the completest satisfaction, in
a manner that will stop the future occurances of like kind." Meanwhile, he
noted, American privateers received "a very warm welcome . . . and the assistance that they needed" in Spanish ports, which made "so much more odious the deed under discussion." The chief minister was irate. He could not
believe "how indecorous it [was] for the crowns of Spain and France to tolerate such excesses, and how unjust it would be to leave their respective subjects exposed in peacetime to tricks of like nature." Something had to be
done before "the American privateers turned into pirates" and the law of nations broke down completely.[65]

A month later, the Count of Aranda replied, telling the chief minister, "[Mr. Grand, speaker for the American deputies,] assured me that they
would take the first opportunity to write to Congress to return the spoils,
make compensation for damages, and impose due restraint on the privateers." "Also, to remedy the situation as soon as possible," Aranda continued, "they would order their correspondents posted throughout Europe to
inform all arriving American ships and charge them, when they meet others from their nation sailing, to warn them of the conduct they must observe to avoid committing an act of this type." Floridablanca returned a
note that stated, "[The American ambassadors'] deference and disposition
have earned the approval of His Majesty as much as the attack of the privateer has caused him displeasure." "He goes on to say," relayed Floridablanca,
"they should recommend that Congress firmly enforce the orders given their
privateers to respect the Spanish flag, and not hinder Spanish commerce in
any way, and that His Majesty would not in any way tolerate the contrary."
While Floridablanca and Spain's king, Charles III, urged Congress to action,
Congress was trying to control American privateers, as discussed in chapter
4. But no matter the number of proclamations, instructions, or ordinances
issued, these mariners operated and acted under their own authority.[66]

The American commissioners to France—Benjamin Franklin, Silas
Deane, and Arthur Lee—tried to rein in privateers sailing in the Atlantic waters. In November 1777, they issued a warning that stated, "Complaint
having been made of Violences done by American armed Vessels, to neutral
Nations . . . contrary to the usage and custom of Nations: This is therefore to
warn and request you, not to commit any such Violation of the Laws of Nations." Captures should be confined to "enemy Vessels when not within the
protection of a neutral River, Fort or Coast, and of all others whatsoever that
shall be carrying, Soldiers, Arms, Ammunitions, Provisions, or other contra-

band Goods, to any British Armies, or Ships employed against the united States." In all other encounters, privateers were ordered, "[Act]with the utmost kindness and Friendship, for the honour of your Country and of your selves."[67]

The American diplomats attempted to defend the actions of Congress to the French and Spanish courts, both of which were displeased with American privateers' behavior. Franklin, Deane, and Lee apologized and assured the courts that the States had "the greatest personal Respect for their most Christian & Catholic Majesties with the strongest Desire of meriting & cultivating their Friendship." In addition, though the Congress granted commissions to privateers, the American trio averred, "[Delegates] have not authorized any Act that may be contrary to the Law of Nations." The commissioners assured the French and Spanish that every action would be taken to prevent American privateers from taking neutral vessels in the future.[68]

Yet the American representatives declared themselves "much troubled with Complaints of our armed Vessels taking the Ships and Merchandize of neutral Nations." Franklin, Deane, and Lee noted, "The European Maritime Powers embarras themselves as well as us by the double Part their Politicks oblige them to act. Being in their Hearts our Friends and wishing us Success, they would allow us every Use of their Ports consistent with their Treaties, or that we can make of them without giving open Cause of Complaint to England." The commissioners suggested drastic measures: "It being so difficult to keep our Privateers within those Bounds, we submit it to Consideration whether it would not be better to forbear Cruizing on these Coasts and bringing Prizes in here, till an open War takes place."[69]

The atmosphere surrounding privateers at the time caused the price of prizes sold in European ports to decrease. Privateers subsequently complained of ill-treatment by the French and Spanish, but the commissioners explained to the committee, "We cannot set our Folks right by acquainting them with the essential Services our Cause is continually receiving from this Nation: And we are apprehensive that Resentment of that supposed unkind Usage, may induce some of them to make Reprisals, and thereby occasion a deal of Mischief." Privateers put these American diplomats in a compromising situation. Franklin, Deane, and Lee faced the prospect of losing European support during the war if they could not control their captains and crews, but that type of control was a feat beyond even the Continental Congress, and one that was never successfully accomplished. By acting out of turn and making decisions based on personal interest, privateers became the omnipresent problem of the Atlantic World.[70]

Though privateers created problems in the long run, in the short term their cruises were quite effective in harassing, delaying, and upsetting the British navy, the functioning of the British government, and public commerce. Lord George Germain received a report stating, "Some of our Merchant Ships will be ready to sail from Jamaica by the latter end of March." However, the traders were reluctant to sail due to the lack of protection available on the open seas. Merchants requested "such reinforcement of the Squadron, as . . . to give convoys thro' the Gulph & the Windward passage into latitudes of security from the American Privateers." In July 1776, news of nine English ships taken by privateers "raised the insurance on all Jamaica ships, and ships from the West-India islands 20 per cent. more than it was before." The *Public Advertiser* reported, "Many of the underwriters even refuse to enter their names on a policy; for they look upon it a very hazardous venture, as there are a vast number of privateers out to intercept our homeward bound West-India ships." Garnier reported to Vergennes in the fall of 1776, "The English islands are suffering more and more from scarcity and the cost of victuals, as from the multiple takings of the American corsairs." "The news of three new ships taken on their return from the West Indies was received this week," Garnier continued, "and the most moderate calculations place the value of losses during this year by English commerce at 600 thousand pounds Sterling."[71]

The British, well aware of the situation they faced, tried to account for American privateers. The Lords Commissioners of the Admiralty ordered Commodore Sir Edward Vernon to "keep along the Coast of Brasil," warning him, "His Majts Rebellious Subjects in North America have fitted out a great number of Vessels this Year for the Whale Fishery on the Coast of Brasil, and . . . several Rebel Privatiers are to cruize in those parts with a view of making Capture of the Ships fitted out from Great Britain for that Fishery." Captain George Murray reported, "There are near four hundred Commissions given out by the Congress for Privateers; a Number of which it is said will Cruize on the banks of Newfoundland, Coasts of Guinea, Portugal & Spain." In response to intelligence such as this, Lord Germain, on behalf of the king, ordered the Lords Commissioners of the Admiralty "to engage Transports" for conveying clothes for the troops under William Howe. Germain deemed the Navy Board vessels "capable of being sufficiently armed to make a good Defence, against any Rebel Cruizers it may be expected they might meet with in case of Separation from the Convoy." Vice Admiral James Young, stationed in Antigua, learned of "five American privateers from Boston . . . arrived at the French Islands." He told correspondent

Philip Stephens, "[The privateer ships] are intended to Cruize to Windward of the Islands to intercept the Convoys expected soon to arrive . . . from England and Ireland, [so] I shall therefore directly send the *Yarmouth* to Cruize to Windward of the Island Barbados to look out for the Trade that may be coming here from Europe." Lord George Germain ordered Lieutenant General Sir Henry Clinton "to destroy all Wharfs and Stores, and Materials for Ship-building, so as to incapacitate them [the colonists] from raising a Marine, or continuing their Depredations upon the Trade of this Kingdom, . . . already so much annoyed by their Ships of War and Privateers." Despite these efforts, privateers continued to impact British shipping and trade.[72]

Merchants throughout England shared intelligence of privateer movements, for their livelihoods were at stake. One merchant from Dunkirk relayed news from a captain who told him "there were no fewer than twenty privateers out from Charlestown, from 6 to 20 guns, and from 50 to 300 men aboard." Within the span of a few months, "upwards of thirty-five vessels had been taken from the British, and . . . some of the best and largest were fitting out as privateers . . . and would be ready to sail in a few weeks on their cruises." Worst of all, said the merchant, "No English ships of war have been on their coast cruising since Sir Peter Parker's fleet left them." One month later, the *Public Advertiser* reported, "On Account of the Number of Captures of Vessels from Portugal, Insurance has risen greatly, consequently Wines will increase in Price, and what generally happens in the Country, treble the Advance will be laid on."[73]

The following day, the same paper printed a story about the capture of the *Orange* packet. The account's author called it "a complete Refutation of what we have been so often told concerning the reduced State of the Americans." British fleets that were supposed to protect England's coast and trade "seem to be literally *Fleets of Observation* only," the piece remarked. In addition, the article stated, "The greatest Encouragement is given not only there [at Dunkirk] but all over France, to the fitting out Privateers against the English." According to the *Public Advertiser*, the British government was not being truthful about the state of affairs on the waters of the Atlantic.[74]

A letter from Dublin reprinted in the *Gazetteer and New Daily Advertiser* added more fuel to the fire. Its writer asserted, "Our trade with Waterford, Corke, Belfast, and Derry, is entirely at a stand, in consequence of the swarms of American privateers, which infest our coast." Privateers did more than stop trade. As the correspondent wrote, "The appearance of the rebels, in a manner at our doors, has given spirits to the Whiteboys and other

disaffected persons; and, in truth, not only commerce, but all legal authority, seems annihilated." One writer from Kirkwall predicted, "If these pirates
will have the patience to stay a couple of weeks longer, they may pick up a
good many of our hemp, and flax loaded ships; for, it is certain, we have not
so much as a single sloop of war on the coast to protect the trade."[75]

The merchants, traders, and shipowners of London wrote a memorial to
Lord Weymouth seeking his assistance with the privateer situation, for they
saw no other recourse or way of protecting their trade. Weymouth's petitioners highlighted the "many and various Cases of the Depredations committed against the Trade of this Kingdom, by American Privateers being permitted to carry British Ships and Cargos into French and Spanish Ports."
Traders and shipowners also complained of practices whereby inhabitants of
France and Spain, despite orders to the contrary, openly aided privateers in
unloading their cargoes and selling their goods at port. The memorialists argued these deeds "could not be executed if the Court of France were sincere
in their Proffessions to the Court of Great Britain, or serious in those Orders issued to their own Subjects."[76]

The main issue was that both France and Spain were acting against the
law of nations, encouraging "practices which must be productive of general
Piracy, and leave a Train of that most dangerous and worst of Crimes, for
Years to come, even after a Reduction of the present Rebellion." In other
words, the actions of France, Spain, and the American privateers would have
far-reaching consequences beyond the conclusion of the war if this type of
conduct was allowed to continue; legalized piracy, in a sense, would be the
order of the day. The memorial closed with a plea to stop these practices, for
if they were not ended, they "must sap the Vitals of this Kingdom." Weymouth's petitioners declared, "To such a Price has the Premium of Insurance already arisen, in Contemplation of those Hazards, that many of the
most valuable Branches of the Navigation of the Kingdom cannot support
so heavy a Charge and must therefore be greatly impaired in their Extent, if
not totally foregone and laid aside."[77]

Alderman Wooldridge appeared before the Lords of Parliament in proceedings held to examine the commercial losses caused by the American rebellion. Wooldridge reported that "the number of ships lost by capture, or
destroyed, by American privateers, since the commencement of the war, to
be 733, of which, after deducting for those retaken and restored, there remained 559." The total value of the losses, "including the ships, cargoes, &c.
amounted, upon a very moderate calculation, to 1,800,633l. 18s." Wooldridge

also noted "that insurance to America, Africa, and the West Indies, was now more than double, even with the convoy, and without convoy, unless the ship was a ship of force, 15 per cent." The price of goods such as sugar, tobacco, pitch, and tar had also increased due to the actions of privateers. William Creighton claimed, "The losses suffered by the merchants, in consequence of the captures made by the American privateers . . . have amounted to at least two millions in October last."[78]

Though privateers' effects on the British economy were clear, the Earl of Suffolk opposed a motion to affirm the known facts "on the impropriety of acknowledging what ought not to be acknowledged at so critical a period, the weakness of the nation." The British Parliament might not have wanted to recognize the privateer issue, but Edmund Burke notified Lord Weymouth of merchants' fears, observing, "If the American privateers continue to receive countenance & assistance in the Spanish Ports, the Trade of our City, already overloaded with high Insurances, & the exorbitant wages paid to Seamen, maybe totaly ruined; and particularly that valuable Branch to Newfoundland."[79]

While the British public fumed over the lack of protection against privateers, American patriots rejoiced in the news of England's suffering. The *Maryland Journal* reported, "The Captures of so many Jamaica Ships by American armed Vessels, have caused the Stoppage of several capital Jamaica Houses in the City of London where it was expected, some months since, that the Price of Sugar would rise to near Three Pounds Sterling per Hundred Weight. Many more Failures are also expected." Franklin and Deane professed to "see the great Effect" privateering "had in raising the Insurance in Britain to a Pitch that would ruin much of her Commerce." However, the ambassadors also contended, "[The] advantage to us [is] not equivalent to the Loss of the King's Favour and the Prejudice to his Honour if permitted."[80]

Privateers were making headway against British shipping, but their actions continued to cause problems in terms of relations with France and Spain. Arthur Lee wrote to Robert Morris that English merchants were forced to ship their goods in French vessels to protect their possessions from privateers. "They have been driven to this necessity," Lee said, "by the number & success of our Cruisers in & about the channel; which has raised Insurance so high, that their Manufactures are in danger of being augmented thereby in their Price too much for the European Markets." Lee supported the efforts of privateers and told Morris of "the utility of continuing & encouraging Cruisers in these seas." However, for the majority of Americans, privateers posed a problem rather than a solution, a problem that continued in the postwar period.[81]

Gustavus Conyngham, whose actions during the war caused a national incident, returned home after his exploits and escapes from prison to find an American nation unprepared—and unwilling—to accept him as a war hero. Conyngham petitioned Congress for "a New Commission to be Granted him," as he had surrendered his original commission to the French government when he was taken at Dunkirk. He argued his commission from Benjamin Franklin in 1777 accorded him the position of captain in the Continental navy. Whether or not Conyngham truly believed he was a naval captain versus a privateer captain is irrelevant at this juncture. What is important is that if Conyngham admitted he was a privateer, he would have no pension and no job following the war. If, however, he could receive a new commission or be reinstated to his "former Situation," Conyngham would receive all the accolades and dues worthy of a Continental officer.[82]

In its typical fashion, Congress took months to return a decision on Conyngham's memorial. Finally, in January 1784, a committee of Congress charged with resolving Conyngham's petition determined "that such Commissions" as the one granted him "were intended for temporary expeditions only & not to give rank in the Navy." In other words, Conyngham was not a captain in the Continental navy; he was the captain of a commissioned, semi-privately owned vessel, or what one might call a privateer. Conyngham continued to petition Congress and members of the new government for recognition and monies owed for years following the war. In July 1793, Secretary of the Treasury Alexander Hamilton responded "to assure [Conyngham] that a report on the Petition, which was referred to [him], will be made to Congress next session." A year later, Congress was still silent on the issue. Conyngham wrote Hamilton again in December 1794 of "his great anxiety to have this tedious business determined if possible in the Course of the present session—it being . . . of serious importance."[83]

Three years later, in December 1797, Conyngham filed another petition with the Congress "to request . . . that his claim, of compensation for services rendered to his country, during her revolutionary War; should be decided on." At this point, Conyngham dropped the question of a commission and simply sought prize money he felt he was owed. The former captain responded to a report concerning his claim filed by Benjamin Walker to the Board of Treasury. Conyngham argued that he was commissioned by Franklin, as a representative of the Continental Congress, and that he sailed only under orders from the commissioners in France. The mariner claimed ignorance as to the private interest held in the vessels he commanded. He maintained that he only changed his articles of agreement in Bilbao in 1778 because he took on a new crew. Though Conyngham conceded that his "command . . . was intricate in its nature," he adamantly held that he was never "under the direction of any private person or persons." All of these efforts and petitions were to no avail. Gustavus Conyngham died in Philadelphia on November 27, 1819, without any pomp or circumstance—and without a military pension.[84]

Considering the vacillating, opportunistic manner in which the Founders had perceived privateers' necessity and virtues during the war, the lack of postwar recognition for Conyngham is not surprising. Congress had no other option. Conyngham, and privateers like him, acted out of turn during the war: seizing neutral vessels, terrorizing friendly coasts, and taking advantage of covert allies and friends. Early in the conflict, when victories were few and morale flagging, news of privateering activities had thrilled colonists. As the Continental army struggled, privateers struck blows against the British Empire in locales throughout the Atlantic World that most colonists could only imagine. However, with the Revolutionary War won and the task of defining a glorious, civilized—and legal—legacy of the nation's founding at hand, Congress could not publicly acknowledge such activities. Nor did the triumphant crafters of the new nation have use for a narrative of the conflict that overflowed the borders of the colonies themselves and detracted from the leadership of Washington or the valorous sacrifices of American soldiers.

More was at stake than the glory of combatants, though. The newly united states were still in a vulnerable position in the immediate aftermath of the Revolution. Trade had to be reestablished with Great Britain and revised with the other major powers of Europe. Diplomatic relations had to resume, albeit in a different form, between Britain and its former colonies. All these tasks needed to be accomplished quickly lest the British Crown perceive the United States as weak and exposed. In short, one wrong step in any of these directions could jeopardize the entire enterprise.

Without a doubt, privateers aided in the war effort. But the shady reputations they had gained as the colonies' most effective form of waterborne warfare came with a price: the fashion in which these mariners had helped achieve victory made them a necessary commemorative afterthought in the postwar period. Privateers faced collective judgment from their government, their champions and foes, their European allies and enemies, and their passengers and peers. In the end, the presence of these ultimate rebels became unwelcome as the rebellion's legacy transformed into the story of a successful revolution. The wartime records of privateers exposed both the reputations of the Founders—admittedly self-interested men like Washington and Jones—and postwar efforts toward diplomacy and trade to a higher degree of risk than the elite overseers of the Revolution's story deemed acceptable.

The sources contained in this chapter bring the story of privateers full circle. These vessels and sailors were the first to outfit and bring the war to the coasts of Britain, but they were also the first to be pushed aside and drowned out of the triumphant narrative of a new nation whose independent spirit they actually personified best. While seeking the favor of European courts, particularly Great Britain, after the war, American representatives could not—and did not want to—remind their recently reconciled relations of the depredations and illegal actions privateers carried out during the conflict. In the end, John Paul Jones seemed to get exactly what he wanted: a strong, patriotic focus on the navy without the pesky presence of privateers. Though, as the conclusion will illustrate, when military and political developments in the nineteenth century made their stories useful once more, the legacy of privateers and their significant role in fostering the spirit of 1776 would be cast in a different light, albeit only temporarily.

Conclusion

*T*he *Calhoun* made its way down the Mississippi River in the evening hours of May 16, 1861. The ship's captain, John Wilson, and his crew spied an unsuspecting vessel drawing near. The *Ocean Eagle* was its name, and it became the first prize taken during the American Civil War by privateers in service of the Confederate States of America.[1]

Wilson and his men took control of the *Ocean Eagle*, which had originally sailed from Rockland, Maine, with a cargo hold containing 3,144 barrels of Thomaston lime. The captain consigned the captured vessel to a towboat; the prize was ultimately carried into New Orleans, Louisiana. Meanwhile, the *Calhoun* returned to the river, where the Confederate privateer could stalk additional prizes.[2]

In the days that followed their encounter with the *Ocean Eagle*, the crew of the *Calhoun* took two more prizes: the *Milan* from Liverpool, England, and the *Ella* from Tampico, Mexico, the latter on a course to Pensacola, Florida. Combined, these ships carried 1,500 sacks of salt and tropical fruits, among other wares and cargo. Wilson and the *Calhoun* escorted these new captures into New Orleans, but he did not stay long. Soon, the *Calhoun* was again cruising down the Mississippi River, sailing once more into the Gulf and back on the hunt.[3]

The trip was another success. Wilson and his privateers eventually seized three more enemy ships: the *Panama*, the *Mermaid*, and the *John Adams*. After a close encounter with the USS *Brooklyn*—a more capable warship and one that Wilson had no interest in engaging—he steered his own vessel and his recently acquired prizes back up the river to New Orleans, where he entered libels in the Confederate States District Court for Louisiana. When all was said and done, the *Ocean Eagle*, the *Milan*, the *Panama*, the *Mermaid*, and the *John Adams* sold for a total of $26,650. Despite the successes of Wilson and a myriad of other Confederate privateers, the tides of maritime warfare were changing; as a result, the American Civil War would be the last conflict in which raiders of Wilson's ilk influenced the outcome. The tradition of privateering in North America, implemented during the Seven Years' War and perfected during the American Revolution, would die out along with the Confederacy. How did this happen?[4]

❊⊱◉◉◉⊰❊

With the conclusion of the Treaty of Paris in 1783, the American War for Independence officially ended. Without the necessity of purpose that war created and thereby with no legitimate enemy cargo to plunder, privateering fell out of favor and out of use. In the immediate postwar period, privateers returned to their former lives as merchants, sailors, carpenters, and surgeons, among other professions. The cheers that had accompanied news of prizes successfully captured faded from memory as the new nation attempted to establish a solid foothold among already-tenured world powers. Once viewed as a destroyer of colonists' liberties, Great Britain for some of these same merchants and ship captains was no longer an enemy, but a potential ally and valuable partner in commerce for the American nation.

During the presidency of John Adams, the United States built up its navy, so by 1798 it included fifty ships and more than five thousand sailors and officers. Adams's efforts notwithstanding, Thomas Jefferson allowed the fleet to decline during his residency in the White House. He decommissioned officers and sat by as ships rotted in their dock slips. Thus, at the outbreak of the War of 1812, the United States Navy consisted of a paltry seven vessels. With maritime combat looming and no navy to speak of, privateers were called to action once more for the American cause.[5]

Following the declaration of war Congress enacted in 1812, the government passed another act. This one authorized then president James Madison to commission privateers, who immediately took to the seas on the lookout for British merchant vessels. The colonial tradition, it seemed, had not been entirely forgotten. The privateers of the War of 1812 sailed the waters of the Atlantic just as their Revolutionary forebears had done three decades earlier. In New England, the great hotbed of privateering during the Revolution, the town of Marblehead, Massachusetts, "supplied 120 men to the American navy but six times that number to the privateers that sailed from the port" during the War of 1812. One vessel, the *Yankee* from Bristol, Rhode Island, accrued prize money in the amount of $5 million during its five cruises. Another privateer, the *True-Blooded Yankee*, "captured twenty-seven vessels, took 270 prisoners . . . and returned to France with twelve thousand pounds of silk, eighteen bales of Turkey carpets, and two thousand swan skins, among her other booty."[6]

Baltimore, Maryland, sent "some 6,000 seamen . . . onto the 122 privateers and letters of marque that set out from that city in the course of the war." Privateer vessels such as these captured more than 500 prizes and brought in 1,600 prisoners of war. In the early months of the conflict, privateers met with great success; "at least 150 British ships had been taken." The United States Navy, meanwhile, had only taken eight merchantmen. As was the case with the American Revolution, privateers were initially lauded for their efforts and for the havoc and destruction they wreaked on British commerce.[7]

Though privateers such as the *Yankee* and the *True-Blooded Yankee* were highly successful, three hundred of the five hundred vessels commissioned during the conflict never captured a prize. Nonetheless, the reputation of American raiders preceded them, and the number of British merchant vessels upon the sea dwindled. Only "heavily escorted convoys and aggressive British cruisers" chanced sailing the Atlantic waters. Great Britain gradually clamped down on the actions of American privateers and their naval brethren over the course of the war. The blockade closed a number of ports, which made the return of vessels and their prizes very difficult. To compensate, the United States' naval strategy shifted toward burning and destroying enemy ships, rather than taking them into port as prizes. Without the potential for profit, the number of American privateer vessels dwindled. Though "517 privateers took 1,345 prizes" by war's end, virtually all of which were labeled as "merchant craft," records show that nearly half of the prizes taken by American privateers were recaptured by the British. Privateers were not nearly as successful during the War of 1812 as they had been during the American Revolution, but they served a vital purpose as substitutes for a competent navy—again. Even so, as the conflict took its place in the national memory, a narrative predominated in which "gloriously the tiny American navy had triumphed" over the Royal Navy, with privateers relegated to a secondary role.[8]

Yet the practice of outfitting privateers continued to hold sway over people as a potential profit maker. During the Napoleonic Wars and the Crimean War, privateers from European countries continued to harass enemy vessels. The effects of this practice began to wear on Great Britain and France, the two largest powers with the most to lose from loose laws concerning maritime raiding. Following the signing of the Treaty of Paris of 1856, fifty-five states ratified the Paris Declaration Respecting Maritime Law. The Paris declaration was "an international agreement" that abolished privateering and sought to protect vessels sailing under neutral flags and carrying neutral goods. The government of the United States, however, still lacking a strong navy, refused to accede to the declaration. Americans believed the pronouncement firmly favored European powers that already possessed large fleets, while the United States still relied, as it always had, on privateering as one of its wartime instruments.[9]

Five years later, the American Civil War began. While the Union government retained control over the country's small antebellum navy, the Confederate States of America did not possess any navy at all. Thus, it turned to privateers. Initially, merchants harkened back to their predecessors of the Revolution and the War of 1812, men who had outfitted private vessels to disrupt their enemies' trade and help shape the outcomes of these wars. Confederate sailors followed in these footsteps, but times had changed, and privateers—though they themselves were not conscious of it at the time—would soon fade from the accepted ranks of nineteenth-century combatants.

In August 1861, the Confederate Congress passed a resolution concerning privateering that delineated specific rules about the practice. These regulations were quite similar to those set forth by the Continental Congress in 1776. Confederate representatives ordered privateers to show respect to neutral vessels. In addition, congressmen established an Admiralty Court system in which the majority of the prize's value fell to the owners, commanders, and crew. The Confederacy also encouraged engagements with enemy war vessels by setting a bounty and additional compensation in the amount of twenty-five dollars for each Union prisoner brought into port. The potential profits of captured prizes still lured privateers to the waters of the Atlantic.[10]

Union president Abraham Lincoln responded to the Confederacy's call for privateering with a proclamation of his own: "Any person molesting United States shipping 'under the pretended authority' of the seceded states would be treated as a pirate." Lincoln refused to recognize the legitimacy of the rebellious states, just as Great Britain had refused to recognize its rebellious colonies. Without recognition and a legitimate government, privateers were often viewed as pirates, despite definitions to the contrary. Nevertheless, Confederate merchants outfitted vessels.[11]

As British ones had before them, Union businessmen in the North feared "the prospect of attacks by hundreds of 'piratical' cruisers, a panic that remained more or less in effect throughout the war." However, the ultimate number of privateers was small, and prizes were few. Though Confederate privateers could slip through the Union blockade in pursuit of prizes, they often faced difficulties in returning to port with the ships postcapture. Great Britain declared a policy of neutrality, a move that effectively closed its ports to any privateers or their prizes. Without an Admiralty Court to libel their captured vessels, privateers could not profit from their efforts, and without profits, the privateering system could not function as it was designed. Two years into the war, the Confederacy turned to commerce raiding rather than privateering; "the last of the Confederate privateers, the *Retribution*, was sold in Nassau in early 1863." After the Civil War, the United States gradually developed a more stable, permanent, and mechanized navy and had no need for a force of privately outfitted vessels. The age of privateering was at an end.[12]

In the age of revolutions that marked the final quarter of the eighteenth century, privateering was always first and foremost a weapon to weaken the enemy's commerce. Privateers prevented imperial providers from supplying their colonial outposts. They intercepted raw materials from those bases that were meant for the foe's metropolitan merchants. Privateering therefore cut the economic sinews of the enemy, making it harder for them to wage war. The main purpose of empire focused on overseas commerce and a favorable balance of trade; successful privateering undermined the very rationale for the adversary's wartime exertions.

Effective privateers conferred benefits on the weaker combatant as well. The capture and repurposing of prize ships and the cargoes they carried stimulated the economy of the privateer nation. Former imperial masters used blockades and other naval tactics to cripple these economies. Privateers could not lift these barricades or directly confront the enemy's naval forces, but their efforts put goods into the economy that were valuable in and of themselves and in short supply because of the war.

Privateer victories gave these struggling combatants something to cheer. The privateer represented the vigorous masculinity, the daring, and the pluck that Americans valued and hoped would help them defeat the British. While not always convincing, the attempt to add a moral dimension to the captures and prizes fit the privateer venture into the larger principled narrative of the Revolution. The American privateer was thus distinguished from his predecessors; he was the people's weapon against oppression, not an imperial tool.

Yet the very qualities that distinguished the Revolutionary privateer did not really fit the use of such sailors in the War of 1812. While the ships' captains, the crews, and the merchants who bankrolled the voyages might have been the same men, or at least have come from the same places and culture of the Revolutionary privateers, it was clear that the later mariners were simply mercenaries seeking to profit from the war. The blockade runners of the Confederate States of America might claim the mantle of the Revolutionary privateer, and many of them were motivated by patriotism rather than greed, but they performed an entirely different wartime function. The Confederate government recognized as much by retiring their privateers in 1863.

On April 9, 1930, George G. Wolkins rose before the Beverly Historical Society at an unveiling of commemorative tablets to give remarks titled "Beverly Men in the War of Independence." On this solemn occasion, Wolkins praised the "tillers of the soil, graziers, fishermen, sailors, the merchants, the professional men, the mechanics, and the tradesmen" who "proved they could resist" the power of Great Britain. The tablets were inscribed with 506 names in recognition of the "sacrifice" and "achievement" these men had made during the American Revolution. Toward the end of his speech, Wolkins observed that "a very considerable number" of Beverly men "sailed on privateers and picked off both private merchant ships and armed men of war." Here, it seemed, privateers would finally receive their due recognition.[13]

Wolkins noted, "The privateersmen sought prizes in the British Channel, in the North Sea, off the coast of Spain, in the West Indies, along the Atlantic coast, everywhere capturing and disposing of ships and cargoes." In this one sentence, Wolkins captured the Atlantic World underpinnings of privateer operations during the American Revolution. Yet the old stigma against privateers was still present; he disclaimed these remarks by adding, "There is something further to be said against the practice that was then permitted." "Men were attracted from the army," Wolkins opined, "and from ships of the navy, as well as from civil life." Regardless of the many victories and captures perpetrated by privateers, they would never be as righteous or as noble as members of the Continental army and navy. As George G. Wolkins shows us, even in the best light, privateers would likely never be an attractive component of the Revolution's legacy.[14]

The privateering experience nevertheless broadens our understanding of how the war was fought and by whom. Privateer owners were prominent merchants and relative unknowns. Investors came in multiple guises, whether as main financiers who paid to actually outfit the vessel or as traders and entrepreneurs who bought and sold crew members' shares. Privateers planned for multiple contingencies, as the fate of a venture could prove triumphant or tragic. Once at sea, they experienced the American Revolution in their own way. They fought in foreign waters and on foreign soil, and they remind us that the Atlantic was a theater of the conflict itself. Privateers expand our understanding of the war's global reach, and they highlight an oft-forgotten aspect of the American martial effort.

Some scholars overlook privateers. Some ignore them. Some claim we have been there and done that. Some argue that privateers are simply the same as other sailors, and that studies focused on the merchant marine have covered their experiences. But this is not true. Privateers of the Revolution served in a new capacity. Indeed, they built upon a legacy of the practice, but they added to that practice too. No previous sailor had sailed or served in a fight for American independence. No seafarers had operated as a new American nation was on the verge of creation. Privateers may share some similar characteristics, experiences, and traits with sailors. It is true that numerous privateers were merchant sailors before the war and returned to sailing after the war. But this does not change their wartime experiences. Privateers are their own subset of sailors—they deserve recognition as such.

The numerous and varied ventures of privateers weave a new thread into the complex story of the American Revolution; they add weight to the current trend that posits the war in its global context. Privateers encountered the conflict in a unique way, one that adds depth and texture to the founding narrative and ultimately expands our knowledge of the American experience. Regardless of their methods, these sea raiders fulfilled a need in the American war effort. Now knowing their story, we cannot go back. Their actions require reckoning and a place in the Revolutionary narrative; when their efforts are minimalized, a key portion of not only the war, but also the history of its history is overlooked.

Privateers are as much a part of the Revolutionary story as George Washington and his troops, or John Adams, Thomas Jefferson, and the Continental Congress, or John Paul Jones and the navy. Though it was in the elite parties' best interests to ensure that privateers were left out of the master narrative, by examining their undertakings and then reintegrating them into the Revolution's history, this study reminds us that it took all kinds of men with all kinds of motives to win the war. It always does.

Abbreviations

AFC: L. H. Butterfield et al., eds., *Adams Family Correspondence*, 14 vols. (Cambridge, Mass.: Belknap Press of Harvard University Press, 1963–).

HFBR: Heard Family Business Records, 1734–1901, John Heard 1st (1744–1834), Privateering Papers, Carton of Schooner *Friendship* before Vice Admiralty Court of Dominica, 1776–1799, Baker Library Special Collections, Harvard Business School, Boston.

JCC: Worthington Chauncey Ford, ed., *Journals of the Continental Congress 1774–1789*, 34 vols. (Washington: Government Printing Office, 1904–1937).

JPP: John Palmer Papers, Collection 53, Manuscripts Collection, G. W. Blunt White Library, Mystic Seaport Museum, Mystic, Conn.

Letters and Papers: Robert Wilden Neeser, ed., *Letters and Papers Relating to the Cruises of Gustavus Conyngham: A Captain of the Continental Navy, 1777–1779* (Port Washington, N.Y.: Kennikat, 1970).

LMCC: Edmund C. Burnett et al., eds., *Letters of Members of the Continental Congress*, 8 vols. (Washington, D.C.: Carnegie Institute of Washington, 1921–1936).

NDAR: William Bell Clark et al., eds., *Naval Documents of the American Revolution*, 13 vols. (Washington: Naval History Division, Department of the Navy, 1964–).

PJA: Robert J. Taylor et al., eds., *Papers of John Adams*, 20 vols. (Cambridge, Mass.: Belknap Press of Harvard University Press, 1996).

RWC: Revolutionary War Collection, 1770–1856, 1901–1911, 1932, 1961, undated, Phillips Library, Peabody Essex Museum, Salem, Mass.

RWPC: United States Court of Appeals in Cases of Capture, *The Revolutionary War Prize Cases: Records of the Court of Appeals in Cases of Capture, 1776–1787* (Washington, D.C.: National Archives and Records Service, 1949), microfilm.

Waterman Family Papers MSS: Richard Waterman Family Papers, MSS 789, Rhode Island Historical Society, Providence.

Notes

1. United States Court of Appeals in Cases of Capture, *Revolutionary War Prize Cases* (hereafter cited as *RWPC*), roll 6, case 57. Note citations include the roll and case numbers in an effort to aid in identifying key sources used.

2. *RWPC*, roll 6, case 57.

3. *RWPC*, roll 6, case 57.

4. *RWPC*, roll 6, case 57.

5. *RWPC*, roll 6, case 57.

6. See Fowler, *Rebels under Sail*; Miller, *Sea of Glory*; Volo, *Blue Water Patriots*.

7. In addition to these published histories, several unpublished master's theses also address the position of privateers in the Revolution. James Richard Wils argues for "the vital importance of American privateers during the early years of the Revolutionary War," while Michael Scott Casey provides a quantitative analysis of privateers compared against the Continental navy. Casey posits that "privateering was the most cost-effective of the naval options available to Congress." Combined, these works assert the importance of privateers operating during the war, the role of elite men in outfitting and encouraging operations, and the impact of these ventures. Yet none of them examine the broader scope of privateer actions and their experiences. Wils, "'In Behalf of the Continent'"; Casey, "Rebel Privateers."

8. Perl-Rosenthal, *Citizen Sailors*, 4; Rouleau, *With Sails Whitening Every Sea*, 3.

9. Little, *Pirate Hunting*, 89; Kert, *Trimming Yankee Sails*, 12–13; Andrews, *Elizabethan Privateering*, 4–5; McDermott, *Martin Frobisher*, 54.

10. Andrews, *Elizabethan Privateering*, 10–11, 21; Lane, *Pillaging the Empire*, 5; Butler, *Pirates, Privateers, & Rebel Raiders*, 5–12.

11. Truxes, *Defying Empire*, 223; Swanson, *Predators and Prizes*, 30; Lane, *Pillaging the Empire*, 5; Andrews, *Elizabethan Privateering*, 5; Kert, *Trimming Yankee Sails*, 13; Butler, *Pirates, Privateers, & Rebel Raiders*, 5; Little, *Pirate Hunting*, 4–5, 8.

12. Chapin, *Privateer Ships and Sailors*, 25–29.

13. Chapin, *Privateer Ships and Sailors*, 56, 63, 116–117.

14. Chapin, *Privateer Ships and Sailors*, 136–137.

15. Butler, *Pirates, Privateers, & Rebel Raiders*, 8; Chapin, *Privateering in King George's War*, 6–9, 44–45; Robert C. Ritchie, "Government Measures against Piracy and Privateering in the Atlantic Area, 1750–1850," in Starkey, van Heslinga, and de Moor, *Pirates and Privateers*, 18–20; Chapin, *Rhode Island Privateers*, 8–9; Swanson, *Predators and Prizes*, 1–2, 134, 223.

16. Anderson, *Crucible of War*, 785n7; Truxes, *Defying Empire*, 34–35, 54.

17. Maclay, *History of American Privateers*, 506, viii; Allen, *Massachusetts Privateers of the Revolution*, 13; Casey, "Rebel Privateers," 59, 63–69.

18. This study falls in with recent scholarship seeking to globalize the American Revolution. See, for example, Allison and Ferreiro, *American Revolution*; DuVal, *Independence Lost*; Gould, *Among the Powers*; Armitage, *Declaration of Independence*.

19. *Manly. A favorite new song.*

CHAPTER I. HARDY SONS OF MARS

1. Cohen, *Commodore Abraham Whipple*, 31–33.

2. The exact makeup of the colonists involved in the *Gaspee* affair is unknown, though Sheldon S. Cohen argues John Brown headed the assembly meeting. In addition to Abraham Whipple, several other experienced commanders, including Benjamin Dunn and John Hopkins, were involved as steersmen. King George III responded to the incident by issuing a proclamation on August 26, 1772, that denounced the colonists' actions, demanded punishment, and offered a reward for anyone willing to assist in the inquiry. A committee was appointed to investigate, but ultimately reported on June 22, 1773, that they could not find the perpetrators; Cohen, *Commodore Abraham Whipple*, 34–40.

3. Elbridge Gerry to John Adams, Water Town, December 4, 1775, in Clark et al., *Naval Documents* (hereafter cited as *NDAR*), 2:1263.

4. "Massachusetts Act Authorizing Privateers and Creating Courts of Admiralty," in *NDAR*, 2:834; Winslow, *"Wealth and Honour,"* 16; Upton, *Revolutionary New Hampshire*, 107–108.

5. George Washington to John Hancock, Cambridge, November 8, 1775, in Philander D. Chase, ed., *Revolutionary War Series, September–December 1775*, vol. 2 of Abbott et al., *Papers of George Washington*, 331. George Washington understood the importance of a colonial presence on the seas. He outfitted his own flotilla of schooners and sent them on a mission to harass the British and capture supplies for his Continental troops. For further information, see Nelson, *George Washington's Secret Navy*; Beattie and Collins, *Washington's New England Fleet*; Hearn, *George Washington's Schooners*; Ford, *Journals of the Continental Congress* (hereafter cited as *JCC*), 3:372.

6. James Warren to John Adams, Watertown, October 20, 1775, in *NDAR*, 2:539; *JCC*, 3:373.

7. "Extract of a Letter from the Camp at Roxbury, November 10, 1775," in *NDAR*, 2:967; "Extract of a Letter from Salem, November 22, 1775," in *NDAR*, 2:1098; *Boston Gazette*, Watertown, Monday, December 11, 1775, in *NDAR*, 3:48; *Providence Gazette*, Saturday, January 27, 1776, in *NDAR*, 3:1010.

8. James Otis to John Hancock, November 11, 1775, in *NDAR*, 2:981; James Warren to Samuel Adams, Watertown, December 5, 1775, in *NDAR*, 2:1286; [Smith], "Diary of Richard Smith in the Continental Congress, 1775–1776," 301; [Smith], "Diary of Richard Smith in the Continental Congress, 1775–1776. II," 499.

9. Josiah Quincy to George Washington, Braintree, February 19, 1776, in *NDAR*, 4:6–8.

10. Butterfield, Faber, and Garrett, *Diary and Autobiography*, 3:328; John Adams to James Warren, November 5, 1775, in *NDAR*, 2:897.

11. [Smith], "Diary of Richard Smith in the Continental Congress, 1775–1776. II," 502; *JCC*, 4:147–150; Josiah Bartlett to John Langdon, February 21, 1776, in *NDAR*, 4:31.

12. [Smith], "Diary of Richard Smith in the Continental Congress, 1775–1776. II," 506; Oliver Wolcott to Mrs. Wolcott, March [9?], 1776, in Burnett et al., *Letters of Members* (hereafter cited as *LMCC*), 1:384.

13. "Journal of the New York Provincial Congress," in *NDAR*, 4:320.

14. [Smith], "Diary of Richard Smith in the Continental Congress, 1775–1776. II," 511.

15. Major Joseph Ward to John Adams, March 14, 1776, in *NDAR*, 4:332; *Essex Journal*, Friday, March 15, 1776, in *NDAR*, 4:347.

16. Oliver Wolcott to Samuel Lyman, Philadelphia, March 17, 1776, in *LMCC*, 1:397; [Smith], "Diary of Richard Smith in the Continental Congress, 1775–1776. II," 512.

17. [Smith], "Diary of Richard Smith in the Continental Congress, 1775–1776. II," 512–514.

18. *JCC*, 4:229.

19. *JCC*, 4:230.

20. John Adams to Brigadier General Horatio Gates, Philadelphia, March 23, 1776, in *NDAR*, 4:481; Major Joseph Ward to John Adams, Boston, April 3, 1776, in *NDAR*, 4:641; William Whipple to Josiah Bartlett, March 24, 1776, in *LMCC*, 1:407; Continental Congress, "In Congress March 23, 1776"; "In Congress," *Pennsylvania Gazette*, March 27, 1776.

21. John Adams to Cotton Tufts, Philadelphia, March 29, 1776, in Butterfield et al., *Adams Family Correspondence* (hereafter cited as *AFC*), 1:367–368; Robert Morris to John Langdon, Philadelphia, April 4, 1776, in *NDAR*, 4:664.

22. United States Continental Congress, *In Congress, April 3, 1776: resolved, that blank commissions for private ships of war, and letters of marque and reprisal, signed by the president, be sent to the general assemblies, conventions, and councils or committees of safety of the United Colonies[. . .^]* (n.p., 1776), Massachusetts Historical Society; *JCC*, 4:247–248, 251. American privateer commissions granted by Congress resembled commissions granted by the British government. Both gave authorization to attack shipping of a specific enemy nation. They also included information about the captain, the vessel, its tonnage, and its weaponry. For examples of a British commission, see *Letters of Marque*; Great Britain, Sov-

ereign (George III), *Instructions given with a commission for seizing the ships, &c.: belonging to the inhabitants of the rebellious colonies, &c.* (n.p., 1777), Massachusetts Historical Society.

23. *JCC*, 4:253–254.

24. *JCC*, 4:253–254.

25. "The President of Congress to the New Hampshire Assembly, April 12, 1776," in *LMCC*, 1:418.

26. For a detailed list of owners and investors in Massachusetts, see Allen, *Massachusetts Privateers of the Revolution*.

27. Hedges, *Browns of Providence Plantations*, 48–49, 279, 282; Nicholas and John Brown to Captain William Chace, Providence, July 7, 1776, in *NDAR*, 5:960; Hedges, 284.

28. Mayo, *John Langdon of New Hampshire*, 130, 135, 137.

29. Mayo, *John Langdon of New Hampshire*, 130, 135, 137.

30. Robert Morris to William Bingham, December 4, 1776, in Smith et al., *Letters of Delegates*, 5:573.

31. Rappleye, *Robert Morris*, 105; Robert Morris to William Bingham, Philadelphia, April 25, 1777, in Smith et al., *Letters of Delegates*, 6:651. For further information about Robert Morris and his role in the American Revolution, see Wagner, *Robert Morris*; and Oberholtzer, *Robert Morris*.

32. Hunt, *Lives of American Merchants*, 2:21, 29, 32–34.

33. Winslow, *"Wealth and Honour,"* 24; Patton, *Patriot Pirates*, 115; Allen, *Massachusetts Privateers of the Revolution*, 65–331; *RWPC*, roll 6, case 57; Benedict Arnold to Thomas Mumford, Philadelphia, June 8, 1777, Benedict Arnold Letters, 1775–1777, Connecticut Historical Society.

34. Richard Ellis to Governor Richard Caswell of North Carolina, New Bern, June 28, 1778, in *NDAR*, 13:216. In a reply dated June 30, 1778, Caswell told Ellis he planned to be in New Bern around July 10 and would render a decision regarding purchasing a part in the privateer at that time, as long as Ellis had not sold all of the shares. However, Caswell told Ellis not to wait on the governor if an opportunity presented itself to sell those shares. See Governor Richard Caswell of North Carolina to Richard Ellis, Dobbs County, June 30, 1778, in *NDAR*, 13:229; Joseph Williams to William Coit, Norwich Merchant, May 3, 1776, in *NDAR*, 4:1389; Privateering Account Book, June 1781–May 1783, Patrick Tracy Jackson Papers, 1766–1869, Massachusetts Historical Society; *New-York Journal*, Thursday, March 14, 1776, in *NDAR*, 4:335.

35. John Broome to Jonathan Trumbull Sr., Hartford, May 13, 1777, Jonathan Trumbull Sr. Papers, Correspondence, January–June, 1777, Connecticut Historical Society; John Broome to Jonathan Trumbull Sr., Hartford, July 25, 1777, Jonathan Trumbull Sr. Papers, Correspondence, June–December 1777, Connecticut Historical Society; John Broome to Jonathan Trumbull Sr., July 30, 1777, Hartford, Jonathan Trumbull Sr. Papers, Correspondence, June–December 1777, Connecticut Historical Society; John Heard to David Pearce, Receipt, Ipswich, November 4, 1778, Heard Family Business Records, 1734–1901, John Heard 1st (1744–1834), Privateering Papers, Carton of Schooner *Friendship* before Vice Admiralty Court of Dominica, 1776–1799, Baker Library Special Collections, Harvard Business School (hereafter cited as HFBR). John Heard to David Pearce, Receipt, Glocester, January 28, 1779, HFBR.

36. Wilbur, *Picture Book*, 8; *Boston-Gazette and Country Journal*, November 13, 1780; Joshua Huntington to Thomas Mumford Esq., Norwich, July 8, 1779, Huntington-Wolcott Papers, 1698–1911, Massachusetts Historical Society.

37. For further information concerning types of vessels, rigging, outfitting, and ship-building, see Coggins, *Ships and Seamen*; Millar, *American Ships*; Hahn, *Ships of the American Revolution*.

38. John Broome to Jonathan Trumbull Sr., July 30, 1777, Hartford, Jonathan Trumbull Sr. Papers, Correspondence, June–December 1777, Connecticut Historical Society; Privateering Account Book, June 1781–May 1783, Patrick Tracy Jackson Papers, 1766–1869, Massachusetts Historical Society.

39. John Broome to Jonathan Trumbull Sr., July 30, 1777, Hartford, Jonathan Trumbull Sr. Papers, Correspondence, June–December 1777, Connecticut Historical Society; Privateering Account Book, June 1781–May 1783, Patrick Tracy Jackson Papers, 1766–1869, Massachusetts Historical Society; "Adam Babcock's Certificate of the Stores &c. of a Privateer, May 13, 1776," Jonathan Trumbull Sr. Papers, Correspondence, 1776, Connecticut Historical Society; "Nathaniel Shaw Junior Certificate of the Stores &c. of a Privateer, June 15, 1776," Jonathan Trumbull Sr. Papers, Correspondence, 1776, Connecticut Historical Society; John Broome to Jonathan Trumbull Sr., Hartford, May 13, 1777, Jonathan Trumbull Sr. Papers, Correspondence, January–June 1777, Connecticut Historical Society; John Broome to Jonathan Trumbull Sr., Hartford, July 25, 1777, Jonathan Trumbull Sr. Papers, Correspondence, June–December 1777, Connecticut Historical Society.

40. Sloop *Fairplay* Journal, John Palmer Papers, Collection 53, Manuscripts Collection, G. W. Blunt White Library, Mystic Seaport Museum (hereafter cited as JPP); *Boston-Gazette and Country Journal*, November 13, 1780; "Advertisement for Seamen for Connecticut Privateer Sloop *Revenge*," in *NDAR*, 13:207.

41. *New-Hampshire Gazette, or, State Journal, and General Advertiser*, May 11, 1779. The same advertisement was also printed May 18 and May 25, 1779; Dyson, *Now Fitting for a Privateer*, *Washington* (Brigantine), Advert for Privateer, 1776, Revolutionary War Collection, 1770–1856, 1901–1911, 1932, 1961, undated, Phillips Library, Peabody Essex Museum (hereafter cited as RWC).

42. John Whiting to Thomas Harris, Martinique, September 13, 1777, Harris Family Papers, 1721–1859, Connecticut Historical Society; Painter, *Autobiography of Thomas Painter*, 10, 16; Sands, "Christopher Vail, Soldier and Seaman," 53–73, 53, 55, 59.

43. Articles of Agreement of the Privateer Ship *Independence*, RWC; "Adam Babcock's Certificate of the Stores &c. of a Privateer, May 13, 1776," Jonathan Trumbull Sr. Papers, Correspondence, 1776, Connecticut Historical Society; *Terrible Creature* Appointment of Agents, April 4, 1778, RWC.

44. Cashbook, 1781, Thomas A. Biddle Records, 1771–1837, Historical Society of Pennsylvania.

45. "Sloop *Revenge* Privateer Abstract Log, July–September 1777, and Journal, February–June 1778," JPP; "Sloop *Revenge* Privateer Journal, Nathan Post, Master," JPP.

46. "In the House of Representatives, December 11, 1775," in *NDAR*, 3:51.

47. William Vernon Sr. to John Adams, Boston, December 17, 1778, in Taylor et al., *Papers of John Adams*, 7:280.

48. Coggins, *Ships and Seamen*, 66.

49. Coggins, *Ships and Seamen*, 66. Christopher Magra argues that mariners, including privateers, were "defending their lives and liberties from tyranny" as early as the Knowles Riot in 1747 and certainly by the outbreak of the American Revolution. Magra, *Poseidon's Curse*, 284.

50. Articles of Agreement of the Privateer Ship *Independence*, RWC; *Pilgrim* (Ship), Articles of Agreement, 1778, RWC; Schooner *Hawk*, July 29, 1777, RWC; "Sloop *Revenge* Privateer Abstract Log," JPP.

51. Articles of Agreement of the Privateer Ship *Independence*, RWC; *Pilgrim* (Ship), Articles of Agreement, 1778, RWC; Schooner *Hawk*, July 29, 1777, RWC; "Sloop *Revenge* Privateer Abstract Log," JPP.

52. *Junius Brutus* (Ship), Officers, Crew and Shares, ca. 1781, RWC; Schooner *Hawk*, July 29, 1777, RWC; Articles of Agreement of the Privateer Ship *Independence*, RWC.

53. *Terrible Creature* (Privateer), Captain Robert Richardson, 1778, RWC; Marblehead, Payment Receipt, September 23, 1778, RWC; Boston, Receipt from *Minerva*, February 9, 1780, Cushing and White Papers, 1773–1852, Phillips Library, Peabody Essex Museum; Receipt from *Minerva*, November 26, 1779, Cushing and White Papers, 1773–1852, Phillips Library, Peabody Essex Museum.

54. Receipt, *General Mifflin*, July 17, 1779, Beriah Brown Papers, Rhode Island Historical Society; Receipt, *General Mifflin*, June 21, 1779, Beriah Brown Papers, Rhode Island Historical Society; Receipt, *General Mifflin*, June 20, 1779, Beriah Brown Papers, Rhode Island Historical Society; Cashbook, 1781, Thomas A. Biddle Records, 1771–1837, Historical Society of Pennsylvania.

55. John Smith, Power of Attorney, June 2, 1777, HFBR.

56. Will of John Shine, August 14, 1778, John Shine Collection, New-York Historical Society.

57. Daniel Lakeman to John Heard, Sale of Shares, May 17, 1778, HFBR; Abraham Perkins to John Heard, Sale of Shares, May 17, 1778, HFBR; Jonathan Wells to John Heard, Sale of Shares, June 24, 1778, HFBR; Thomas Spiller to John Heard, Sale of Shares, June 24, 1778, HFBR; John Smith to John Heard, Sale of Shares, June 24, 1778, HFBR; William Smith to John Heard, Sale of Shares, July 4, 1778, HFBR; William Wise to John Heard, Sale of Shares, December 30, 1777, HFBR; Joseph Pirkins to John Heard, Sale of Shares, April 9, 1781, HFBR.

58. Nathaniel Mansfield to John Heard, Sale of Shares, April 8, 1778, HFBR; John Wait Junior and Robert Farley, Exchange of Shares, April 11, 1781, HFBR.

59. David Ross to John Heard, Sale of Shares, December 29, 1777, HFBR; Boston, Receipt, *General Mifflin*, December 29, 1779, Beriah Brown Papers, Rhode Island Historical Society.

60. Joshua Fisher to John Heard, Sale of Shares, May 31, 1777, HFBR; John Lee's Surety for Samuel Harris, HFBR; Samuel Harris to John Heard, Sale of Shares, May 27, 1777, HFBR.

61. Isaac and Thorowgood Smith to Robert Morris, Accomack, August 21, 1778, Robert Morris Papers, 1756–1782, Historical Society of Pennsylvania; Lieutenant James Campbell to Daniel of St. Thomas Jenifer, Baltimore, May 1, 1776, in *NDAR*, 4:1369.

62. Sturgis Gorham and Others to Massachusetts Council, Cohassett, January 12, 1776, in *NDAR*, 3:748; Robert Palmer, Privateersman's Bond, May 2, 1777, Massachusetts Historical Society.

63. Jonathan Titcomb and Others to Benjamin Greenleaf, Newburyport, December 8, 1775, in *NDAR*, 3:4–5; "Commission of Captain Peter Roberts to Command Massachusetts Private Sloop *Gamecock*," in *NDAR*, 3:52.

64. Governor William Livingston of New Jersey to Henry Laurens, President of the Continental Congress, Princeton, June 11, 1778, in *NDAR*, 13:84; Governor William Greene of Rhode Island to Governor Jonathan Trumbull of Connecticut, Providence, June 12, 1778, in *NDAR*, 13:96.

CHAPTER 2. A PRIVATEERING WE WILL GO

1. [Bartlett], "Log of the *Pilgrim*," 105.

2. [Bartlett], "Log of the *Pilgrim*," 105–106.

3. "Sloop *Revenge* Privateer Abstract Log, July–September 1777, and Journal, February–June 1778," JPP. [Drowne], *Journal of a Cruise in the Fall*, 4. Paul Gilje notes the differences between official logbooks and personal diaries kept aboard seagoing vessels. For the purposes of this study, the distinction between the two is not specifically noted, as the experiences chronicled therein are the significant factor, not the logbook or diary as medium. As Gilje argues, "The form and content in such personal diaries and journals were similar to the basic logbook . . . and cover the same sort of information." Gilje, *To Swear Like a Sailor*, 85–95.

4. [Drowne], *Journal of a Cruise in the Fall*, 5–6.

5. [Boardman], *Log-Book of Timothy Boardman*, 65–66; "Sloop *Revenge* Privateer Journal, Nathan Post, Master," JPP; Painter, *Autobiography of Thomas Painter*, 17–18.

6. Sands, "Christopher Vail, Soldier and Seaman," 53–73, 59. John Palmer and Christopher Vail both sailed aboard a sloop named *Revenge*. Palmer served on the vessel during three cruises from 1777 to 1778, and Christopher Vail served on a cruise in 1779. Nathan Post commanded the latter cruise for Palmer and the one for Vail. Thus, it is quite likely that Palmer and Vail sailed on the same vessel, albeit at different times. Shipton and Swain, *Rhode Islanders Record the Revolution*, 97.7. [Bartlett], "Log of the *Pilgrim*," 99, 121; Shipton and Swain, *Rhode Islanders Record the Revolution*, 104, 125.

8. [Boardman], *Log-Book of Timothy Boardman*, 63; "Sloop *Revenge* Privateer Journal, Nathan Post, Master," JPP; [Drowne], *Journal of a Cruise in the Fall*, 4; "Journal of a Cruise in 1777," 45:247; [Drowne], 7.

9. [Bartlett], "Log of the *Pilgrim*," 98; "Sloop *Revenge* Privateer Journal, Nathan Post, Master," JPP; "Journal of a Cruise in 1777," 45:255. Note that this particular *Oliver Cromwell* is different from the one Timothy Boardman sailed on. Timothy Boardman's *Oliver Cromwell* sailed from New London, Connecticut, while the *Oliver Cromwell* mentioned here sailed from Beverly, Massachusetts. Shipton and Swain, *Rhode Islanders Record the Revolution*, 75.

10. Wilbur, *Picture Book*, 90.

11. [Bartlett], "Log of the *Pilgrim*," 109; "Sloop *Revenge* Privateer Abstract Log, July–

September 1777, and Journal, February–June 1778," JPP; *General Pickering* (Brigantine), Logbook, typescript, 1778, undated, RWC.

12. [Bartlett], "Log of the *Pilgrim*," 103–104.

13. [Bartlett],"Log of the *Pilgrim*," 105; "Sloop *Revenge* Privateer Abstract Log," JPP; [Drowne], *Journal of a Cruise in the Fall*, 10–11; [Bartlett], 120; Shipton and Swain, *Rhode Islanders Record the Revolution*, 121; [Bartlett], 100; Shipton and Swain, 107; [Boardman], *Log-Book of Timothy Boardman*, 64.

14. Robertson, *Spanish Town Papers*, 53; [Olmsted], *Journal of Gideon Olmsted*, 70; Shipton and Swain, *Rhode Islanders Record the Revolution*, 104, 119; [Bartlett], "Log of the *Pilgrim*," 122; "Journal of a Cruise in 1777," 45:252; *General Pickering* (Brigantine), Logbook, typescript, 1778, undated, RWC.

15. *General Pickering* (Brigantine), Logbook, typescript, 1778, undated, RWC; "Sloop *Revenge* Privateer Abstract Log," JPP; "Log of Rhode Island Privateer Ship *Marlborough*, Captain George Wait Babcock, Commander," in *NDAR*, 12:825; Shipton and Swain, 129.

16. [Drowne], *Journal of a Cruise in the Fall*, 7; [Bartlett], "Log of the *Pilgrim*," 121; "Sloop *Revenge* Privateer Abstract Log," JPP.

17. Shipton and Swain, *Rhode Islanders Record the Revolution*, 72–73; Dr. Zuriel Waterman, Privateer Journal, 1779–1781, Richard Waterman Family Papers, MSS 789, Rhode Island Historical Society (hereafter cited as Waterman Family Papers MSS).

18. [Drowne], *Journal of a Cruise in the Fall*, 10; "Sloop *Revenge* Privateer Abstract Log," JPP; Shipton and Swain, *Rhode Islanders Record the Revolution*, 72; Waterman Family Papers MSS.

19. Waterman Family Papers MSS; Shipton and Swain, *Rhode Islanders Record the Revolution*, 107; [Drowne], *Journal of a Cruise in the Fall*, 14; Shipton and Swain, 123, 95.

20. [Bartlett], "Log of the *Pilgrim*," 111; "Sloop *Revenge* Privateer Journal, Nathan Post, Master," JPP.

21. [Bartlett], "Log of the *Pilgrim*," 97, 123, 104, 119.

22. "Journal of a Cruise in 1777," 45:251–253; [Bartlett],"Log of the *Pilgrim*," 118; "Journal of a Cruise in 1777," 45:251; Shipton and Swain, *Rhode Islanders Record the Revolution*, 105; "Sloop *Revenge* Privateer Abstract Log," JPP; Shipton and Swain, 77.

23. Shipton and Swain, *Rhode Islanders Record the Revolution*, 90; [Bartlett], "Log of the *Pilgrim*," 118.

24. "Log of Rhode Island Privateer Ship *Marlborough*," in *NDAR*, 12:818; [Bartlett], "Log of the *Pilgrim*," 100, 123.

25. [Bartlett], "Log of the *Pilgrim*," 104.

26. [Bartlett], 110.

27. [Bartlett], 110.

28. [Bartlett], 115.

29. [Bartlett], 119.

30. [Bartlett], 119–120.

31. Shipton and Swain, *Rhode Islanders Record the Revolution*, 75. Clamtown has since been renamed Tuckerton, New Jersey.

32. Shipton and Swain, 88–89.

33. Shipton and Swain, 89.

34. "Introduction," in *Letters and Papers*, xxxvi; [Boardman], *Log-Book of Timothy Boardman*, 73.

35. [Boardman], *Log-Book of Timothy Boardman*, 73–74.

36. [Boardman], *75–76*.

37. [Boardman], *73–77*. Unfortunately, the logbook does not include the name of the Gunner aboard the *Oliver Cromwell* of New London, Connecticut.

38. [Boardman], *77–79*.

39. [Boardman], *76, 78–79*.

40. For the experiences of the Continental Congress, see Beeman, *Our Lives, Our Fortunes*; and McCullough, *John Adams*.

41. Shipton and Swain, *Rhode Islanders Record the Revolution*, 69–70, 75, 100.

42. "Sloop *Revenge* Privateer Abstract Log," JPP.

43. Shipton and Swain, *Rhode Islanders Record the Revolution*, 76; "Log of Rhode Island Privateer Ship *Marlborough*," in *NDAR*, 12:826; Waterman Family Papers MSS.

44. Shipton and Swain, *Rhode Islanders Record the Revolution*, 129; "Sloop *Revenge* Privateer Abstract Log," JPP.

45. See Fenn, *Pox Americana*, particularly 92–103; "Journal of a Cruise in 1777," 45:250–252.

46. "Journal of a Cruise in 1777," 45:250–252.

47. "Sloop *Revenge* Privateer Abstract Log," JPP.

48. Fenn, *Pox Americana*, 32; "Journal of a Cruise in 1777," 45:250–251.

49. "Journal of a Cruise in 1777," 45:250–252.

50. "Sloop *Revenge* Privateer Abstract Log," JPP; [Boardman], *Log-Book of Timothy Boardman*, 51; *General Pickering* (Brigantine), Logbook, typescript, 1778, undated, RWC; "Log of Rhode Island Privateer Ship *Marlborough*," in *NDAR*, 12:817.

51. "Sloop *Revenge* Privateer Abstract Log," JPP; Shipton and Swain, *Rhode Islanders Record the Revolution*, 92, 80; Waterman Family Papers MSS; "Log of Rhode Island Privateer Ship *Marlborough*," in *NDAR*, 12:826.

52. [Drowne], *Journal of a Cruise in the Fall*, 15; "Journal of a Cruise in 1777," 45:254–255.

53. [Fairbanks], "John Fairbanks—His Journal," 6:142; [Olmsted], *Journal of Gideon Olmsted*, 18–21.

54. Freneau, *Some Account of the Capture*, 21; "Sloop *Revenge* Privateer Abstract Log," JPP.

55. [Bartlett], "Log of the *Pilgrim*," 109; [Boardman], *Log-Book of Timothy Boardman*, 51; "Sloop *Revenge* Privateer Abstract Log," JPP.

56. Shipton and Swain, *Rhode Islanders Record the Revolution*, 95; "Log of Rhode Island Privateer Ship *Marlborough*," in *NDAR*, 12:817.

57. Wilbur, *Picture Book*, 54–56; [Bartlett], "Log of the *Pilgrim*," 124; Shipton and Swain, *Rhode Islanders Record the Revolution*, 94; [Drowne], *Journal of a Cruise in the Fall*, 11, 5.

58. *Peggy* (Sloop) Logbook, 1779, Log 1059, Phillips Library, Peabody Essex Museum; Shipton and Swain, *Rhode Islanders Record the Revolution*, 99; "Sloop *Revenge* Privateer Abstract Log," JPP.

59. Shipton and Swain, *Rhode Islanders Record the Revolution*, 92–93.

60. [Bartlett], "Log of the *Pilgrim*," 100.

61. [Bartlett], "Log of the *Pilgrim*," 109.

62. [Bartlett], "Log of the *Pilgrim*," 100; "Journal of a Cruise in 1777," 45:246; "Sloop *Revenge* Privateer Journal, Nathan Post, Master," JPP; Sands, "Christopher Vail, Soldier and Seaman," 59.

63. Shipton and Swain, *Rhode Islanders Record the Revolution*, 74, 104. Note the *Revenge* mentioned here is not the same vessel noted in earlier paragraphs. *Revenge* was a common name for privateer vessels. [Bartlett], "Log of the *Pilgrim*," 117; "Log of Rhode Island Privateer Ship *Marlborough*," in *NDAR*, 12:818–819; [Boardman], *Log-Book of Timothy Boardman*, 65.

64. "Sloop *Revenge* Privateer Journal, Nathan Post, Master," JPP.

65. Shipton and Swain, *Rhode Islanders Record the Revolution*, 101, 120; [Bartlett], "Log of the *Pilgrim*," 120.

66. Shipton and Swain, *Rhode Islanders Record the Revolution*, 109.

CHAPTER 3. WHEN CANNON BALLS DO FLY

1. In a recent study, Benjamin Armstrong makes the case for three forms of "naval activity": *guerre de course, guerre d'escadre*, and *guerre de razzia*. Armstrong posits that guerre de razzia—or war by raiding—has been overlooked as a "lens" of study regarding American naval history. Armstrong notes that he "does not include the more traditional naval operations of privateers, since they tended to be open-water operations and ship-versus-ship engagements and were a part of classically defined guerre de course." The vignette above, in addition to examples and encounters throughout this chapter, illustrates that privateers did indeed engage in war raiding at times. As such, their actions deserve consideration in Armstrong's third category of naval strategy. See Armstrong, *Small Boats and Daring Men*, 5–6.

2. Some historians argue that Gustavus Conyngham was a commissioned captain in the Continental navy. This historian begs to differ. The main thrust of the opposition's argument relies on a commission granted to Gustavus Conyngham by Benjamin Franklin. The commission states that Conyngham is appointed "commander . . . in the service of the Thirteen United Colonies of North-America." The term "service" is an important one. In the commission given to John Paul Jones, a man known as the "Father of the United States Navy," "service" is crossed out and the word "Navy" inserted. Conyngham's commission has no such edit. Some scholars bolster their argument with a certificate issued by Franklin stating that he gave "a Commission of Congress appointing [Conyngham] a Captain in the Navy of the said States" when the former captain was petitioning for recognition from Congress. The issue here is twofold. First, in earlier correspondence, Franklin specifically referred to Conyngham as a privateer. He defended Congress's actions concerning Conyngham by explaining there were set rules "in the commission given to privateers" that Conyngham received and disobeyed. Second, the Continental Congress ruled "that such Commissions" as the one granted to Conyngham by Franklin "were intended for temporary expeditions only & were not to give rank in the Navy." These facts, coupled with the actions of Gustavus Conyngham explored in this

chapter, clearly illustrate that the captain was a privateer, regardless of his (and historians') protestations otherwise.

3. "Attestation of Gustavus Conyngham," in Neeser, *Letters and Papers* (hereafter cited as *Letters and Papers*), 159.

4. "A Narrative respective Lugger surprize & Cutter revenge," in *Letters and Papers*, 1.

5. [Bartlett], "Log of the *Pilgrim*," 101, 105, 112.

6. John Adams to James Warren, Philadelphia, March 31, 1777, in *LMCC*, 2:313.

7. George Lupton to William Eden, Paris, May 13, 1777, in *Letters and Papers*, 23; Lord Stormont to Lord Weymouth, Paris, May 8, 1777, in *Letters and Papers*, 17.

8. Comte de Vergennes to the Marquis de Noailles, Versailles, May 31, 1777, in *Letters and Papers*, 38.

9. William Carmichael to Gustavus Conyngham, Dunkerque, July 15, 1777, in *Letters and Papers*, 65.

10. "Extract of a Letter from Dunkirk, June 26, [1777]," in *Letters and Papers*, 50; Marquis de Noailles to the Comte de Vergennes, London, August 1, 1777, in *Letters and Papers*, 74; "A Narrative respective Lugger surprize & Cutter revenge," in *Letters and Papers*, 3.

11. "Log of Rhode Island Privateer Ship *Marlborough*, Captain George Wait Babcock, Commander," in *NDAR*, 12:820, 822.

12. [Bartlett], "Log of the *Pilgrim*," 97, 98, 101; Shipton and Swain, *Rhode Islanders Record the Revolution*, 127–128; "Sloop *Revenge* Privateer Abstract Log, July–September 1777, and Journal, February–June 1778," JPP.

13. [Bartlett], "Log of the *Pilgrim*," 101; "Journal of a Cruise in 1777," 45:246.

14. "Sloop *Revenge* Privateer Abstract Log," JPP.

15. [Drowne], *Journal of a Cruise in the Fall*, 11–12. Note there are two ships named *Oliver Cromwell* discussed in this chapter—one from Beverly, Massachusetts, and one from New London, Connecticut.

16. [Drowne], *Journal of a Cruise in the Fall*, 14; [Boardman], *Log-Book of Timothy Boardman*, 63, 65; "Sloop *Revenge* Privateer Abstract Log," JPP.

17. Shipton and Swain, *Rhode Islanders Record the Revolution*, 73–74.

18. [Boardman], *Log-Book of Timothy Boardman*, 66, 51–52.

19. Freneau, *Some Account of the Capture*, 17–18.

20. [Bartlett], "Log of the *Pilgrim*," 97, 107.

21. "Sloop *Revenge* Privateer Abstract Log," JPP.

22. "Sloop *Revenge* Privateer Abstract Log," JPP; Shipton and Swain, *Rhode Islanders Record the Revolution*, 91. Note: Fort Royal Harbor has since been renamed Fort-de-France, Martinique.

23. [Olmsted], *Journal of Gideon Olmsted*, 22–33.

24. [Olmsted], *Journal of Gideon Olmsted*, 22–33.

25. "Sloop *Revenge* Privateer Abstract Log," JPP; "Journal of a Cruise in 1777," 45:247–248.

26. "Journal of a Cruise in 1777," 45:247–248.

27. "Log of Rhode Island Privateer Ship *Marlborough*," in *NDAR*, 12:820.

28. "Log of Rhode Island Privateer Ship *Marlborough*," in *NDAR*, 12:821–822.

29. "Journal of a Cruise in 1777," 45:248.

30. [Olmsted], *Journal of Gideon Olmsted*, 33, 29–30, 37–38; Shipton and Swain, *Rhode Islanders Record the Revolution*, 72; "Log of Rhode Island Privateer Ship *Marlborough*," in *NDAR*, 12:823.

31. "Sloop *Revenge* Privateer Journal, Nathan Post, Master," JPP.

32. [Boardman], *Log-Book of Timothy Boardman*, 53; "Log of Rhode Island Privateer Ship *Marlborough*," in *NDAR*, 12:825; "Journal of a Cruise in 1777," 45:249–250.

33. "Journal of a Cruise in 1777," 45:246; Shipton and Swain, *Rhode Islanders Record the Revolution*, 91.

34. Shipton and Swain, *Rhode Islanders Record the Revolution*, 129, 113.

35. "St. George's, Oct. 11, 1777," *New-York Gazette, and the Weekly Mercury*, December 15, 1777; [Bartlett], "Log of the *Pilgrim*," 100.

36. [Bartlett], "Log of the *Pilgrim*," 120.

37. Shipton and Swain, *Rhode Islanders Record the Revolution*, 123.

38. Shipton and Swain, *Rhode Islanders Record the Revolution*, 89; [Drowne], *Journal of a Cruise in the Fall*, 8, 15–16.

39. [Bartlett], "Log of the *Pilgrim*," 109, 112.

40. [Bartlett], "Log of the *Pilgrim*," 108, 121, 124.

41. [Bartlett], "Log of the *Pilgrim*," 111; Shipton and Swain, *Rhode Islanders Record the Revolution*, 111.

42. "Journal of a Cruise in 1777," 45:247.

43. "Extract of a Letter, Dated Southampton, (Long-Island) June 25, 1776," *Connecticut Gazette; and the Universal Intelligencer*, July 5, 1776.

44. [Drowne], *Journal of a Cruise in the Fall*, 12; "Log of Rhode Island Privateer Ship *Marlborough*," in *NDAR*, 12:825.

45. [Bartlett], "Log of the *Pilgrim*," 102, 98, 123.

46. "Journal of a Cruise in 1777," 45:249; [Boardman], *Log-Book of Timothy Boardman*, 53; Shipton and Swain, *Rhode Islanders Record the Revolution*, 128.

47. [Bartlett], "Log of the *Pilgrim*," 107.

48. [Drowne], *Journal of a Cruise in the Fall*, 14; "Philadelphia, Dec. 30," *Boston-Gazette and Country Journal*, January 18, 1779.

49. "London, April 20," *Pennsylvania Packet, or, The General Advertiser*, July 16, 1778; Lord Stormont to Lord Weymouth, Paris, May 14, 1777, in *Letters and Papers*, 26.

50. Silas Deane to John Ross, Paris, January 15, 1778, in *Letters and Papers*, 118.

51. Silas Deane to Gustavus Conyngham, Paris, January 21, 1778, in *Letters and Papers*, 120.

52. "London, April 20," *Pennsylvania Packet, or, The General Advertiser*, July 16, 1778.

53. "London, May 11. Extract of a Letter from an Officer on Board the Monarch, Lately Arrived at Portsmouth," *New Jersey Gazette*, September 16, 1778; "Extract of a letter from Cadiz, May 6," *Pennsylvania Packet, or, The General Advertiser*, September 24, 1778; "Extract of a Letter from Dublin, May 22," *Pennsylvania Packet, or, The General Advertiser*, September 22, 1778.

54. [Bartlett], "Log of the *Pilgrim*," 106, 117.

55. Shipton and Swain, *Rhode Islanders Record the Revolution*, 71, 127.

56. Shipton and Swain, *Rhode Islanders Record the Revolution*, 103–104; "Attestation by the Crew of the *Revenge*, On board the Sloop *Revenge*, May 31, 1778," in *Letters and Papers*, 133.

57. Comte de Creutz to Comte de Vergennes, October 1, 1778, in *Letters and Papers*, 138–139.

58. Benjamin Franklin to Ferdinand Grand, Passy, October 14, 1778, in *Letters and Papers*, 146–147; Benjamin Franklin to Ferdinand Grand, Passy, November 3, 1778, in *Letters and Papers*, 149.

59. Arthur Lee to the Committee of Foreign Affairs, Paris, November 15, 1778, in *Letters and Papers*, 150.

60. "St. Peirre (Martinico) Dec. 10.," *New-Hampshire Gazette, or, State Journal, and General Advertiser*, February 16, 1779.

61. "From the St. Christopher's Journal, November 21, 1778, to the Dutch Admiral Commanding at St. Eustatius," *Norwich (Conn.) Packet*, March 15, 1779.

62. Robertson, *Spanish Town Papers*, 50–52.

63. "By the Ship Martha, Captain Hutchinson, in 11 Weeks from Whitehaven, We Have the following Advices, Viz.," *Supplement to the Royal Gazette*, (New York City), June 23, 1779.

64. [Bartlett], "Log of the *Pilgrim*," 100–101.

65. [Bartlett], "Log of the *Pilgrim*," 111–112.

66. Bowen-Hassell, Conrad, and Hayes, *Sea Raiders of the American Revolution*, 39–40.

67. Shipton and Swain, *Rhode Islanders Record the Revolution*, 121.

68. "Journal of a Cruise in 1777," 45:249, 254.

69. [Bartlett], "Log of the *Pilgrim*," 103.

70. [Bartlett], "Log of the *Pilgrim*," 109, 111, 117–118.

71. Freneau, *Some Account of the Capture*, 31–33; Shipton and Swain, *Rhode Islanders Record the Revolution*, 126.

72. Sands, "Christopher Vail, Soldier and Seaman," 71–72.

73. Sands, "Christopher Vail, Soldier and Seaman," 72.

74. Shipton and Swain, *Rhode Islanders Record the Revolution*, 84; Sands, "Christopher Vail, Soldier and Seaman," 60.

75. Painter, *Autobiography of Thomas Painter*, 22; Sands, "Christopher Vail, Soldier and Seaman," 63. T. Cole Jones argues Britain treated all American maritime prisoners as "rebels and traitors without any legal standing." Jones notes, though, that "American sailors serving on board private ships of war, or privateers, were the principal targets of the High Treason Act and consequently suffered the most at the hands of their capturers." T. Cole Jones, "'Dreadful Effects of British Cruilty,'" 436, 438.

76. [Olmsted], *Journal of Gideon Olmsted*, 61, 53; Sands, "Christopher Vail, Soldier and Seaman," 64–67.

77. Sands, "Christopher Vail, Soldier and Seaman," 66.

78. Sands, "Christopher Vail, Soldier and Seaman," 67.

79. "A Narrative respective Lugger surprize & Cutter revenge," in *Letters and Papers*, 11.

80. Cutter, "Yankee Privateersman in Prison," *New England Historical and Genealogical Register* 30 (July 1876): 343; [Widger], "Diary of William Widger," 73:315–316; Cutter, "Yankee Privateersman in Prison," *New England Historical and Genealogical Register* 32 (January 1878): 72.

81. George Thompson Diary, 1777–1781, DIA 184, Phillips Library, Peabody Essex Museum; [Widger], "Diary of William Widger," 73:319. For further information about American prisoners of war during the Revolution, see Bowman, *Captive Americans*; Cohen, *Yankee Sailors in British Gaols*; Cogliano, *American Maritime Prisoners*; Metzger, *Prisoner in the American Revolution*.

82. Painter, *Autobiography of Thomas Painter*, 21–46.

83. Painter, 21–46.

84. Painter, 21–46.

85. Sands, "Christopher Vail, Soldier and Seaman," 60–62.

86. Sands, 60–62.

87. Sands, 60–62.

88. Cutter, "Yankee Privateersman in Prison," *New England Historical and Genealogical Register* 32 (January 1878): 70; [Widger], "Diary of William Widger," 73:328.

89. Cutter, "Yankee Privateersman in Prison," *New England Historical and Genealogical Register* 30 (July 1876): 347; Sands, "Christopher Vail, Soldier and Seaman," 63–64.

90. [Foot], "Reminiscences of the Revolution," 26:97, 100. Each jail kept a list for prisoner exchange in order of captives' imprisonment. However, as Foot notes, if prisoners were caught attempting to escape, or succeeded and were returned to jail, their names were moved to the bottom of the exchange list.

CHAPTER 4. MAKE YOUR FORTUNES NOW, MY LADS

1. Bourguignon, *First Federal Court*, 88–89; *RWPC*, roll 1, case 7.

2. Bourguignon, *First Federal Court*, 75.

3. Fitzpatrick, *Writings of George Washington*, 4:81–82. George Washington had his own motives in addressing John Hancock. A fleet Washington had outfitted was sending in prizes, and he needed to know how these vessels should be disposed of legally. See Nelson, *George Washington's Secret Navy*; Hearn, *George Washington's Schooners*. The in-depth process of establishing a legal system to support privateers' activities has never been fully outlined. While this examination and timeline of how the necessary committees and courts were created at the state and national levels is admittedly tedious, it is also a vital component of the social history of privateering. This analysis underscores two critical points. First, the process of creation was lengthy and complicated for the men *actually undertaking it*. Congress quickly established a structure, then spent years making alterations, tweaks, and variations, leading to an oftentimes complex and changing court system. Second, in that real-time complexity, privateers were thrown into a tangled and at times twisted legal system. Without a knowledgeable maritime attorney, they could lose their prize before ever even presenting their case. To comprehend the nature of privateers in port and court, an understanding of the establishment of this legal system is critical.

4. *Acts and Resolves*, 5:437–441.

5. See chapter 1 for a discussion of how these resolutions affected the commissioning of privateers, 15–16; *JCC*, 3:373–375.

6. *Acts and Resolves*, 5:462–468, 474–477.

7. Bourguignon, *First Federal Court*, 61–78. The states quickly created new courts to hear cases concerning captures, but the main model they had was the provincial Vice-Admiralty Court. Though it seems hypocritical to call those provincial courts tyrannical and then, in the same breath, build new ones based upon that dismissed "old" version, that is exactly what colonists did. However, one important change included a provision for trial by jury. Carl Ubbelohde notes that "the new state courts attempted to do away with the most hated feature of the old provincial vice-admiralty courts—trial without jury." However, this experiment in jury trials did not work, especially considering the complex nature of maritime law. Eventually, "the pattern soon emerged of local juries being overruled by appeals to the committee created by Congress." Ubbelohde, *Vice-Admiralty Courts*, 195, 199.

8. Bourguignon, *First Federal Court*, 61–78.

9. Bourguignon, *First Federal Court*, 61–78.

10. "Advertisement of Libels Against Six British Prizes," *New England Chronicle*, August 15, 1776, in *NDAR*, 6:192; *Pennsylvania Evening Post*, Tuesday, September 3, 1776, in *NDAR*, 6:668; *Connecticut Gazette*, Friday, September 6, 1776, in *NDAR*, 6:723; "Libels in New Hampshire Admiralty Court Against the Prize Schooners *Glasgow* and *Neptune*," *Freeman's Journal*, October 29, 1776, in *NDAR*, 6:1172–1173.

11. "Advertisement of Sale of Prize Schooner *Peter* and Cargo," *Pennsylvania Gazette*, September 18, 1776, in *NDAR* 6:895; "Advertisement of Sale of the Prize Ship *Caroline* at Chincoteague, Virginia," *Maryland Gazette*, October 17, 1776, in *NDAR*, 6:1140–1141.

12. *JCC*, 5:747, 848.

13. *JCC*, 7:75.

14. *JCC*, 7:336–337, 348.

15. *JCC*, 8:607, 640.

16. *JCC*, 7:172, 9:936; Bourguignon, *First Federal Court*, 90.

17. *JCC*, 5:605–606.

18. *JCC*, 10:112, 196, 225.

19. *JCC*, 11:486.

20. *JCC*, 14:508–509.

21. *JCC*, 14:508–510.

22. *JCC*, 14:635.

23. *JCC*, 14:1002, 15:1220–1223. Congress was supposed to resume discussion on November 8, 1779. Monday, November 8, came and went. Another week passed before Congress "took into consideration the report of the committee on the plan for the establishment of courts of appeals for determining captures on water." After spending "some time" on the subject, the "farther consideration . . . [was] postponed" yet again.

24. *JCC*, 15:1271–1272, 1349–1350, 1356. On December 6, Congress once again "took into consideration the report of the committee on a plan for establishing a court of appeals." While "some progress" was made, "the farther consideration" was once again postponed.

The following day, Tuesday, December 7, 1779, Congress met as a whole to devote further attention to the report. However, having "made some progress therein, but not having come to a conclusion," the Congress "desire[d] leave to sit again" until "Friday next."

25. *JCC*, 16:17–18.

26. *JCC*, 16:18, 29–32.

27. *JCC*, 16:32.

28. *JCC*, 16:61–64, 79, 100, 121.

29. In *The First Federal Court*, Henry J. Bourguignon makes the case that the Court of Appeals in Cases of Capture was established in February 1780. On the other hand, the introduction included at the beginning of each reel of microfilm of *The Revolutionary War Prize Cases* sets the date of establishment on January 15, 1780. *JCC*, 17:458–459.

30. *JCC*, 16:322, 411, 403–408; "In Congress, May 2, 1780, Instructions to the Captains and Commanders . . . ," Hector McNeill Papers, 1765–1821, Massachusetts Historical Society.

31. *JCC*, 16:322, 411, 403–409, 17:721, 744; "In Congress, May 2, 1780, Instructions to the Captains and Commanders . . . ," Hector McNeill Papers, 1765–1821, Massachusetts Historical Society.

32. *JCC*, 19:66–67, 200.

33. *JCC*, 19:360–364, 374–375, 21:861, 961, 985, 1147, 1152, 23:765.

34. *JCC*, 26:126, 343, 28:209, 230, 413, 29:491–493, 30:60–61.

35. *RWPC*, introduction.

36. *RWPC*, roll 1, case 4. Note in the microfilm housed at the University of Georgia's Alexander Campbell King Law Library, the papers for case 4, *Barry v. The Sloop Betsey*, and papers for case 5, *Joyne v. The Sloop Vulcan*, seem to be misfiled. The papers for each are interchanged and filed under the other's case title. However, it appears that both cases are complete in terms of the papers contained therein. In terms of legal terminology used, a few definitions might provide clarity. The libelants in a case are those who bring a suit via a libel. The claimants are those who make a claim, in this case, a claim of ownership, in court.

37. *RWPC*, roll 1, case 4; "Advertisement," *Pennsylvania Packet, Published as Dunlap's Packet, or, The General Advertiser*, September 10, 1776.

38. *RWPC*, roll 1, case 4.

39. *RWPC*, roll 1, case 4.

40. *RWPC*, roll 1, case 4.

41. *RWPC*, roll 1, case 4.

42. *RWPC*, roll 2, case 11.

43. *RWPC*, roll 2, case 11.

44. *RWPC*, roll 2, case 11.

45. *RWPC*, roll 2, case 11. Titus Hosmer, justice of the peace, took a deposition from Sylvanus Waterman due to the distance from the court, an illness the captain contracted, and Waterman's inability to attend the court session in person.

46. *RWPC*, roll 2, case 11.

47. *RWPC*, roll 2, case 11.

48. *RWPC*, roll 2, case 11.

49. *RWPC*, roll 2, case 11; *JCC*, 7:297.

50. *RWPC*, roll 2, case 11.

51. *RWPC*, roll 3, case 25.

52. *RWPC*, roll 3, case 25.

53. *RWPC*, roll 3, case 25.

54. *RWPC*, roll 3, case 25.

55. *RWPC*, roll 3, case 25.

56. *RWPC*, roll 3, case 25.

57. *RWPC*, roll 3, case 25.

58. *RWPC*, roll 3, case 25.

59. *RWPC*, roll 3, case 25.

60. *RWPC*, roll 3, case 25.

61. *RWPC*, roll 3, case 25.

62. *RWPC*, roll 9, case 75. Throughout the papers relating to this case, the names Thomas Griffien and Moses Welch are spelled various ways; in point, one version of the story claims the men were indeed two different people. In the case of Griffien, his name is spelled Griffiey, Griffieu, Grieffin, and Griffien. In the case of Welch, his name is spelled Welch and Welsh. For the sake of consistency, the names used here are Griffien and Welch.

63. *RWPC*, roll 9, case 75.

64. *RWPC*, roll 9, case 75.

65. *RWPC*, roll 9, case 75.

66. *RWPC*, roll 9, case 75.

67. *RWPC*, roll 9, case 75.

68. *RWPC*, roll 9, case 75.

69. *RWPC*, roll 9, case 75.

70. *RWPC*, roll 9, case 75. Throughout the papers relating to this case, various spellings appear for the name of the broker involved, Habertus Hallewaand. These include the first name Hybertus, Huibertus, Habertus, Hybertios, and Hubertius, as well as the last name Hallward, Hallewaerd, Hallewaand, and Hallewaard. For sake of consistency, the name used here is Habertus Hallewaand. The papers also contain different names for the owners involved: the Brothers Antichan and two separate men, Brother and Antichan. For the sake of consistency, the names used here are Antichan and Brother.

71. *RWPC*, roll 9, case 75.

72. *RWPC*, roll 9, case 75.

73. *RWPC*, roll 9, case 75.

74. *RWPC*, roll 9, case 75.

75. *RWPC*, roll 9, case 75.

CHAPTER 5. TO GLORY LET US RUN

1. Mansel Alcock to Timothy Pickering Jr. [Beverly or Salem, Mass., April 1778], in *NDAR*, 12:5.

2. Mansel Alcock to Timothy Pickering Jr. [Beverly or Salem, Mass., April 1778], in *NDAR*, 12:5.

3. See Breen, *American Insurgents, American Patriots*; Countryman, *American Revolution*; Ellis, *His Excellency: George Washington*; Fisher, *Washington's Crossing*; McCullough, *1776*. In the years preceding the U.S. Civil War, privateers took on the mantle of romantic characters in fictional works. Whereas privateers were taken out of the Revolutionary wartime narrative in an effort to keep the republic pure, they were found elsewhere in the public's imagination. See, for example, Buntline, *Seawaif*; Burdick, *Sea Lion*; Cobb, *Golden Eagle*; Cobb, *Maniac's Secret*.

4. Elbridge Gerry to Samuel Adams, Water Town, October 9, 1775, in *NDAR*, 2:369–370

5. Jack Thompson to S. Burling, St. Eustatia, April 13, 1775, in *NDAR*, 4:805–807.

6. William Hunt to Elbridge Gerry, Watertown, May 18, 1776, in *NDAR*, 5:141; D. Ingraham Jr. to Samuel Phipps Savage, Boston, May 18, 1776, in *NDAR*, 5:141–142.

7. Robert Morris, for the Committee of Secret Correspondence, to Silas Deane, Philadelphia, June 5, 1776, in *NDAR*, 5:384; William Whipple to John Langdon, Philadelphia, June 5, 1776, in *NDAR*, 5:385; "Copy of a Letter from Philadelphia, Dated June 5," in *NDAR*, 5:386.

8. Captain Lambert Wickes to Samuel Wickes, Cape May Rhode, July 2, 1776, in *NDAR*, 5:882; Josiah Bartlett to John Langdon, Philadelphia, August 5, 1776, in *NDAR*, 6:63; Committee of Secret Correspondence of the Continental Congress to Silas Deane, Philadelphia, August 7, 1776, in *NDAR*, 6:103. Note: at this time the committee consisted of Benjamin Franklin, Benjamin Harrison, and Robert Morris. David Cobb to Robert Treat Paine, Boston, September 9, 1776, in *NDAR*, 6:755; Samuel Cooper to Benjamin Franklin, Boston, September 17, 1776, in *NDAR*, 6:871.

9. William Bingham to Benjamin Franklin, St. Pierre, Martinique, September 29, 1776, in *NDAR*, 6:1046; Silas Deane to John Jay, Paris, December 3, 1776, in *NDAR*, 7:777.

10. John Adams to Benjamin Rush, Amsterdam, September 20, 1780, in Taylor et al., *Papers of John Adams* (hereafter cited as *PJA*), 10:165; John Adams to Major Joseph Ward, Philadelphia, July 17, 1776, in *PJA*, 4:387; Joseph Ward to John Adams, Boston, June 16–17, 1776, in *PJA*, 4:319.

11. James Warren to John Adams, Watertown, June 5, 1776, in *PJA*, 4:240; James Warren to John Adams, Boston, August 11, 1776, in *PJA*, 4:445.

12. James Warren to John Adams, Boston, August 11, 1776, in *PJA*, 4:445; John Adams to James Warren, Philadelphia, August 21, 1776, in *PJA*, 4:482.

13. John Adams to Samuel Adams, Paris, February 28, 1780, in *PJA*, 8:374; Benjamin Hichborn to John Adams, Cambridge, November 25, 1775, in *PJA*, 3:324; John Adams to Henrik Calkoen, Amsterdam, October 27, 1780, in *PJA*, 10:251; Isaac Smith Sr. to John Adams, Salem, September 11, 1776, in *PJA*, 5:23; John Adams to Isaac Smith Sr., Amsterdam, December 6, 1780, in *AFC*, 4:26.

14. John Adams to Abigail Adams, August 12, 1776, in *AFC*, 2:89; Abigail Adams to John Adams, Boston, August 25, 1776, in *AFC*, 2:107–108; John Adams to Abigail Adams, Philadelphia, May 7, 1777, in *AFC*, 2:234.

15. "NEW-YORK, May 22. Extract of a Letter from Philadelphia, May 18," *Constitutional Gazette* (New York City), May 22, 1776; "Extract of a Letter, Dated Southamp-

ton, (Long-Island) June 25, 1776," *Connecticut Gazette; and the Universal Intelligencer,* July 5, 1776; "SALEM, July 2," *American Gazette, or The Constitutional Journal* (Salem, Mass.), July 2, 1776; "Extract of a Letter from an Officer in New-York, Dated August 30," *Providence (R.I.) Gazette; and Country Journal,* September 7, 1776.

16. "Portsmouth, July 13, 1776," *Freeman's Journal, or New-Hampshire Gazette,* July 13, 1776; "Portsmouth, Nov. 5, 1776," *Freeman's Journal, or New-Hampshire Gazette,* November 5, 1776; *Independent Chronicle and the Universal Advertiser* (Boston), January 2, 1777; "New-London, December 20," *Continental Journal, and Weekly Advertiser* (Boston), January 2, 1777.

17. "Boston, Jan. 19," *Boston-Gazette and Country Journal,* January 19, 1778.

18. "Boston, July 30," *Pennsylvania Evening Post,* August 18, 1778; "Philadelphia, September 1," *Connecticut Journal,* September 16, 1778; "Boston, January 28," *Providence (R.I.) Gazette; and Country Journal,* January 30, 1779.

19. *Gazette of the State of South-Carolina,* Tuesday, December 2, 1777, in *NDAR,* 10:656.

20. "Kingston, May 16," *Pennsylvania Evening Post,* August 6, 1778; "Philadelphia, April 21," *Connecticut Journal,* May 10, 1781; *Public Advertiser,* Friday, August 30, 1776, in *NDAR,* 6:578.

21. *Public Advertiser,* Wednesday, July 10, 1776, in *NDAR,* 6:472; *Public Advertiser,* Monday, July 15, 1776, in *NDAR,* 6:476; "Extract of a Letter from Bristol, August 31," in *NDAR,* 6:578.

22. "Letter from Plymouth, July 28, 1776," in *NDAR,* 6:512; "Extract of an Authentic Letter from Captain Underwood, Dated Lisbon, Oct. 2," in *NDAR,* 6:627; "Letter from Dominica, [December 13], 1776," in *NDAR,* 7:479.

23. *London Chronicle,* Saturday, October 5 to Tuesday, October 8, 1776, in *NDAR,* 7:680; *Public Advertiser,* Thursday, October 10, 1776, in *NDAR,* 7:685.

24. *Public Advertiser,* Friday, October 18, 1776, in *NDAR,* 7:701; *Public Advertiser,* Wednesday, January 1, 1777, in *NDAR,* 8:500; *Public Advertiser,* Friday, March 14, 1777, in *NDAR,* 8:676; *New-York Gazette,* Monday, April 7, 1777, in *NDAR,* 8:287.

25. "Memorandum Book of the Pennsylvania Committee of Safety," in *NDAR,* 5:773.

26. Isaac Smith Sr. to John Adams, Salem, August 6, 1776, in *PJA,* 4:436–437; Brigadier General Benedict Arnold to Major General Horatio Gates, Isle La Motte, September 18, 1776, in *NDAR,* 6:884; John Langdon to John Hancock, Portsmouth, November 4, 1776, in *NDAR,* 7:31.

27. John Langdon to William Whipple, Portsmouth, November 6, 1776, in *NDAR,* 7:56–57; John Langdon to Willing, Morris & Co., Portsmouth, November 19, 1776, in *NDAR,* 7:205.

28. Commodore Esek Hopkins to the Continental Marine Committee, Providence, September 10, 1776, in *NDAR,* 6:770; Commodore Esek Hopkins to the Continental Marine Committee, Providence, September 22, 1776, in *NDAR,* 6:949.

29. Commodore Esek Hopkins to the Continental Marine Committee, Providence, September 30, 1776, in *NDAR,* 6:1056; Commodore Esek Hopkins to the Continental Marine Committee, Newport, October 24, 1776, in *NDAR,* 6:1399.

30. Commodore Esek Hopkins to the Continental Marine Committee, Providence,

November 2, 1776, in *NDAR*, 7:17; Commodore Esek Hopkins to the Continental Marine Committee, Providence, November 8, 1776, in *NDAR*, 7:85.

31. Major General Charles Lee to Meshech Weare, Camp Philipsburg, November 27, 1776, in *NDAR*, 7:306–307.

32. Benjamin Rush to Richard Henry Lee, Near Bristol, December 21, 1776, in *NDAR*, 7:543–544.

33. In this letter, Trumbull referred to a meeting held months earlier regarding the defense of New England. Governor Jonathan Trumbull to George Washington, Lebanon, February 21, 1777, in *NDAR*, 7:1255; Commodore Esek Hopkins to the Continental Marine Committee, Providence, March 18, 1777, in *NDAR*, 8:143; Captain Thomas Thompson to the New Hampshire Committee of Safety, Portsmouth, February 6, 1777, in *NDAR*, 7:1115.

34. John Adams to James Warren, Philadelphia, April 6, 1777, in *PJA*, 5:145.

35. "Order of the Massachusetts Council, Boston, January 27, 1777," in *NDAR*, 7:1042; "Acts and Resolves of the Massachusetts General Court, Boston, Wednesday, March 26, 1777," in *NDAR*, 8:203.

36. "Minutes of the New Hampshire Committee of Safety, May 19, 1777," in *NDAR*, 8:992; Portsmouth Committee of Safety to New Hampshire Committee of Safety, Portsmouth, July 7, 1777, in *NDAR*, 9:230.

37. "Ordinance of the South Carolina Legislature, January 26, 1778," in *NDAR*, 11:209; "Journal of the New Hampshire Council, March 9, 1778," in *NDAR*, 11:547; "Journal of the Massachusetts Council, April 10, 1778," in *NDAR*, 12:77.

38. Captain Thomas Thompson to the New Hampshire General Assembly, Portsmouth, June 4, 1777, in *NDAR*, 9:16; William Whipple to Robert Morris, Portsmouth, July 21, 1777, in *NDAR*, 9:308; Captain Nicholas Biddle to Robert Morris, September 1, 1777, in *NDAR*, 9:863–864.

39. William Whipple to Josiah Bartlett, Portsmouth, June 1, 1778, in *NDAR*, 13:15–16.

40. Josiah Bartlett to William Whipple, York Town, June 20, 1778, in *NDAR*, 13:165–166.

41. William Whipple to Josiah Bartlett, Portsmouth, July 12, 1778, in *NDAR*, 13:355–356.

42. Captain Hector McNeill to the Continental Marine Committee, Boston, October 9, 1777, in *NDAR*, 10:85; John Bradford to the Continental Marine Committee, Boston, March 25, 1778, in *NDAR*, 11:782; William Whipple to Robert Morris, Portsmouth, July 6, 1777, in *NDAR*, 11:1148.

43. "'Memoire' of Chevalier de Beaudot de Sainneville, Lieutenant Commandant, French Navy, Brest, June 15, 1778," in *NDAR*, 13:924–925.

44. Robert Morris to Silas Deane, Philadelphia, September 12, 1776, in *NDAR*, 6:794.

45. William Rotch to Nicholas Brown, Nantucket, November 26, 1776, in *NDAR*, 7:292–293.

46. Esek Hopkins to the Continental Marine Committee, Providence, April 8, 1777, in *NDAR*, 8:294; William Whipple to Josiah Bartlett, Portsmouth, May 3, 1778, in *NDAR*, 12:253; "Proclamation of the Continental Congress, May 9, 1778," in *NDAR*, 12:312n2.

47. Alline, *Life and Journal*, 143; [Drowne], *Journal of a Cruise in the Fall*, 9.

48. Painter, *Autobiography of Thomas Painter*, 47.

49. George Washington to Lieutenant Colonel Joseph Reed, Cambridge, November 20, 1775, in Philander D. Chase, ed., *Revolutionary War Series, September–December 1775*, vol. 2 of Abbott et al., *Papers of George Washington*, 409; John Paul Jones to Robert Morris, Newport, October 17, 1776, in *NDAR*, 6:1303.

50. John Paul Jones to Joseph Hewes, Rhode Island, October 31, 1776, in *NDAR*, 6:1474; John Paul Jones to Robert Morris, Nantes, December 11, 1777, in *NDAR*, 10:1091–1092.

51. John Paul Jones to Robert Morris, Nantes, December 11, 1777, in *NDAR*, 10:1091–1092.

52. "Vice Admiral Samuel Graves's Order to Captain James Wallace, Boston, September 17, 1775," in *NDAR*, 2:129–130.

53. Major General William Howe to Lord Dartmouth, Boston, December 13, 1775, in *NDAR*, 3:82.

54. "Intelligence Conveyed from New York to Vice Admiral Molyneux Shuldham, [New York, January 23, 1776]," in *NDAR*, 3:941; "Intelligence Received the 25th December 1777," in *NDAR*, 11:35.

55. "Intelligence Summary of French Assistance to American Naval Vessels and Privateers, Admiralty Office, July 3, 1777," in *NDAR*, 9:453–457; "Intelligence Regarding Martinique Received from Arthur Pigott, July 3, 1777," in *NDAR*, 9:457–461; Governor Valentine Morris to Lord George Germain, St. Vincent, December 4, 1777, in *NDAR*, 10:667.

56. Captain John Jervis, R.N., to Philip Stephens, Causand Bay, August 10, 1777, in *NDAR*, 9:560; "Intelligence from Captain John Macartney, R.N., at Halifax, March 13, 1778," in *NDAR*, 11:626.

57. "Narrative of Vice Admiral Samuel Graves, [Boston, January] 27, [1776]," in *NDAR*, 3:1006; Vice Admiral James Young to Philip Stephens, Antigua, April 7, 1776, in *NDAR*, 4:703; Major Francis Hutcheson to Major General Frederick Haldimand, Staten Island, August 8, 1776, in *NDAR*, 6:124; Captain Sir George Collier, R.N., to Massachusetts Commissary of Prisoners, Halifax, January 17, 1778, in *NDAR*, 11:148.

58. Lord Grantham to Lord Weymouth, [Madrid], December 2, 1776, in *NDAR*, 7:774; "Statement Concerning the Employment of Lieut. Col. Edward Smith with Regard to Captain Hynson and a Sketch of the Information Obtained, [London, March 31, 1777]," in *NDAR*, 8:727; Major General Eyre Massey to General Sir William Howe, Halifax, January 10, 1778, in *NDAR*, 11:83.

59. Governor John Dalling of Jamaica to Lord George Germain, Jamaica, April 25, 1778, in *NDAR*, 12:194–195; Lord Stormont to Lord Weymouth, Paris, December 10, 1777, in *NDAR*, 10:1081.

60. M. Garnier to Vergennes, London, June 11, 1776, in *NDAR*, 6:416; Vergennes to M. Garnier, Marly, June 21, 1776, in *NDAR*, 6:431.

61. "Extract of a Letter from William Bingham, St. Pierre Martinico, March 15, 1777," in *PJA*, 5:111.

62. Lacoste Cassenave & Co. to Benjamin Franklin, Cadiz, October 24, 1777, in *NDAR*, 10:940; "Verbal Instruction Given to Jean Holker, November 25, 1777," in *NDAR*, 10:1029.

63. Jean Holker to Henry Laurens, President of the Continental Congress, York Town,

June 16, 1778, in *NDAR*, 13:127–128; Comte de Vergennes to the American Commissioners in France, Versailles, May 15, 1778, in *NDAR*, 12:697.

64. Lord Weymouth to Lord Grantham, St. James's, August 1, 1777, in *NDAR*, 9:544.

65. Conde de Floridablanca to Conde de Aranda, San Lorenzo, October 23, 1777, in *NDAR*, 10:937–938.

66. Conde de Aranda to Conde de Floridablanca, Paris, November 26, 1777, in *NDAR*, 10:1039–1040; Conde de Floridablanca to Conde de Aranda, Madrid, December 9, 1777, in *NDAR*, 10:1079–1080.

67. American Commissioners in France to Commanders of Armed American Vessels, Paris, November 21, 1777, in *NDAR*, 10:1012–1013.

68. American Commissioners in France to the French and Spanish Courts, Paris, November 23, 1777, in *NDAR*, 10:1020.

69. American Commissioners in France to the Committee of Commerce, Passy, November 30, 1777, in *NDAR*, 10:1052–1053.

70. American Commissioners in France to the Committee of Commerce, Passy, November 30, 1777, in *NDAR*, 10:1052–1053.

71. Stephen Fuller to Lord George Germain, Jamaica, January 27, 1776, in *NDAR*, 3:1023; *Public Advertiser*, Monday, July 29, 1776, in *NDAR*, 6:512; M. Garnier to Vergennes, London, October 18, 1776, in *NDAR*, 7:698.

72. Lords Commissioners, Admiralty, to Commodore Sir Edward Vernon, October 26, 1776, in *NDAR*, 7:712; Captain George Murray, R.N., to Captain William Hay, H.M.S. *Alarm*, Gibraltar Bay, March 14, 1777, in *NDAR*, 8:677; Lord George Germain to Lords Commissioners, Admiralty, Whitehall, April 10, 1777, in *NDAR*, 8:757–758; Vice Admiral James Young to Philip Stephens, Antigua, December 21, 1777, in *NDAR*, 10:774; Lord George Germain to Lieutenant General Sir Henry Clinton, Whitehall, March 8, 1778, in *NDAR*, 11:1070–1071.

73. "Extract of a Letter from a Merchant in Dunkirk, to his Friend in Leith, Dated Dunkirk, 10th April, 1777," in *NDAR*, 8:758; *Public Advertiser*, Wednesday, May 14, 1777, in *NDAR*, 8:846.

74. *Public Advertiser*, Thursday, May 15, 1777, in *NDAR*, 8:847.

75. "Extract of a Letter from Dublin, July 9, 1777," in *NDAR*, 9:475; "Extract of a Letter from Kirkwall, July 26, 1777," in *NDAR*, 9:534.

76. "Memorial of the Merchants, Traders, and Ship Owners of London to Lord Weymouth, London, November 24, 1777," in *NDAR*, 10:1023.

77. "Memorial of the Merchants, Traders, and Ship Owners of London to Lord Weymouth, London, November 24, 1777," in *NDAR*, 10:1023.

78. "Proceedings in the Lords Respecting the Commercial Losses Occasioned by the American War," February 6, 1778, in *NDAR*, 11:967–969.

79. "Proceedings in the Lords Respecting the Commercial Losses Occasioned by the American War, February 11, 1778," in *NDAR*, 11:995; Edmund Burke to Lord Weymouth, Westminster, February 16, 1778, in *NDAR*, 11:1007.

80. *Maryland Journal*, Tuesday, May 6, 1777, in *NDAR*, 8:921; Benjamin Franklin and Silas Deane to Ferdinand Grand, Paris Banker, Passy, August 15, 1777, in *NDAR*, 9:571.

81. Arthur Lee to Robert Morris, Chairman of the Secret Committee, Paris, September 9, 1777, in *NDAR*, 9:636.

82. "Memorial of Gustavus Conyngham to Congress," in *Letters and Papers*, 207.

83. "Report of Committee of Congress on Conyngham Memorial," in *Letters and Papers*, 209; Alexander Hamilton to Gustavus Conyngham, Treasury Department, July 5, 1793, in *Letters and Papers*, 213; "Endorsements by Conyngham, Philadelphia, December 8, 1794," in *Letters and Papers*, 214.

84. "Petition of Gustavus Conyngham to Congress, Philadelphia, December 26, 1797," in *Letters and Papers*, 215; "Observations on the Report of Benjamin Walker Esq. to the late Board of Treasury on the Subject of Capt. Gustavus Conyngham's claim against the United States, as commander of the Lugger Surprize & the Cutter Revenge," in *Letters and Papers*, 216–223. The final word on Conyngham came from a member of his crew, Ebenezer Gilbert, surgeon on board the *Revenge*, who wrote Timothy Pickering in 1828 asking for recognition of Conyngham's and the vessel's service to Congress and the nation during the Revolution. At the time, Gilbert was in need of money himself, and he hoped for back pay from the government. Pickering responded, "I was a member of the Continental *Board of War* & not of the Navy Board, & know nothing of the subject of the inquiry." Thus ended the story of Captain Gustavus Conyngham. Ebenezer Gilbert to Timothy Pickering, Middletown, June 10, 1828, in *Letters and Papers*, 223–225.

CONCLUSION

1. Robinson, *Confederate Privateers*, 38.

2. Robinson, 38.

3. Robinson, 38.

4. Robinson, 39–40.

5. Weber, *Neither Victor nor Vanquished*, 188. See also Kert, *Privateering*, 70. Kert contends there were seventeen vessels in the U.S. Navy in June 1812.

6. Robinson, *Confederate Privateers*, 303; Budiansky, *Perilous Fight*, 287–288.

7. Budiansky, *Perilous Fight*, 287; Lambert, *Challenge*, 208–209, 89; Dudley, *Splintering the Wooden Wall*, 74.

8. Budiansky, *Perilous Fight*, 288, xi; Lambert, *Challenge*, 428; Butler, *Pirates, Privateers, & Rebel Raiders*, 15; Kert, *Privateering*, 8, 24–26.

9. Butler, *Pirates, Privateers, & Rebel Raiders*, 16; Robinson, *Confederate Privateers*, 2.

10. Robinson, *Confederate Privateers*, 19–23.

11. Robinson, *Confederate Privateers*, 25.

12. Roberts, *Now for the Contest*, 15, 122.

13. Wolkins, "Beverly Men in the War," 22–23.

14. Wolkins, "Beverly Men in the War," 22–23.

Bibliography

MANUSCRIPT COLLECTIONS

American Philosophical Society, Philadelphia

Benjamin Franklin Papers
Lusanna Prize Case Records

Baker Library Special Collections, Harvard Business School, Boston

Heard Family Business Records

Connecticut Historical Society, Hartford

Benedict Arnold Letters, 1775–1777
Harris Family Papers, 1721–1859
Jonathan Trumbull Sr. Papers

Historical Society of Pennsylvania, Philadelphia

Ball Families Papers, 1676–1879
Charles A. Tracy Collection of Hardie Family Papers, 1777–1902
Clifford Family Papers, 1722–1832
Reed and Forde Papers, 1759–1823
Robert Morris Papers, 1756–1782
Thomas A. Biddle Records, 1771–1837
Thomas Truxtun Correspondence, 1779–1946

The Mariners' Museum, Newport News, Va.

Records of Stewart, Nesbitt and Company, 1757–1940

Massachusetts Historical Society, Boston

Dering Family Papers, 1627–1898
Dolbeare Family Papers, 1665–1830
Edward Payne Shipping Record, 1778–1790
Frost Family Papers II, 1754–1848
Hector McNeill Papers, 1765–1821
Huntington-Wolcott Papers, 1698–1911
Josiah Bartlett Diary and Logbook, 1781–1782
Josiah Bartlett Reminiscences, 1778–1782
Patrick Tracy Jackson Papers, 1766–1869
Privateersman's Bond, May 2, 1777

Mystic Seaport Museum, Mystic, Conn.

John Palmer Papers
Records of the Sloop *Hancock*

New-York Historical Society, New York City

Charles Nicoll Ledger A, 1758–1774
James Robertson (1717–1788) (Lt. Gen.) Letters, 1782–1788
Will of John Shine, 1778

Phillips Library, Peabody Essex Museum, Salem, Mass.

Ann (Sloop) Logbook, 1783
Cushing and White Papers, 1773–1852
Derby Family Papers, 1716–1921
Dispatch (Ship) Logbook Abstract, 1781
George Thompson Diary, 1777–1781
John Hancock Papers, 1775–1776, 1791
Joseph Peabody Family Papers, 1721–1936
Oliver Cromwell (Brigantine) Logbook, 1777
Peggy (Sloop) Logbook, 1779
Revolutionary War Collection, 1770–1856, 1901–1911, 1932, 1961, Undated
Success (Schooner) Journal, 1778–1779

Rhode Island Historical Society, Providence

Beriah Brown Papers
Jeremiah Olney Papers
Rhode Island State Records Collection
Richard Waterman Family Papers
William Greene Papers

South Carolina Historical Society, Charleston

Benjamin H. Rutledge Family Papers, 1675–1967
Gabriel Manigault Papers
Jean Holker, 1745–1822
John Mauroumet, Letters of Administration, 1765
Thomas J. Tobias Papers

NEWSPAPERS AND PERIODICALS

American Gazette, or The Constitutional Journal
Boston-Gazette and Country Journal
Connecticut Gazette; and the Universal Intelligencer
Connecticut Journal
Constitutional Gazette (New York City)
Continental Journal, and Weekly Advertiser (Boston)
Freeman's Journal, or New-Hampshire Gazette
Independent Chronicle and the Universal Advertiser (Boston)
New-Hampshire Gazette, or, State Journal, and General Advertiser
New Jersey Gazette
New-York Gazette, and the Weekly Mercury
Norwich (Conn.) Packet
Pennsylvania Evening Post
Pennsylvania Packet, or, The General Advertiser
Pennsylvania Packet, Published as Dunlap's Packet, or, The General Advertiser
Providence (R.I.) Gazette; and Country Journal
Supplement to the Royal Gazette (New York, N.Y.)

PUBLISHED PRIMARY SOURCES

Abbott, W. W., et al., eds. *The Papers of George Washington: Revolutionary War Series*. 22 vols. Charlottesville: University Press of Virginia, 1985–.

The Acts and Resolves, Public and Private, of the Province of the Massachusetts Bay: To Which Are Prefixed the Charters of the Province. Boston: Wright and Potter, 1886.

Alline, Henry. *The Life and Journal of the Rev. Mr. Henry Alline*. Boston: Gilbert and Dean, 1806.

[Bartlett, Josiah]. "Log of the *Pilgrim*, 1781–1782." In *Transactions 1922–1924*, 94–124. Vol. 25 of *Publications of the Colonial Society of Massachusetts*, edited by Albert Matthews. Boston: Colonial Society of Massachusetts, 1924.

[Boardman, Timothy]. *Log-Book of Timothy Boardman; Kept On Board The Privateer Oliver Cromwell, During A Cruise From New London CT., to Charleston, S.C., And Return In 1778; Also A Biographical Sketch Of The Author By The Rev. Samuel W. Boardman, D.D.* Albany, N.Y.: Joel Munsell's Sons, 1885.

Buntline, Ned. *Seawaif, or The Terror of the Coast.* New York: F. A. Brady, [1859].

Burdick, Austin C. *The Sea Lion, or, The Privateer of the Penobscot: A Story of Ocean Life and the Heart's Love.* New York: Samuel French, 1853.

Burnett, Edmund C., ed. *Letters of Members of the Continental Congress.* 8 vols. Washington, D.C.: Carnegie Institute of Washington, 1921–1936.

Butterfield, L. H., et al., eds. *Adams Family Correspondence.* 14 vols. Cambridge, Mass.: Belknap Press of Harvard University Press, 1963–.

Butterfield, L. H., Leonard C. Faber, and Wendell D. Garrett, eds. *Diary and Autobiography of John Adams.* 4 vols. Cambridge, Mass.: Belknap Press of Harvard University Press, 1961.

Clark, William Bell, et al., eds. *Naval Documents of the American Revolution.* 13 vols. Washington: Naval History Division, Department of the Navy, 1964–.

Cobb, Sylvanus, Jr. *The Golden Eagle: or, The Privateer of '76; A Tale of the Revolution.* Boston: F. Gleason, 1850.

———. *The Maniac's Secret, or, The Privateer of Massachusetts Bay: A Story of the Revolution.* New York: Samuel French, [185–?].

Continental Congress. "In Congress March 23, 1776. Whereas the petitions of these United Colonies to the King, for the redress of great and manifest grievances [...] resolved, that the inhabitants of these colonies be permitted to fit out armed vessels to cruise on the enemies of these United Colonies ..." Philadelphia: John Dunlap, [1776].

[Drowne, Solomon]. *Journal of a Cruise in the Fall of 1780 in the Private-Sloop of War, Hope. By Solomon Drowne, M.D. of Providence, R.I. with "Notes" By Henry T. Drowne.* New York: Charles L. Moreau, 1872.

Dyson, John. *Now Fitting for a Privateer, in the harbour of Beverly, the brigantine* Washington [...]. Newburyport, Mass.[?]: John Mycall[?], 1776.

[Fairbanks, John]. "John Fairbanks—His Journal." In *Collections and Proceedings of the Maine Historical Society,* 6:139–144. Second Series. Portland: Maine Historical Society, 1895.

Fitzpatrick, John C., ed. *The Writings of George Washington from the Original Manuscript Sources, 1745–1799.* 39 vols. Washington, D.C.: U.S. Government Printing Office, 1931–1944.

[Foot, Caleb]. "Reminiscences of the Revolution. Prison Letters and Sea Journal of Caleb Foot: Born, 1750; Died, 1787. Compiled by his Grandson and Namesake, Caleb Foote." In *The Essex Institute Historical Collections,* 26:90–122. Salem, Mass.: Salem Press, 1889.

Ford, Worthington Chauncey, ed. *Journals of the Continental Congress, 1774–1789.* 34 vols. Washington, D.C.: Government Printing Office, 1904–1937.

Freneau, Philip. *Some Account of the Capture of the Ship* Aurora. New York: M. F. Mansfield and A. Wessels, 1899.

Great Britain, Sovereign (George III), *Instructions given with a commission for seizing the ships, &c.: belonging to the inhabitants of the rebellious colonies, &c.* (n.p., 1777).

Jameson, J. Franklin, ed. *Privateering and Piracy in the Colonial Period: Illustrative Documents.* New York: Macmillan, 1923.

"Journal of a Cruise in 1777 in the Privateer Brig *Oliver Cromwell*." In *The Essex Institute Historical Collections*, 45:245–255. Salem, Mass.: Printed for the Essex Institute, 1909.

Letters of Marque, Declarations against France, Spain and the United Provinces, 1777–1783, in the Public Record Office. East Ardsley, Wakefield, Yorkshire, U.K.: Microform Academic, 1985. Microfilm.

Manly. A new favorite song, in the American fleet. Salem: Printed by Ezekiel Russell, [1776].

Neeser, Robert Wilden, ed. *Letters and Papers Relating to the Cruises of Gustavus Conyngham: A Captain of the Continental Navy, 1777–1779*. Port Washington, N.Y.: Kennikat, 1970.

[Olmsted, Gideon]. *The Journal of Gideon Olmsted: Adventures of a Sea Captain during the American Revolution*. Washington, D.C.: Library of Congress, 1978.

Painter, Thomas. *Autobiography of Thomas Painter: Relating His Experiences during the War of the Revolution*. n.p.: printed for private circulation, 1910.

Sands, John O. "Christopher Vail, Soldier and Seaman in the American Revolution." *Winterthur Portfolio* 11 (1976): 53–73.

[Sherburne, Andrew]. *Memoirs of Andrew Sherburne: A Pensioner of the Navy of the Revolution. Written by Himself*. 2nd ed. Providence, R.I.: H. H. Brown, 1831.

Shipton, Nathaniel S., and David Swain, eds. *Rhode Islanders Record the Revolution: The Journals of William Humphrey and Zuriel Waterman*. Providence: Rhode Island Publications Society, 1984.

Smith, Paul H., et al., eds. *Letters of Delegates to the Continental Congress, 1774–1789*. 25 vols. Washington, D.C.: Library of Congress, 1976–2000.

[Smith, Richard]. "Diary of Richard Smith in the Continental Congress, 1775–1776." *American Historical Review* 1, no. 2 (January 1896): 288–310.

[Smith, Richard]. "Diary of Richard Smith in the Continental Congress, 1775–1776. II." *American Historical Review* 1, no. 3 (April 1896): 493–516.

Taylor, Robert J., et al., eds. *Papers of John Adams*. 20 vols. Cambridge, Mass.: Belknap Press of Harvard University Press, 1977–.

[Thompson, George]. "Diary of George Thompson of Newburyport, Kept at Forton Prison, England, 1777–1781." In *The Essex Institute Historical Collections*, 76:221–242. Salem, Mass.: Newcomb and Gauss, 1940.

Tyson, George F., Jr. *Powder, Profit & Privateers: A Documentary History of the Virgin Islands during the Era of the American Revolution*. Charlotte Amalie, St. Thomas, Virgin Islands: Bureau of Libraries, Museums & Archaeological Services, 1977.

United States Court of Appeals in Cases of Capture. *The Revolutionary War Prize Cases: Records of the Court of Appeals in Cases of Capture, 1776–1787*. Washington, D.C.: National Archives and Records Service, 1949. Microfilm.

[Widger, William]. "Diary of William Widger of Marblehead, Kept at Mill Prison, England, 1781. Introduction by William Hammond Bowden." In *The Essex Institute Historical Collections*, 73:311–347. Salem, Mass.: Newcomb and Gauss, 1937.

Wolkins, George G. "Beverly Men in the War of Independence." Remarks, Beverly Historical Society on the Occasion of the Unveiling of Commemorative Tablets, Beverly, Mass., April 9, 1930.

SECONDARY SOURCES

Alberts, Robert C. *The Golden Voyage: The Life and Times of William Bingham, 1752–1804*. Boston: Houghton Mifflin, 1969.

Alexander, John K. "'American Privateersmen in the Mill Prison during 1777–1782': An Evaluation." In *The Essex Institute Historical Collections*, 102:318–340. Salem, Mass.: Newcomb and Gauss, 1966.

———. "Forton Prison during the American Revolution: A Case Study of British Prisoner of War Policy and the American Prisoner Response to That Policy." In *The Essex Institute Historical Collections*, 103:365–389. Salem, Mass.: Newcomb and Gauss, 1967.

Allen, Gardner Weld. *Massachusetts Privateers of the Revolution*. Vol. 77 of Massachusetts Historical Society Collections. Cambridge, Mass.: Harvard University Press, 1927.

———. *A Naval History of the American Revolution*. Vols. 1 and 2. New York: Russell and Russell, 1962.

Allison, David K., and Larrie D. Ferreiro, eds. *The American Revolution: A World War*. Washington, D.C.: Smithsonian Books, 2018.

Anderson, Fred. *Crucible of War: The Seven Years' War and the Fate of Empire in British North America, 1754–1766*. New York: Alfred A. Knopf, 2000.

Andrews, Kenneth R. *Elizabethan Privateering: English Privateering during the Spanish War, 1585–1603*. Cambridge: Cambridge University Press, 1964.

Applegate, Howard Lewis. "American Privateersmen in the Mill Prison during 1777–1782." In *The Essex Institute Historical Collections*, 97:303–320. Salem, Mass.: Newcomb and Gauss, 1961.

Armitage, David. *The Declaration of Independence: A Global History*. Cambridge, Mass.: Harvard University Press, 2007.

Armstrong, Benjamin. *Small Boats and Daring Men: Maritime Raiding, Irregular Warfare, and the Early American Navy*. Norman: University of Oklahoma Press, 2019.

Bailyn, Bernard. *Atlantic History: Concept and Contours*. Cambridge, Mass.: Harvard University Press, 2005.

Beattie, Donald W., and J. Richard Collins. *Washington's New England Fleet: Beverly's Role in Its Origins, 1775–1777*. Salem, Mass.: Newcomb and Gauss, 1969.

Beeman, Richard R. *Our Lives, Our Fortunes and Our Sacred Honor: The Forging of American Independence, 1774–1776*. New York: Basic Books, 2013.

Bolton, Charles Knowles. *The Private Soldier under Washington*. Port Washington, N.Y.: Kennikat, 1964.

Bourguignon, Henry J. *The First Federal Court: The Federal Appellate Prize Court of the American Revolution, 1775–1787*. Philadelphia: American Philosophical Society, 1977.

Bowen-Hassell, E. Gordon, Dennis M. Conrad, and Mark L. Hayes, eds. *Sea Raiders of the American Revolution: The Continental Navy in European Waters*. Washington, D.C.: Naval Historical Center Department of the Navy, 2003.

Bowman, Larry G. *Captive Americans: Prisoners during the American Revolution*. Athens, Ohio: Ohio University Press, 1976.

Brecher, Frank W. *Securing American Independence: John Jay and the French Alliance*. Westport, Conn.: Praeger, 2003.

Breen, T. H. *American Insurgents, American Patriots: The Revolution of the People*. New York: Hill and Wang, 2010.

Buchanan, John. *The Road to Valley Forge: How Washington Built the Army That Won the Revolution*. Hoboken, N.J.: John Wiley and Sons, 2004.

Budiansky, Stephen. *Perilous Fight: America's Intrepid War with Britain on the High Seas, 1812–1815*. New York: Alfred A. Knopf, 2010.

Buel, Richard, Jr. *In Irons: Britain's Naval Supremacy and the American Revolutionary Economy*. New Haven, Conn.: Yale University Press, 1998.

Burrows, Edwin G. *Forgotten Patriots: The Untold Story of American Prisoners during the Revolutionary War*. New York: Basic Books, 2008.

Butler, Lindley S. *Pirates, Privateers, & Rebel Raiders of the Carolina Coast*. Chapel Hill: University of North Carolina Press, 2000.

Casey, Michael Scott. "Rebel Privateers—The Winners of American Independence." Master's thesis, U.S. Army Command and General College, 1990.

Chadwick, Bruce. *The First American Army: The Untold Story of George Washington and the Men behind America's First Fight for Freedom*. Naperville, Ill.: Sourcebooks, 2005.

Chapin, Howard M. *Privateering in King George's War, 1739–1748*. Providence, R.I.: E. A. Johnson, 1928.

———. *Privateer Ships and Sailors: The First Century of American Colonial Privateering, 1625–1725*. Toulon, France: Imprimerie G. Mouton, 1926.

———. *Rhode Island Privateers in King George's War, 1739–1748*. Providence: Rhode Island Historical Society, 1926.

Chavez, Thomas E. *Spain and the Independence of the United States: An Intrinsic Gift*. Albuquerque: University of New Mexico Press, 2002.

Chidsey, Donald Barr. *The American Privateers*. New York: Dodd, Mead, 1962.

Claghorn, Charles E. *Naval Officers of the American Revolution: A Concise Biographical Dictionary*. Metuchen, N.J.: Scarecrow, 1988.

Clark, William Bell. *Ben Franklin's Privateers: A Naval Epic of the American Revolution*. Baton Rouge: Louisiana State University Press, 1956.

Coggins, Jack. *Ships and Seamen of the American Revolution—Vessels, Crews, Weapons, Gear, Naval Tactics, and Actions of the War for Independence*. Harrisburg, Pa.: Promontory, 1969.

Cogliano, Francis D. *American Maritime Prisoners in the Revolutionary War: The Captivity of William Russell*. Annapolis, Md.: Naval Institute Press, 2001.

Cohen, Sheldon S. *Commodore Abraham Whipple of the Continental Navy: Privateer, Patriot, Pioneer*. Gainesville: University of Florida Press, 2010.

———. *Yankee Sailors in British Gaols: Prisoners of War at Forton and Mill, 1777–1783*. Newark: University of Delaware Press, 1995.

Coleman, Eleanor S. *Captain Gustavus Conyngham, U.S.N.: Pirate or Privateer, 1747–1819*. Washington, D.C.: University Press of America, 1982.

Collier, Thomas S. *The Revolutionary Privateers of Connecticut with an Account of the State Cruisers, and a Short History of the Continental Naval Vessels Built In the State, with Lists of Officers and Crews*. New London, Conn., 1892.

Conway, Stephen. *The British Isles and the War for American Independence*. Oxford: Oxford University Press, 2000.

Cook, Don. *The Long Fuse: How England Lost the American Colonies, 1760–1785.* New York: Atlantic Monthly Press, 1995.

Countryman, Edward. *The American Revolution.* New York: Hill and Wang, 1985.

Cox, Caroline. *A Proper Sense of Honor: Service and Sacrifice in George Washington's Army.* Chapel Hill: University of North Carolina Press, 2004.

Cummins, Light Townsend. *Spanish Observers and the American Revolution, 1775–1783.* Baton Rouge: Louisiana State University Press, 1991.

Cutter, William Richard. "American Prisoners at Forton Prison, England, 1777–1779." *New England Historical and Genealogical Register* 33 (January 1879): 36–41.

———. "A Yankee Privateersman in Prison in England, 1777–1779." *New England Historical and Genealogical Register* 30 (April 1876): 174–177.

———. "A Yankee Privateersman in Prison in England, 1777–1779." *New England Historical and Genealogical Register* 30 (July 1876): 343–352.

———. "A Yankee Privateersman in Prison in England, 1777–1779." *New England Historical and Genealogical Register* 31 (April 1877): 212–213.

———. "A Yankee Privateersman in Prison in England, 1777–1779." *New England Historical and Genealogical Register* 31 (January 1877): 18–21.

———. "A Yankee Privateersman in Prison in England, 1777–1779." *New England Historical and Genealogical Register* 31 (July 1877): 284–288.

———. "A Yankee Privateersman in Prison in England, 1777–1779." *New England Historical and Genealogical Register* 32 (April 1878): 165–168.

———. "A Yankee Privateersman in Prison in England, 1777–1779." *New England Historical and Genealogical Register* 32 (January 1878): 70–73.

———. "A Yankee Privateersman in Prison in England, 1777–1779." *New England Historical and Genealogical Register* 32 (July 1878): 280–287.

Dudley, Wade G. *Splintering the Wooden Wall: The British Blockade of the United States, 1812–1815.* Annapolis, Md.: Naval Institute Press, 2003.

Dull, Jonathan R. *The French Navy and American Independence: A Study of Arms and Diplomacy, 1774–1787.* Princeton: Princeton University Press, 1975.

DuVal, Kathleen. *Independence Lost: Lives on the Edge of the American Revolution.* New York: Random House, 2015.

Elliott, John H. *Empires of the Atlantic World: Britain and Spain in America, 1492–1830.* New Haven, Conn.: Yale University Press, 2006.

Ellis, Joseph J. *His Excellency: George Washington.* New York: Alfred A. Knopf, 2004.

Fenn, Elizabeth A. *Pox Americana: The Great Smallpox Epidemic of 1775–82.* New York: Hill and Wang, 2001.

Fischer, David Hackett. *Washington's Crossing.* Oxford: Oxford University Press, 2004.

Fowler, William M. *Rebels under Sail: The American Navy during the Revolution.* New York: Scribner's, 1976.

Gilje, Paul A. *Liberty on the Waterfront: American Maritime Culture in the Age of Revolution.* Philadelphia: University of Pennsylvania Press, 2004.

———. *To Swear Like a Sailor: Maritime Culture in America, 1750–1850.* Cambridge: Cambridge University Press, 2016.

Gould, Eliga H. *Among the Powers of the Earth: The American Revolution and the Making of a New World Empire*. Cambridge, Mass.: Harvard University Press, 2012.

Hahn, Harold M. *Ships of the American Revolution and Their Models*. Annapolis, Md.: Naval Institute Press, 1988.

Hearn, Chester G. *George Washington's Schooners: The First American Navy*. Annapolis, Md.: Naval Institute Press, 1995.

Hedges, James B. *The Browns of Providence Plantations: Colonial Years*. Cambridge, Mass.: Harvard University Press, 1952.

Howe, Octavius T. "Beverly Privateers in the American Revolution." In *Publications of the Colonial Society of Massachusetts*, 24:318–442. Boston: Colonial Society of Massachusetts, 1923.

Howland, Henry R. "A British Privateer in the American Revolution." *American Historical Review* 7, no. 2 (January 1902): 286–303.

Hunt, Freeman. *Lives of American Merchants*. Vol. 2. New York: Derby and Jackson, 1858.

Johnston, Ruth Y. "Privateers in French Ports, 1776–1778." *Pennsylvania Magazine of History and Biography* 53, no. 4 (1929): 352–374.

Jones, Peter E. "Grant Us Commission to Make Reprisals upon Any Enemies Shipping." *Rhode Island History* 34, no. 4 (November 1975): 104–119.

Jones, T. Cole. "'The Dreadful Effects of British Cruilty': The Treatment of British Maritime Prisoners and the Radicalization of the Revolutionary War at Sea." *Journal of the Early Republic* 36, no. 3 (Fall 2016): 435–465.

Kert, Faye M. *Privateering: Patriots & Profits in the War of 1812*. Baltimore: Johns Hopkins University Press, 2015.

———. *Trimming Yankee Sails: Pirates and Privateers of New Brunswick*. Fredericton, New Brunswick, Canada: Goose Land Editions and the New Brunswick Military Heritage Project, 2005.

Klooster, Wim. *Revolutions in the Atlantic World: A Comparative History*. New York: New York University Press, 2009.

Lambert, Andrew. *The Challenge: America, Britain and the War of 1812*. London: Faber and Faber, 2012.

Lane, Kris E. *Pillaging the Empire: Piracy in the Americas, 1500–1750*. Armonk, N.Y.: M. E. Sharpe, 1998.

Lee, Wayne E. *Barbarians and Brothers: Anglo-American Warfare, 1500–1865*. Oxford: Oxford University Press, 2011.

Lemisch, Jesse. *Jack Tar vs. John Bull: The Role of New York's Seamen in Precipitating the Revolution*. New York: Garland, 1997.

Linebaugh, Peter, and Marcus Rediker. *The Many-Headed Hydra: Sailors, Slaves, Commoners, and the Hidden History of the Revolutionary Atlantic*. Boston: Beacon, 2000.

Little, Benerson. *Pirate Hunting: The Fight against Pirates, Privateers, and Sea Raiders from Antiquity to the Present*. Washington, D.C.: Potomac Books, 2010.

Lutnick, Solomon. *The American Revolution and the British Press, 1775–1783*. Columbia: University of Missouri Press, 1967.

Maclay, Edgar Stanton. *A History of American Privateers*. New York: Burt Franklin, 1899.

Magra, Christopher P. *Poseidon's Curse: British Naval Impressment and Atlantic Origins of the American Revolution*. Cambridge: Cambridge University Press, 2016.

Mayo, Lawrence Shaw. *John Langdon of New Hampshire*. Port Washington, N.Y.: Kennikat, 1970.

McCranie, Kevin D. *Utmost Gallantry: The U.S. and Royal Navies at Sea in the War of 1812*. Annapolis, Md.: Naval Institute Press, 2011.

McCullough, David G. *John Adams*. New York: Simon and Schuster, 2001.

———. *1776*. New York: Simon and Schuster, 2005.

McDermott, James. *Martin Frobisher: Elizabethan Privateer*. New Haven, Conn.: Yale University Press, 2001.

McDonnell, Michael A., Clare Corbould, Frances M. Clarke, and W. Fitzhugh Brundage, eds. *Remembering the Revolution: Memory, History, and Nation Making from Independence to the Civil War*. Amherst: University of Massachusetts Press, 2013.

Metzger, Charles H., S.J. *The Prisoner in the American Revolution*. Chicago: Loyola University Press, 1962.

Millar, John F. *American Ships of the Colonial and Revolutionary Periods*. New York: W. W. Norton, 1978.

Miller, Nathan. *Sea of Glory: A Naval History of the American Revolution*. Annapolis, Md.: Naval Institute Press, 1974.

———. *The U.S. Navy: A History*. 3rd ed. Annapolis, Md.: Naval Institute Press, 1997.

Morgan, William James. "American Privateering in America's War for Independence, 1775–1783." *American Neptune* 36, no. 2 (April 1976): 79–87.

Morison, Samuel Eliot. *John Paul Jones: A Sailor's Biography*. Annapolis, Md.: Naval Institute Press, 1959.

Morse, Sidney G. "State or Continental Privateers?" *American Historical Review* 52, no. 1 (October 1946): 68–73.

Nagy, John A. *Rebellion in the Ranks: Mutinies of the American Revolution*. Yardley, Pa.: Westholme, 2008.

Nelson, James L. *George Washington's Secret Navy: How the American Revolution Went to Sea*. New York: McGraw Hill, 2008.

Nettels, Curtis P. *The Emergence of a National Economy, 1775–1815*. New York: Holt, Rinehart and Winston, 1962.

Oberholtzer, Ellis Paxson. *Robert Morris: Patriot and Financier*. New York: Macmillan, 1903.

Patton, Robert H. *Patriot Pirates: The Privateer War for Freedom and Fortune in the American Revolution*. New York: Pantheon Books, 2008.

Perl-Rosenthal, Nathan. *Citizen Sailors: Becoming American in the Age of Revolutions*. Cambridge, Mass.: Belknap Press of Harvard University Press, 2015.

Rappleye, Charles. *Robert Morris: Financier of the American Revolution*. New York: Simon and Schuster, 2010.

Rediker, Marcus. *Between the Devil and the Deep Blue Sea: Merchant Seamen, Pirates, and the Anglo-American Maritime World, 1700–1750*. Cambridge: Cambridge University Press, 1987.

Resch, John. *Suffering Soldiers: Revolutionary War Veterans, Moral Sentiment, and Political Culture in the Early Republic.* Amherst: University of Massachusetts Press, 1999.

Resch, John, and Walter Sargent, eds. *War and Society in the American Revolution: Mobilization and Home Fronts.* Dekalb: Northern Illinois University Press, 2006.

"Revolutionary Privateering." *Bulletin of the Business Historical Society* 7, no. 3 (May 1933): 7–10.

Roberts, William H. *Now for the Contest: Coastal and Oceanic Naval Operations in the Civil War.* Lincoln: University of Nebraska Press, 2004.

Robertson, E. Arnot. *The Spanish Town Papers: Some Sidelights on the American War of Independence.* New York: Macmillan, 1959.

Robinson, William Morrison, Jr. *The Confederate Privateers.* Columbia: University of South Carolina Press, 1990.

Rouleau, Brian. *With Sails Whitening Every Sea: Mariners and the Making of an American Maritime Empire.* Ithaca, N.Y.: Cornell University Press, 2014.

Schwartz, Stuart B., ed. *Tropical Babylons: Sugar and the Making of the Atlantic World, 1450–1680.* Chapel Hill: University of North Carolina Press, 2004.

Starkey, David J., E. S. van Eyck van Heslinga, and J. A. de Moor, eds. *Pirates and Privateers: New Perspectives on the War on Trade in the Eighteenth and Nineteenth Centuries.* Exeter: University of Exeter Press, 1997.

Swanson, Carl E. *Predators and Prizes: American Privateering and Imperial Warfare, 1738–1748.* Columbia: University of South Carolina Press, 1991.

Syrett, David. *The Royal Navy in European Waters during the American Revolutionary War.* Columbia: University of South Carolina Press, 1998.

Thompson, Mack. *Moses Brown: Reluctant Reformer.* Chapel Hill: University of North Carolina Press, 1962.

Thomson, Buchanan Parker. *Spain: Forgotten Ally of the American Revolution.* North Quincy, Mass.: Christopher, 1976.

Toth, Charles W., ed. *The American Revolution and the West Indies.* Port Washington, N.Y.: Kennikat, 1975.

Truxes, Thomas. *Defying Empire: Trading with the Enemy in Colonial New York.* New Haven, Conn.: Yale University Press, 2008.

Ubbelohde, Carl. *The Vice-Admiralty Courts and the American Revolution.* Chapel Hill: University of North Carolina Press, 1960.

Upton, Richard Francis. *Revolutionary New Hampshire: An Account of the Social and Political Forces Underlying the Transition from Royal Province to American Commonwealth.* Port Washington, N.Y.: Kennikat, 1970.

Vickers, Daniel. *Young Men and the Sea: Yankee Seafarers in the Age of Sail.* With Vince Walsh. New Haven, Conn.: Yale University Press, 2005.

Volo, James M. *Blue Water Patriots: The American Revolution Afloat.* Westport, Conn.: Praeger, 2007.

Wagner, Frederick. *Robert Morris: Audacious Patriot.* New York: Dodd, Mead, 1976.

Weber, William. *Neither Victor nor Vanquished: America in the War of 1812.* Washington, D.C.: Potomac Books, 2013.

Wilbur, C. Keith. *Picture Book of the Revolution's Privateers*. Harrisburg, Pa.: Stackpole Books, 1973.

Wils, James Richard. "'In Behalf of the Continent': Privateering and Irregular Warfare in Early Revolutionary America, 1775–1777." Master's thesis, East Carolina University, 2012.

Winslow, Richard E., III. *"Wealth and Honour": Portsmouth during the Golden Age of Privateering, 1775–1815*. Portsmouth: Published for the Portsmouth Marine Society by Peter E. Randall, 1988.

Index